Protest Is Not Enough

Protest Is Not Enough

The Struggle of Blacks and Hispanics
for Equality in Urban Politics

by
Rufus P. Browning
Dale Rogers Marshall
David H. Tabb

UNIVERSITY OF CALIFORNIA PRESS

Berkeley / Los Angeles / London

To Lucy Beckett Browning
and Robert Hamilton Browning
Donald Jay Marshall
Connie Tabb

University of California Press
Berkeley and Los Angeles, California

University of California Press, Ltd.
London, England

First Paperback Printing 1986
ISBN 0-520-05730-9

Printed in the United States of America

2 3 4 5 6 7 8 9

Library of Congress Cataloging in Publication Data
Browning, Rufus P.
    Protest is not enough.
    Bibliography: p.
    Includes index.
    1. Afro-Americans—California—Politics and governemnt. 2. Hispanic Americans—California—Politics and government. 3. California—Politics and government—1951–   4. Political participation—California. 5. Municipal government—California. I. Marshall, Dale Rogers. II. Tabb, David H. III. Title.
E185.93.C2B76   1984   323.1 '196073 '0794   83-15552

The paper used in this publication meets the minimum requirements of American National Standard for Information Sciences—Permanence of Paper for Printed Library Materials, ANSI Z39.48–1984. ∞

Contents

List of Figures and Tables

TABLES

Acknowledgments

The intellectual and personal origins of this book are manifold. We are white political scientists who were touched in various ways by the civil rights movement—by growing up in *de jure* segregated communities in the South and in families where the pain of oppression was deeply felt though not experienced firsthand, by exposure to Quaker education, and by teaching urban politics—in short by observing many who had experienced inequality or participated in protest.

Having followed separate paths, in the early seventies we were all newly arrived in the San Francisco Bay Area looking for appropriate research projects. The vagaries of the job market resulted in Rufus and Dale sharing a car pool to U. C. Davis and passing the time by designing an urban research project that would capitalize on the proximity of many comparable cities within easy traveling distance. Entranced with the Davis commute, we decided to expand it to include ten cities in northern California.

Dale had the original idea, and Rufus and Dale carried out a pilot project in the summer of 1974. Soon thereafter David joined the effort to develop a fundable proposal. Eventually this proposal was funded by the National Science Foundation, and we began operations in early 1976 as the Policy Implementation Project at the Institute of Governmental Studies, U.C. Berkeley—a convenient and hospitable home.

At that stage the project was designed to examine the impact of the implementation of federal programs on blacks and Hispanics in the ten selected cities, thus its title. But delving into the local histories of federal programs soon convinced us that their implementation was intricately linked with larger political developments in the cities and the nation, and we expanded our focus to encompass minority protest, electoral politics, and other aspects of urban political change. A continuation grant for 1979–1980 was based on a proposal that placed much more emphasis on quantitative analysis and on the evolution of local political systems in response to the minority mobilization movement.

Broadening the scope of the project multiplied the difficulties we faced. The frustration was summed up when one of us showed the finally completed manuscript to a young family member and was greeted with a look of utter disbelief: "It took you ten years to write this?" And each of us has heard the incredulous voices of family members and friends echoing that question. Given our work styles, there is something of an infinite regress in the research process. We have never stopped finding points to polish, errors to correct, and implications to explore. But now it is time to expose the work to wider scrutiny.

Along the way, we have had a lot of help. The research was supported by two generous grants from the Division of Social Sciences, National Science Foundation: SOC 75–18656/57 and SOC 79–07121. We also received support from the Institute of Governmental Affairs, University of California at Davis; the Institute of Governmental Studies, University of California at Berkeley, and the Frederic Burk Foundation and School of Behavioral and Social Sciences, San Francisco State University.

We acknowledge with great appreciation extraordinary special assistance from the Institute of Governmental Studies at U.C. Berkeley and its director, Eugene Lee. IGS provided a home for the project and "bail outs" when the frequent crises arose. David Leege and Gerald Wright at the National Science Foundation were also especially supportive.

All field researchers know that their fate depends on the forbearance of their respondents and we are no exception. The candor and generosity of our respondents, who generally suppressed their understandable hostility toward academics, were highlights of the project.

We wish to thank our many research assistants: Stephanie Arbuckle, Susan Bain, Eileen Bleeker, Marla Browning, Leah Brumer, Jim Desveaux, Barbara Dietrick, Noelle Farner, Mario Herrera, Gerald Korshak, Michael MacDonald, Brian Miller, Walter Park, Burleigh Randolph, Margaret Rands, Dale Scott, Diane Shearer, Bob Waste, Bruce Wallin, and Margaret Wrightson. Thanks also go to the efficient interviewing team of Jule Anderson, Ellen Hodghead, Bob Sweeney, and Joan Sweeney; our project secretary, Linda Grant, and our super typist and word processing expert, Vickie Zinner. For all of you who years ago started asking why you had not gotten your free copy of the book yet, now you understand.

Several colleagues kindly supported our efforts and offered helpful suggestions, including Richard DeLeon, Aaron Wildavsky, Todd LaPorte, Victor Jones, Frances Fox Piven, Judith May, Fred Wirt, and Eugene Lee.

We also wish to thank the reviewers for U. C. Press and those who commented on an earlier version of this book: Terry Clark, Rich DeLeon, Chris Garcia, William Keech, Eugene Lee, Larry Nitz, Paul Peterson, and Francine Rabinovitz.

Many good hands at U.C. Press contributed to the quality of this book. William McClung, sponsoring editor, encouraged us in our endeavor early on. Mary Lamprech managed the publication process, and her good judgment and meticulous attention are evident to us throughout. Jonas Weisel's copyediting alerted us to points in the manuscript that were improved with rewriting. Barbara Roos prepared an astonishingly thorough index that makes all the right connections. Patricia Malango worked closely with us to make sure the book received appropriate publicity. To all, our thanks.

Rufus Browning thanks Patricia and Elizabeth, Marla, Ross, Charles, and Mark—whose patience allowed him to dedicate himself to this work and whose impatience helped keep it in perspective; his mother, whose concern for the disadvantaged impressed itself on him as a boy; and his coauthors, who supplied balance and a broader view, invested their own skill and energy where his left off, tolerated the arrogance of his specialization, and insisted on stopping.

Dale Marshall thanks the Bay Area Faculty Women's Research Forum, her parents, three brothers, and three sisters-in-law, who reacted favorably to the manuscript at one of the annual family reunions at Tahoe, and her children—Jessica, Cynthia, and Clayton—who grew up while their mother was busy with the project and who will hopefully understand someday how much their mother appreciates their tolerance, however grudging, and how unusual Donald Jay Marshall was to support such an enterprise before it was fashionable.

David Tabb acknowledges the patience of his children, Kevin and Lisa, and colleagues, Rufe and Dale. When Connie, the beacon of his life, struggled against unyielding odds, they provided encouragement and silent understanding, reaffirming that family and friends can make a critical difference.

Introduction

The Struggle for Political Equality

The gradual development of the equality of conditions is therefore a providential fact . . . it is universal, it is durable, it constantly eludes all human interference, and all events as well as all men contribute to its progress. . . . [it is an] irresistible . . . revolution, which has advanced for centuries in spite of such amazing obstacles. (Alexis de Tocqueville, *Democracy in America*)

The idea of political equality has exerted extraordinary force in human history, even if progress toward equality is not so irresistible or universal as de Tocqueville believed. In many societies a gradual reduction of ascriptive barriers to political participation, such as birth, wealth, race, religion, and more recently gender, has been achieved. In spite of defeats and setbacks, the quest for equality has been a central concern of many social movements that have challenged existing political systems, insisted on access to the powers of government, and, eventually, demanded a broadening of rights to include economic and social as well as political equality.[1]

[1]See Bendix (1964); Lapidus (1978); Marshall (1964).

In the American political system the glaring inequality between blacks and whites has led to a protracted struggle for political equality and access to government at both the national and local levels. Commentators from de Tocqueville to Myrdal have identified racial inequalities as a basic challenge to democratic governance. De Tocqueville wrote, "If there ever are great revolutions there, they will be caused by the presence of blacks upon American soil. That is to say, it will not be the equality of social conditions but rather their inequality which may give rise thereto" (1969, p. 639). More recently, the U.S. National Advisory Commission on Civil Disorders pointed to the dangers of a divided society when it concluded in 1968 that "our nation is moving toward two societies, one black, one white— separate and unequal" (1968, p. 1). Over the long run the existence of a subordinate group in society, whether racial or economic, generates tensions that threaten the stability and legitimacy of democratic governments.

Within twenty years after the end of the Second World War, the "American dilemma" of "an ever-raging conflict" between egalitarian beliefs and the unequal treatment and position of blacks had been brought dramatically and forcefully to national attention and to the forefront of governmental action at the national level.[2] The 1960s witnessed a sustained burst of political mobilization and protest by black people in the United States. The civil rights movement began as an effort to secure the most basic political rights—the right to vote and the right to equal treatment before the law—but rapidly expanded in scope to demand governmental action to end discrimination in employment, public education, housing, and public facilities generally and to alleviate poverty and reduce unemployment, expand health care to blacks and other low income groups, and gain other governmental benefits.

A significant part of this effort by blacks and later Hispanics and other groups was aimed at gaining access to city governments, city jobs, and the benefits of city programs and policy. The civil rights movement and its local manifestations and successors became a critical test of the openness of the American

[2]Myrdal (1944). For a recent account, see Harding (1981).

political system and of the ability of the American political process to respond to the demands of hitherto excluded groups for equal treatment before the law and for equal access to government; the responses of city governments were an important part of governmental responsiveness overall.

The struggle by minority groups for political access and responsive policies at the local level and the responses of city governments are the subjects of this book. We address them by examining the political mobilization of blacks and Hispanics, and its impact on access to policy making and on governmental responsiveness in ten California cities during the tumultuous decades of the sixties and seventies. To what extent did blacks and Hispanics mobilize politically? There were huge differences from city to city in the types and intensity of mobilization and the level of minority political activity. What accounts for these differences and how effective were the different strategies of protest and electoral effort?

Where blacks and Hispanics mobilized, were they successful in achieving some significant part of their demands? Did they in fact secure continuing access to city governments, access that was not just a product of co-optation? And even where representation was achieved, can we point to significant impact on the policies of city governments? Were these governments responsive to minority concerns? If some were but some were not, under what conditions was responsiveness achieved? By tracing closely the linkages between political mobilization, minority group access, and governmental responsiveness, we are able to shed light on these questions.

The Setting

The treatment of blacks and Hispanics has important implications for the future of the American political system because they are the two largest minority groups in the United States, comprising 18.1 percent of the national population in 1980 and much larger proportions in many states and cities. In California blacks and Hispanics constituted 26.9 percent of the population in 1980 (7.7 percent black and 19.2 percent Hispanic), the Hispanic population having almost doubled in the ten years between 1970 and 1980.[3]

The ten cities we study are the largest cities with the largest black and Hispanic populations in northern California. They are San Francisco, San Jose, Oakland, Sacramento, Stockton, Berkeley, Richmond, Hayward, Vallejo, and Daly City. In 1970 they ranged from 67,000 to 715,000 with black populations constituting from 2 to 36 percent and Hispanic populations from 4 to 17 percent of total city populations.[4] Combined black and Hispanic population ranged from 16 to 43 percent. In 1970 the mean population was 231,000; the mean percent black was 16, and Hispanic 11.

Eight of the cities ring San Francisco Bay: San Francisco and its suburb, Daly City, at the west; San Jose at the southern end, Vallejo at the northern; Hayward, Oakland, Berkeley, and Richmond on the eastern side. Two are in the agricultural Central Valley: Sacramento less than 100 miles to the northeast of San Francisco, and Stockton 50 miles south of Sacramento. No city is more than 130 miles by freeway from any other.

In the years between 1960 and 1980 these cities were caught up in the turmoil of protest and demand activity around issues of political equality and social equity for blacks and Hispanics. The assault on traditional patterns was felt to one degree or another in all the cities. First came the civil rights movement, which challenged the exclusion of blacks, etching scenes on the American consciousness—National Guardsmen escorting black children past mobs of taunting white parents, lunch counter sit-ins, Governor Wallace—"segregation today, segregation tomorrow, segregation forever"—blocking the doorway to the University of Alabama to federal officials, Martin Luther King, Jr.'s impassioned plea for equality from the steps of the

[3]U.S. Department of Commerce, Bureau of the Census (1981a, 1981b). Definitions of "Hispanic" differ, and different definitions may lead to different conclusions about Hispanic populations. With two minor exceptions that are clearly noted, we use the 1980 census definition of Hispanics as "persons of Spanish origin," self-identified. See footnotes to appendix A for further discussion of the problem.

[4]Appendix A presents selected demographic and economic characteristics of the cities.

Lincoln Memorial, the marches in Selma and Birmingham, and the murder of civil rights workers. The challenge of the civil rights movement spread to California cities beginning in the late 1950s, leading both to protest and to the organization of more traditional electoral and lobbying efforts. The shock waves were felt in city after city.

Finally violence erupted in American cities during the second half of the sixties. Riots in Los Angeles, Detroit, Newark, and other American cities aroused fear, anger, and hatred as leaders struggled to control events and prevent cities from burning. The riots were followed by recriminations, investigations, and heightened demands.

The federal government initiated programs directed at the problems of poverty, racial inequality, and discrimination. President Johnson pushed aggressively for the passage of the Civil Rights Act of 1964, the Voting Rights Act of 1965, and the war on poverty. These were followed by Model Cities and a great array of other social programs, most of which impacted the agenda and resources of city governments and of minority claimants on their resources. The federal grant system was reorganized but continued to expand with the institution of general revenue sharing and block grants under the Nixon administration.

The civil rights movement, the federal programs, and the riots all had impacts on our ten cities. Some cities experienced years of intense political mobilization and conflict, and remarkable political transformations. There was a clash of ambitions and values between blacks, Hispanics, and whites; between minority leaders and their followers; and between white leaders and their followers. New leaders emerged and others were eclipsed, strategies and ambitions were constantly tested. But in others of our cities there was much less mobilization and less change.

Central Questions

The differences in the struggle for political equality in our ten cities—that is, the variations in the way minority mobilization expressed itself in local settings—are the central focus of this book. The book can be read on two different levels.

It is an empirical study of minority political activity and urban politics and policy in ten cities over twenty years, examining the openness of urban political systems to previously excluded groups. The book also develops a theory of urban political change, a theory of political incorporation and policy responsiveness. We provide an explanation of why so much more change occurred in some cities than in others. We identify the conditions that facilitated or impeded the inclusion of blacks and Hispanics in urban political systems and the conditions that led to policy responsiveness. Our findings are relevant to many specialized areas within urban politics—group mobilization, electoral politics, decision making, policy determinants, and implementation. We integrate components from these areas into a more comprehensive theory of incorporation, of mobilization and response. In regard to minority strategies, we compare the effectiveness of demand-protest with electoral efforts. Concerning group access, we compare the impact of minority representation to what we call minority incorporation in which liberal electoral coalitions replace conservative dominant coalitions on councils. By considering cities in their historical, political, and intergovernmental contexts, the theory attempts to overcome the limitations of studies that isolate components of urban systems from the larger context and from the central concerns of political life.[5]

The three central questions addressed are:

1. How open are urban political systems?

2. How does political incorporation occur?

3. Does political incorporation of minorities make a difference for policy?

How Open Are Urban Political Systems?

Analysts have set forth alternative conceptions of the American political system that imply different assessments of the

---

[5]Recent efforts with similar aims are Katznelson (1981) and Peterson (1981).

possibilities of democracy for blacks and Hispanics. One relatively optimistic view holds that the system both nationally and locally is significantly open to the demands of new or newly mobilized groups—if they are able to articulate their political interests, the system affords opportunities for them to influence government:

> Whenever a group of people believe that they are adversely affected by national policies or are about to be, they generally have extensive opportunities for presenting their case and for negotiations that may produce a more acceptable alternative. In some cases, they may have enough power to delay, to obstruct, and even to veto the attempt to impose policies on them. (Dahl, 1967, p. 23) The institutions [of American government] . . . offer organized minorities innumerable sites in which to fight, perhaps to defeat, at any rate to damage an opposing coalition. (Dahl, 1967, p. 329)

The assertion is that groups typically have many opportunities to influence policy.

Critics have argued that American politics both nationally and locally is much less open than this view suggests. In this perspective the appearance of openness masks a closed system that makes symbolic adaptations to demands from low resource groups without significantly changing the distribution of political power and governmental benefits (Bachrach and Baratz, 1970; Edelman, 1971; Katznelson, 1981; Piven and Cloward, 1971). These writers emphasize the lack of responsiveness and the resistance to change.

Comparative studies of city governments, however, have found significant variation in their openness to the demands of newly mobilized groups. For example, Agger, Goldrich, and Swanson compared four cities over time and observed changes in policies as new city residents generated new issues and successful political challenges, but they found the trend toward reform or good government varied in different cities (1964, chap. 5).[6]

From the analysis of city responses to the mobilization of blacks and Hispanics, then, we might find that the cities were

---

[6]Banfield and Wilson (1963, p. 330) and Dahl (1961, pp. 11–86) also see trends toward reform governments in cities. Other analysts who stress differences in city responsiveness to new demands include Gamson (1975), Greenstone and Peterson (1973), and Mollenkopf (1973, 1983).

open to the forcefully articulated demands of these groups. Or we might conclude that their demands were largely ignored, responsiveness was a sham, and there is little to show for the intense effort and prolonged conflict of the sixties and seventies. Third, we might find significant variation: some cities open and responsive, others closed and resistant.

The findings of this study support the third view. These ten cities responded very differently to the challenge of the national civil rights movement, its local manifestations, and its sequels. In some cities quite remarkable levels of responsiveness to minority interests were achieved, and minority representatives came to occupy positions of substantial authority and respect. In other cities relationships between white and minority leaders were more manipulative and co-optative, though significant concessions to minority interests were made. And in still other cities established interests successfully resisted minority demands and effectively excluded minority representatives from influence. Local polities were sometimes open, sometimes closed.

Assertions about the openness of national and local political systems are sometimes equated with pluralism. A variety of generalizations about openness is found in the writings of Robert Dahl and others associated with pluralism. However, in an important reanalysis of the debates swirling around the label *pluralism*, Nelson Polsby distinguished among three uses of the term (1980). The use that is relevant to our concern with the local communities, "pluralism$_2$," asserts that power is relatively dispersed. Used according to this strict definition, pluralism does not address issues of openness. It characterizes the overall distribution of power in a community across many different issues and in relation to all groups (typically at one point in time, though Polsby and Dahl both acknowledge changes over time). Our work does not attempt to provide a global assessment of power dispersion in our cities. It does not assess "pluralism$_2$." Instead this book examines the change in the political position of two groups (blacks and Hispanics) vis à vis city government and its policies. It asks, in Polsby's terms, whether the dispersion of power to these groups increased over time and what factors were associated with the changes. Whether the dispersion of power prior to these changes or after was great enough to warrant the pluralist label is not addressed.

Parallels are often drawn between the situation faced by blacks and Hispanics and the experiences of earlier migrants to the cities from Europe—the Irish, Italians, Jews, and Poles. The earlier migrants used participation in city governments as a route to political inclusion and socioeconomic mobility; city governments were open to these new groups. Some assume that blacks and Hispanics will follow the same route, that they will be the successors to the earlier claimants and will meet a similar response from city governments (Dahl, 1961; Lowi, 1964; Wolfinger, 1974). Others question whether ethnic succession will continue, arguing that conditions are no longer favorable, that local political systems are not open to blacks and Hispanics (Gronbjerg, Street, and Suttles, 1978, p. 131; Harrigan, 1981, p. 47; Katznelson, 1973 and 1981). When describing the openness of urban political systems to blacks and Hispanics, we are also dealing with the question of ethnic succession.

How Did Political Incorporation Occur and Did It Make a Difference for Policy?

Examining the openness of urban political systems to black and Hispanic efforts to gain political equality leads us to explanations of the mobilization of minorities, their incorporation into city politics, and the impact of incorporation on policy responsiveness. Our work explains the amount of political change that occurred and the differences among the cities in the levels of incorporation and responsiveness achieved.

The study examines the conditions, developments, interactions, and sequence of events associated with efforts to increase the access of minority groups to city governments. How did urban political systems respond to the pressure and conflict generated by these groups? We ask what mobilization strategies and group characteristics were associated with different results for minorities. What was the relative effectiveness of demand-protest strategies compared to electoral strategies? What interaction was there between these two mobilization strategies? How did they evolve over time and with what consequences for incorporation of minorities into city politics? These questions address themes in the literature on group mobilization and conflict (Coleman, 1971; Gamson, 1975; Tarrow, 1981; Tilly, 1978) and on the strategies of minorities in urban politics (Keech, 1968; Kirby, Harris, Crain, and Rossell, 1973; Lipsky, 1970; Mollenkopf, 1983).

We then look at the connection between minority political incorporation and policy responsiveness. Did an increase in minority access to city government result in changes in policy, in the kinds of decisions made in city hall? Did policies become more responsive to the interests of minorities? We assess the relative importance of political variables like minority incorporation for policy responsiveness and the effects of the implementation of federal social programs. In doing so, we address hypotheses in the policy-determinants literature about the importance of socioeconomic and bureaucratic factors in shaping policy (Jones, 1980; Karnig and Welch, 1980; Lineberry, 1977). We also provide evidence about the implementation and effects of federal programs (Greenstone and Peterson, 1973; Mazmanian and Sabatier, 1980; Pressman and Wildavsky, 1979; Williams, 1980b).

Study Design

The analysis is based on a unique combination of time-series data; surveys of officials, activists, and other knowledgeable informants; and historical research. The combination of techniques, the long time span, and the comparison of two minority groups in ten cities increase the usefulness and validity of the findings.

The intensiveness of the empirical work required by our comparative, longitudinal design, including the collection of data over time on many indicators, made it necessary to limit the number of cities to ten. By selecting cities in the same region and state, we control for some structural and political variables. With some variation, all are cities in the reform tradition with nonpartisan elections, city managers, and professional civil service systems. They share the same state political, fiscal, and legal context, thus controlling for the range of functional responsibilities undertaken by local government (except for San Francisco, a combined city and county). They were selected on the variables of city size, percent black, and percent Hispanic. Six were the largest northern California cities in 1970 (San Francisco, San Jose, Oakland, Sacramento, Berkeley, and Stockton). The other four (Richmond, Vallejo, Daly City, and Hayward) were those with the largest black and Hispanic populations among cities with more than 60,000 population.

The choice of cities is not a probability sample; therefore, it is not possible to generalize our findings to all American cities in a simple and direct way. However, the ten cities are illustrative of a certain type of city—cities with 50,000 inhabitants or more and with substantial black and/or Hispanic populations. [7] Intensive study of this purposive sample designed to reduce variation on some factors has enhanced our ability to penetrate behind the gross variables used in large sample studies. We are thus able to analyze political phenomena that are causally much closer to the changes under study, and in this way to develop a fuller understanding of the political processes at work. We think these processes are common to many cities and that our theory and method will be useful for understanding minority group mobilization and political incorporation in many settings.

[7] In 1970 there were 421 U.S. cities with 50,000 or more inhabitants. Approximately 100 of these cities were in each of four geographical regions: the Northeast, North Central, South, and West. Council manager forms of government existed in 224 of these cities. At least 175 of these 421 cities had 10 percent or more black or Hispanic populations. (This is a rough estimate using *1970 Census of Population, General Population Characteristics*, U.S. Summary, table 66.) Our ten cities rank among the largest 266 cities in the United States (U.S. Department of Commerce, Bureau of the Census, *County and City Data Book, 1977*, pp. 804–809, table A-4). In 1975 San Francisco was 16th largest and Vallejo was 266th largest. So our cities are in the upper two-thirds of U.S. cities with 50,000 or more inhabitants. Our cities also rank among those with the largest black populations; 5 of the cities are in the 100 cities with the largest black populations in the United States with Oakland ranking 16th and San Jose ranking 97th (U.S. Department of Commerce, Bureau of the Census, *Data User News*, October 1981). In sum, our cities are not a sharply atypical group of cities in terms of size and percent minority.

The findings are based on both microlevel and aggregate data: 80 structured elite interviews, 300 semistructured interviews, city council election results over a twenty-year period, city budgets and employment figures, program data, newspaper clippings, and aggregate level demographic and fiscal data.[8] The combination of aggregate and microlevel data enables us to develop theory that is finer grained and more political than the findings of large sample studies and yet broader and more general than those emanating from individual case studies.

Organization of the Book

The first part of the book examines the political incorporation of blacks and Hispanics into city politics—the extent to which they have achieved not only representation but positions of influence in local policy making. Chapter 1 discusses changes in minority representation and incorporation, and the preconditions for successful incorporation, stressing the importance of coalitions. Chapter 2 presents historical case studies to illustrate four distinctive patterns—biracial electoral alliance, cooptation, protest and exclusion, and weak minority mobilization. Chapter 3 elaborates on the interpretations introduced in chapters 1 and 2 by systematically analyzing and statistically testing propositions about the conditions that produced significant mobilization and incorporation.

The second part of the book explores the effects of minority political incorporation on the policy responsiveness of city governments. Chapter 4 looks at minority-oriented policies, including police review boards, minority contracting, and commission appointments, to see how they have been influenced by variations between cities in the incorporation of blacks and Hispanics. Chapter 5 examines one form of policy responsiveness, the employment of minorities in city government at all levels and at the top levels.

In the final section of the book chapter 6 considers the implementation and effects of federal programs on minority mobilization and incorporation and on policy responsiveness.

[8]Appendix B describes the data in detail.

Chapter 7 summarizes the findings, discusses their significance for theory and practice, and speculates about future trends. Can we expect continued strengthening of the political position of minorities? What happens to blacks and Hispanics after they have achieved incorporation in local political systems? What are the implications of a new era of fiscal constraint and a much less beneficent federal government?

PART ONE

The Political Incorporation of Blacks and Hispanics

1

Representation and Incorporation: The Importance of Coalitions

Andrew Young: ". . . It's like the old preacher says: We ain't what we oughta be; we ain't what we're gonna be; but thank God we ain't what we was." (Bass and DeVries, 1976)

Tom McCain: "There's an inherent value in office-holding that goes far beyond picking up the garbage. A race of people who are excluded from public office will always be second class." (American Civil Liberties Union, *Civil Liberties*, 1981)

It is all too easy to forget how serious the problem of political inequality was in American cities in the early 1960s and then to jump to the conclusion that whatever inequalities did exist in urban politics have since been solved. Such lapses of memory and selective perception can contribute to dangerous complacency and to unpleasant surprises when new cycles of protest and upheaval occur.

Minority groups were almost totally excluded from city politics in the early 1960s. Much progress toward political equality has been made since then; however, there were great differences among the cities in the rate of progress, and there remain great differences in the extent of the achievement. In this chapter we first document the increase of minority representation on city councils from the early 1960s to the end of the 1970s. However, although essential and of potentially great value, representation may produce little or no influence over public policy. The second section of the chapter, therefore, presents findings on what we call "political incorporation" of minority groups, a dimension more closely related to influence in policy making. Incorporation refers not only to representation but also to the position of minority representatives vis-à-vis the dominant coalition on the city council. We trace changes in minority incorporation between 1960 and the late 1970s, highlighting differences in the political incorporation of blacks and Hispanics and comparing cities.

In the rest of the chapter we analyze three bases for minority mobilization and incorporation: the growth of minority populations, new Democratic majorities among voters and on councils, and electoral support for minority interests. We show that the incorporation of blacks and Hispanics into city government was inextricably bound up with the replacement of conservative coalitions by liberal challenging coalitions. But in several cities conservative dominant coalitions were not replaced by liberal ones, and minority groups did not achieve any incorporation in some cities and attained only low levels of incorporation in others. Liberal coalitions that overthrew conservative predecessors were invariably Democratic, but not all Democratic majorities were liberal on issues of race.

When liberal coalitions that included minority leaders successfully challenged hitherto dominant conservative groups, policy process and content changed significantly in favor of minority interests. Dramatic strengthening of the minority position in these cities was almost always linked to a shift in dominant coalitions. In short, the incorporation of minority interests was accompanied by the rise of liberal coalitions that included whites as well as minorities.

Evidence of the impact of newly dominant liberal coalitions in which minorities played significant roles was overwhelming. At its strongest, the incorporation of minority interests brought with it pervasive changes in the attitudes and behavior of city officials and in the policies and responsiveness of city governments. Although the strength of minority groups and the influence of minority leaders varied greatly from city to city (and remained near zero in several), liberal coalitions in which minorities were less prominent also brought about changes. The combination of minority incorporation and the replacement of conservative dominant coalitions by more liberal ones proved to be a potent force. This major finding of our research is documented at length in the following chapters.

Minority Representation on Councils, 1960–80

The most widely used indicator of a group's position in a political system is the presence of members of that group in elective offices. On that measure, minority representation on city councils in 1960 was zero in every one of our ten cities.

Although the mean minority population in the ten cities was 18.9 percent in 1960, and more than half of the cities had over 20 percent minority population, there were no minority councilmembers in any of the cities. Photographs of councils around 1960 reveal homogeneous groups of middle-aged white men with short hair—the stereotype of the small businessman, which they typically were.

The exclusion of minorities from councils was reflected in the composition of all city government personnel. Longtime city employees, asked to estimate the number of blacks and Hispanics employed by their cities in the early sixties, invariably counted on their fingers—"Let's see, there was Jane, and Jim . . ." —citing names because minority employees were so rare that each one was remembered clearly. One participant in Berkeley politics recalls that in the fifties "one could walk the length and breadth" of the main commercial streets and "scarcely encounter a single minority group employee." In city government, apart from the refuse collection department, there were virtually no minority group employees. Even in the minority neighborhoods, the schools had very few black and Hispanic teachers (Gordon, 1978, p. 273).

Starting from zero, minority representation took off in the 1960s, but not in every city. By the late 1970s minority councilmembers had been elected in seven of the ten cities, and in six of these they held two or more council seats; in two cities, a minority candidate was elected to the mayor's office. Figure 1 shows trends in average minority population and representation from 1960 to 1978. Overall, minority population rose steadily, but minority representation increased even more, in spite of the slight decline at the end of the period.

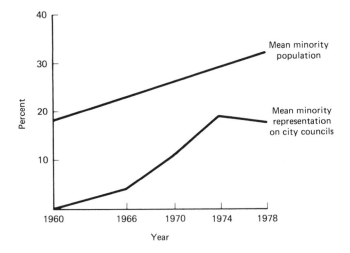

FIGURE 1   Trends in Minority Population and Representation. (Ten cities, means for four-year periods ending in indicated years)

By 1978 the mean minority population was 32.1 percent with 17.6 percent representation, which yields a mean parity ratio of .55. Parity ratios measure the extent of group representation on a council relative to the size of the group in the population and thus measure one aspect of political equality; a ratio of .55 indicates that average minority representation on councils was 55 percent of the average percent minority of city population.[1] This is a dramatic improvement; nevertheless, table 1

[1]The parity ratio is calculated by dividing the proportion of a group on a council by the proportion of that group in the population. It is most meaningful when the group comprises a sizeable proportion of the population and the governmental entity being analyzed is large. When dealing with city councils of five to twelve members, as in table 1, one must interpret the parity ratio with caution because large ratio changes may result from the election or defeat of only a single minority person.

TABLE 1 Minority, Black, and Hispanic Representation on City Councils, 1975–78

City	Size of city council	Minority parity ratio	Blacks Population %	Blacks Representation on city council %	Blacks Parity ratio	Hispanics Population %	Hispanics Representation on city council %	Hispanics Parity ratio
Berkeley	9	1.52	20.8	38.8	1.87	4.8	0	0
Stockton	9	1.10	10.6	22.2	2.09	21.1	11.1	.53
San Francisco	12	.68	12.9	8.3	.64	11.8	8.3	.70
Richmond	7	.61	45.4	27.8	.61	9.5	5.6	.59
Sacramento	9	.60	12.9	11.1	.86	14.8	5.6	.38
San Jose	7	.57	4.3	0	0	20.7	14.3	.69
Oakland	9	.42	44.3	16.7	.38	9.0	5.5	.61
Vallejo	7	0	18.5	0	0	7.6	0	0
Daly City	5	0	9.8	0	0	17.9	0	0
Hayward	7	0	4.9	0	0	19.0	0	0
Mean		.55	18.4	12.5	.65	13.6	5.0	.35

NOTE: Size of and representation on city councils include mayoral positions and their occupants. The three parity ratios are ratios of percent minority of city council (mean, 1975–78) to percent minority of city population (1978, linearly interpolated from 1970 and 1980 data), for blacks and Hispanics combined and separately.

shows that underrepresentation was still a problem. With minority populations of at least 23 percent in all of these cities, three still had no representation in the late 1970s, and in all but two, representation fell substantially short of parity with population. Acknowledgment of the increases in minority representation must not be taken to mean that problems of underrepresentation or no representation have been eliminated.

Even with strong minority representation in some cities, the total number of minority people elected to city council and mayoral positions was not large. Of a total of 223 newly elected officeholders in all ten cities from 1961 to 1977, 32 (14 percent) were blacks or Hispanics. This amounted to an average of 3.2 per city, or 3.6 per city in the nine cities where any minority candidates won election. To be sure, these were not the only minority officeholders; minority candidates also won state legislative seats and positions on county boards of supervisors, boards of education, and boards of community colleges and other special districts. The 30 minority councilmembers and 2 mayors also represent far more than thirty-two terms in office. Many minority officeholders served for more than one term, minority incumbents won reelection at approximately the same rate as white incumbents (80 percent), and length of time in office was also similar. These are further indications of the strength of minority representation.

The changes in minority representation on councils that took place between 1960 and 1980 in our ten cities can be vividly symbolized by three individuals: Lionel Wilson in Oakland, Joe Serna in Sacramento, and Ralph White in Stockton. In the early sixties all three were outside city hall in the vanguard of efforts to improve the status of minorities by pressuring city government. By 1980 they were all inside city hall, all much closer to being "the establishment" than seemed possible twenty years earlier.

MINORITY REPRESENTATION—THREE CAREERS:

Lionel Wilson, black mayor of Oakland. Grew up in Berkeley, recalls having to fight for the right to play tennis on public courts. Lawyer. Appointed to Oakland Municipal Court in 1961, then elevated to Alameda County Superior

Court. Accepted appointment as Chairman of the Board of Oakland Community Action Agency in 1964. Ran for mayor in 1977 and won.

Joe Serna, Hispanic councilmember, Sacramento. Student at Sacramento State University in late 1960s, leader of Chicano organizing efforts focusing on poverty programs, protest activity, and local elections. In 1970s political associate of the mayor and member of the Housing and Redevelopment Commission. Elected to city council in 1981.

Ralph White, black councilmember, Stockton. In 1960s a militant leader standing outside city hall, threatening to burn it down. By 1980, completing almost a decade as councilmember.

Blacks achieved significantly higher levels of representation than Hispanics. A very high proportion of the blacks in the ten cities gained representation on city councils: 93 percent lived in cities with at least one black councilmember in 1980 (all cities except Daly City, Hayward, and Vallejo). Most of the Hispanics (77 percent) also lived in cities with a Hispanic representative on city council—Sacramento, San Jose, San Francisco, and Stockton. Black representation was much closer to the proportion of blacks in the population than Hispanic representation was to the proportion of Hispanics. Table 1 shows that blacks had a mean parity ratio of .65 in 1978, Hispanics only .35. Two of the seven cities with black populations larger than 10 percent were above parity, and three more were at least halfway to it in 1978. The addition of one councilmember in these cities would put them approximately at parity. However, none of the six cities with more than 10 percent Hispanic population was at parity, and three of the six had no Hispanic councilmembers.

The growth in minority representation, the difference between black and Hispanic representation, and the continuing underrepresentation of both groups in these ten cities are all very typical of patterns found throughout the country. For example, in 1976 blacks constituted 23.2 percent of the population in large American cities and had achieved a parity ratio of .50 (Robinson and Dye, 1978). Nationally the number of black officials has more than tripled from 1970 to 1980, but they still accounted for less than 1 percent of the elected officials in the United States, even though blacks constituted more than 11 percent of the nation's population. And the rate of increase has slowed to 8.6 percent per year in 1983 from a high of 27 percent in 1971 (Joint Center, 1980; *New York Times*, Jan. 9, 1984). Typically blacks hold more elected seats and have reached higher parity levels than Hispanics. In California, where Hispanics constituted 19.2 percent of the population and blacks constituted 7.7 percent, blacks held eight seats in the state legislature and three seats in Congress in 1979, whereas Hispanics held six seats in the state legislature and one in Congress (Henry, 1980, p. 7). In the United States Hispanics held only 2.2 percent of all elected city and county government positions in the early 1970s (Garcia and de la Garza, 1977, p. 109). In 1980 there was only one Hispanic big city mayor, but blacks were mayors in such large cities as Detroit, Atlanta, New Orleans, and Washington, D.C. In Los Angeles, which had 18 percent Hispanics and 18 percent blacks, the mayor and three councilmembers were black, but there were no Hispanic members (Henry, 1980). By 1982 Los Angeles had 28 percent Spanish-surnamed population but still no Hispanic councilmembers (*California Journal*, Sept. 1982).

Representation or Incorporation? — A Significant Difference

Although representation of minority persons on councils is clearly an important indicator of a group's position in the political system and is used frequently (Karnig and Welch, 1980), it is only one of many possible indicators. We emphasize two other aspects of political equality: the *policy responsiveness* of government and the degree of *incorporation* of minority groups into the political system. Changes in both of these dimensions increase the probability of outcomes favorable to the interests of minority populations. Policy responsiveness, which is the focus of the second part of the book, refers to changes in city government policies that respond to minority interests. It is responsiveness to the interest of minority groups in the distribution of benefits. Incorporation may be thought of as the responsiveness of the system to the interest of inclusion and substantial authority and influence.[2]

The concept of political incorporation concerns the extent to which group interests are effectively represented in policy making. We measure the political incorporation of black and Hispanic minorities by assessing the extent to which they were represented in coalitions that dominated city policy making on minority-related issues.[3] Our reliance on this measure, rather than on representation alone, stems from our observation that identifiable coalitions typically controlled city policy on issues of central concern to minority groups and that participation in such a dominant coalition produced more important changes in government policy than simple representation did. Minority roles in dominant coalitions determined coalition commitment to minority interests.[4]

The measure of political incorporation is a scale based on three elements of minority position on the city council: the number of minority councilmembers, minority participation in the dominant coalition, and minority control of the mayor's office (table 2). The lowest value on the scale is zero—no minority representation on city council. Scores of one or two points were assigned for minority representation on city council but not in the dominant coalition. Higher scores were assigned if minority representatives were part of the dominant coalition. The highest values depend on factors that are, we hypothesize, related to the prominence of the minority role in the dominant coalition and, therefore, to minority influence in policy making: the number of minority councilmembers in the

[2]This distinction between incorporation and responsiveness is similar to Gamson's delineation of two successful outcomes of group mobilization, acceptance and new advantages (Gamson, 1975, pp. 28–37; see also Crain, 1968 and Coleman, 1971).

[3]Our use of the term *incorporation* and the focus on coalitions were stimulated by Stinchcombe (1968, pp. 177–78). Hinckley (1981) also argues the centrality of coalitions.

[4]By *coalition*, we refer to a wide range of joint actions between councilmembers, ranging from mere voting alliances—groups of councilmembers who typically voted together on a set of issues—to groups of councilmembers who deliberately worked together in election campaigns and on the council. We

TABLE 2   Scale of Minority Political Incorporation

Level of incorporation: minority group position in city council		Scale values[a]	Hypothesized minority influence in policy making
High			*Strong*
	Minority control of mayor's office		
Minority representation on city council and participation in dominant coalition		5 – 9	
	Several minority members		
	1 – 2 minority members	3 – 4	
Minority representation on city council but not in dominant coalition		1 – 2	
No minority representation on city council		0	
Low			*Weak*

[a]Observed in these cities, 1960 – 80. See appendix C – 1 for scoring procedure.

dominant coalition and minority control of the mayor's office. To illustrate, in a city council of nine (including the mayor), a coalition of five members could dominate on minority issues. If minority representatives on the council not only participate in the dominant coalition but also occupy the mayor's office, this indicates a strong minority position in the dominant coalition

consider council coalitions only in regard to minority-related issues involving potentially redistributive policies in areas such as employment, housing, community development, social services, and police protection, which have typically been salient for minority groups. We do not attempt to characterize council coalitions in other policy areas that may involve different coalition structures in some cities.

Council coalitions on minority-related issues varied widely in their stability, cohesiveness, and control over policy. Despite this diversity and the conventional wisdom about the absence of coalitions in reform politics, respondents typically had no difficulty identifying coalitions that voted together on minority issues and the coalition that was usually able to shape policy. (See appendix C, table 1A for documentation of this point.) Our definition of coalitions is more inclusive than Eulau and Prewitt's (1973).

and in policy making. (Seven points would be assigned for this set of conditions. Development, rationale, and application of all measures are explained fully in appendix C.)

Political incorporation is central to our analysis. It encompasses the notion of representation but adds other factors that better reflect minority access to city government and influence within it. As Karnig and Welch say (1980, p. 116), "Black influence on the council is not . . . necessarily proportionate to number" or percentage of black representatives on councils. We show in part II of this book that political incorporation is the better indicator of minority influence in city government policy making.

Dominant coalitions that explicitly included minorities always took at least moderately liberal positions, sympathetic to some redistribution of resources to minorities. Conservative coalitions, those that resisted the redistribution of resources to minorities, never had minority members. (Our use of the terms liberal and conservative with respect to city council ideologies is explained in appendix C-2.)

A group that has achieved substantial political incorporation has taken a major step toward political equality. It is in a position to articulate its interests, its demands will be heard, and through the dominant coalition it can ensure that certain interests will be protected, even though it may not win on every issue. The group will have successfully opened the system and gained the kind of ability to make its interests prevail that other groups have already achieved.[5]

Minority Incorporation, 1960 – 80

In order to compare cities and trace shifts in minority incorporation over time, we assigned scores on the incorporation scale to each city for each year between 1960 and 1980 for blacks, for Hispanics, and for the two groups combined. The trend line in

[5] Arguing that equality is "the most powerful idea of our time," Rae (1981, p. 19), deftly explicates the multiple meanings of that idea. Minority claims for political equality are what Rae calls bloc-regarding claims, "a claim of equality for two or more subject classes, equality being required between these classes (blocs) but not within them" (p. 43). We do not address the issue of what full

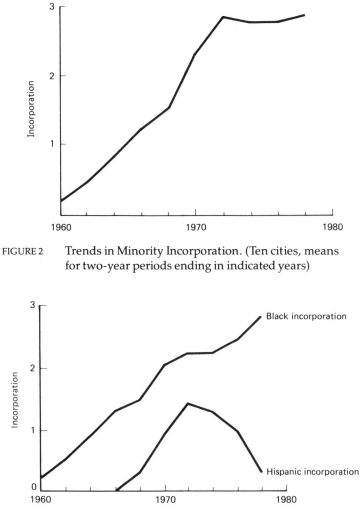

FIGURE 2   Trends in Minority Incorporation. (Ten cities, means
for two-year periods ending in indicated years)

FIGURE 3   Trends in Black and Hispanic Incorporation. (Ten cities,
means for two-year periods ending in indicated years)

political equality for minorities would entail, but we consider generally that
minority mobilization and incorporation as well as governmental responsiveness are relevant to it and that blacks and Hispanics began this period with
very low status relative to the white majority.

figure 2 shows a marked increase in minority incorporation between 1960 and 1980. The average level of minority incorporation in the late 1970s was much higher than in 1960, paralleling the increase in minority representation noted earlier. Incorporation rose steadily between 1960 and 1972, rising most rapidly between 1968 and 1972 and leveling off thereafter.

Figure 3 shows that the trends for average black and Hispanic incorporation were significantly different. Black incorporation started earlier, continued to grow steadily throughout almost the whole period, and reached higher levels. Hispanic incorporation started later and, after an initial rise, fell during the 1970s. By 1978 it was down to the low levels of the mid-1960s. Before 1972 Hispanic incorporation lagged six or seven years behind black incorporation on the average. After 1972 Hispanic incorporation deviated markedly from the black pattern, exhibiting a decline that became progressively steeper toward the end of the decade. Eighty-two percent of the black population as a whole lived in cities where black councilmembers were more or less clearly incorporated into a liberal dominant coalition: Berkeley, Oakland, Richmond, Sacramento, and San Francisco. But only 32 percent of the Hispanics lived in cities where Hispanic councilmembers were part of the dominant coalition at some point in the period 1976–80 (Sacramento, San Francisco).

Table 3 indicates the levels of incorporation achieved in each city by 1978. The highest levels were reached in Berkeley and Oakland; black mayors in both cities were leaders of liberal dominant coalitions. Vallejo, Daly City, and Hayward had the lowest levels of minority incorporation; in 1978 blacks and Hispanics were not represented on their councils. In three cities minority councilmembers participated in more or less liberal dominant coalitions; in two, they sat on the city council, but conservative dominant coalitions stayed in control.

Whereas black councilmembers or mayors in five cities had roles in liberal dominant coalitions, Hispanics in 1978 held such positions in only one city, San Francisco (and that seat was lost in 1979 and not regained as of 1983). Earlier in the seventies Hispanics held council seats in Oakland, Richmond, and Sacramento as well, but they had lost those positions by 1978. (The Sacramento seat was regained in 1981.)

TABLE 3   Minority, Black, and Hispanic Incorporation in Ten City Councils, 1978

| City | | Incorporation scores | | |
		Minority (blacks and Hispanics combined)	Blacks	Hispanics
Minority control of mayor's office	Berkeley	7	7	0
	Oakland	6	6	0
Several minority councilmembers in dominant coalition	Richmond	5	5	0
1–2 minority councilmembers in dominant coalition	San Francisco	4	3	3
	Sacramento	3	3	0
Minority representation on city council but not in dominant coalition	Stockton	2	2	1
	San Jose	1	0	1
No minority representation on city council	Hayward	0	0	0
	Daly City	0	0	0
	Vallejo	0	0	0

SOURCE: See text and appendix C-1 for scoring procedure.

The Bases for Incorporation:
Minorities, Democrats, Liberals

The trends in incorporation just described resulted from minority mobilization that took place in diverse demographic and political contexts. For mobilization and incorporation the most important contextual factors were the growth of minority populations, new Democratic majorities among voters and on councils, and electoral support for minority interests.

The Growth of Minority Populations

The migration of large numbers of minority people into these cities was, of course, a necessary condition for the surge of minority political mobilization in the sixties and subsequent incorporation: first blacks, mainly from the South, during and after World War II; then Hispanics, mainly Mexican Americans, in a wave starting in the fifties and sixties. Although the great bulk of this population movement took place after 1940, small black populations (3,000−9,000) and the beginnings of a black middle class and black political leadership were already in place in several of the cities before 1940—in Berkeley, San Francisco, and Oakland in particular.

The growth of minority populations was extremely rapid in some cities. Richmond went from 1 percent black in 1940 to 48 percent in 1980, Oakland from 3 percent to 47 percent over the same period. But although black populations grew rapidly in most of these cities, the period of explosive growth had ended by the 1970s in some cities and the black population actually declined slightly in San Francisco, Berkeley, and Stockton, according to census data. Simultaneously, smaller cities with very small black populations in 1970, such as Daly City and Hayward, began to experience rapid growth in their black populations.

Hispanics tended to concentrate in different cities than blacks. Whereas black populations concentrated in Oakland, San Francisco, Richmond, and Berkeley, all with stable or declining populations by 1970, Hispanics tended to concentrate in cities that experienced very rapid growth overall in the 1970s—San Jose, Stockton, and Daly City. In San Francisco both groups were large in numbers but modest in percentage terms (12–13 percent) by 1980. As proportions of total city population, Hispanic groups increased in size in every city between 1970 and 1980. (See appendix A for city-by-city data.)

An obvious factor in the greater incorporation of blacks into city governments was the greater size of black populations, in three respects. First, the immigration of blacks had started earlier, therefore sizeable black populations had been in place for a longer period of time by the 1960s. Leadership, mobilization, and organization are facilitated by time. A population recently arrived and preoccupied with settling in is not likely to mobilize itself immediately. Studies of individual political activity show substantial relationships with length of time in place (Milbrath, 1965).

Second, black populations were larger than Hispanic populations throughout this period, on the average. Blacks were 15.6 percent of city population in 1970, Hispanics 10.6; in 1980 blacks constituted an average 19.2 percent, Hispanics 14.4 percent. Thus in terms of average percentage of city population, Hispanics were perhaps twelve to thirteen years behind blacks.

Furthermore, the distribution of the black population favored stronger political mobilization by blacks. To the extent that a group's percentage of city population is an indicator of potential strength, blacks were stronger than Hispanics because blacks were more heavily concentrated in a few cities, whereas Hispanics were more evenly dispersed over the ten cities. This is readily seen in figure 4. The graphs compare the distributions of black populations in 1970 with Hispanic populations in 1980, when average percentages over the ten cities were about equal. Clearly black population percentages were more likely to be very large or very small. In no city did Hispanics in 1980 even approach the larger black population sizes of 1970, in spite of similar average size.

Whatever the differences in the distribution of blacks and Hispanics, it is clear that by 1970 there were substantial minority populations in all of these cities. In no city was there less than 17 percent minority population (black and Hispanic) in 1970; the average was 26 percent. If size were the only criterion, this was surely enough to support substantial political roles in every city,

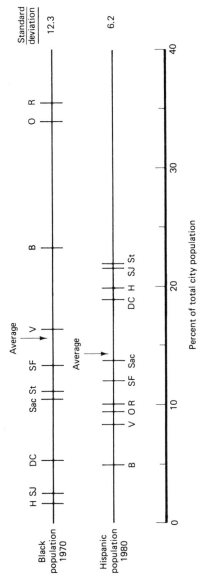

FIGURE 4   Distributions of Black and Hispanic Populations

(B = Berkeley; DC = Daly City; H = Hayward; O = Oakland; R = Richmond;
Sac = Sacramento; SF = San Francisco; SJ = San Jose; St = Stockton; V = Vallejo)

but not enough in any city to control city government without a coalition with other segments of the population.

(The reader who insists on knowing immediately the answer to the obvious question about the importance of minority population relative to other factors may turn to chapter 3, where such questions are answered with a cross-sectional statistical analysis. Here and in chapter 2 we describe the actors who struggled to achieve and to prevent minority incorporation and the diverse patterns of mobilization and incorporation they produced between 1960 and 1980. The analysis of chapter 3 condenses an enormous amount of political organization and conflict into a few numbers; the preliminary analyses and historical descriptions of chapters 1 and 2 provide essential grounding for them, indeed establish their meaning.)

The New Democratic Majorities

As minority populations were growing to a point where they could be potent forces in city politics, so too was Democratic strength increasing in local electorates. And at the same time the civil rights movement was building momentum nationally in the 1950s and 1960s, Democrats in the ten cities were moving to capitalize on Democratic majorities among voters. In these formally nonpartisan cities the party affiliation of voters and candidates remained important, even though it did not appear on local ballots.

Table 4 shows the dramatic change in the partisan composition of council and mayoral offices in our ten cities from 1962 to 1977. In the early 1960s Republicans constituted a majority on half the city councils, even though majorities of the voters in every city were Democrats. In 1962 registered Democrats constituted, on the average, 40 percent of the councilmembers and 63 percent of the voters. By 1977 Democratic registration of councilmembers and mayors had shot up 40 points to an average 80 percent, even though Democratic voter registration had increased only seven points to 70 percent. In short, the so-called Republican bias of nonpartisan elections appears to have been overcome and reversed in these ten cities over the last two decades (Hawley, 1973; Lee, 1960). As one respondent explained, "We have nonpartisan elections of Democrats."

TABLE 4   Changes in Partisan Composition of Council and Mayoral Offices

Cities	Percent Democratic officeholders[a] 1962	1977	Percentage points difference, 1962–77	Percent Democratic voter registration[b] 1962	1977	Percentage points difference, 1962–77
All cities (mean)	40	80	+40	63	70	+ 7
Berkeley	56	100	+44	53	73	+20
Daly City	60	80	+20	66	70	+ 4
Hayward	14	86	+72	67	67	0
Oakland	11	67	+56	60	71	+11
Richmond	56	56	0	71	79	+ 8
Sacramento	56	89	+33	63	68	+ 5
San Francisco	58	83	+25	62	77	+15
San Jose	29	86	+57	55	58	+ 3
Stockton	22	100	+78	61	64	+ 3
Vallejo	38	57	+19	73	74	+ 1

[a]Councilmembers and mayors; party registration was determined from voter lists at the offices of county registrars of voters.
[b]California Secretary of State, *Report of Registration, 1962–1977* (Sacramento, 1978).

Local Democratic officeholders were not necessarily linked to Democratic party organizations, which varied in strength from city to city. Nevertheless, Democratic councilmembers were commonly supported by local liberal Democrats and by Democratic clubs, labor unions, minority organizations, and other liberal elements; and they were, on the average, more liberal on minority issues than their predecessors.

Averages, to be sure, conceal variation. The rise of Democratic majorities in every city did not bring liberal coalitions to power in every city council. In Vallejo and Daly City the shift to Democratic majorities did not appreciably alter the ideological stance of city government on minority issues. Democrats opposed to redistributive programs controlled city councils in these cities and were prominent in others. Individual Democratic councilmembers in many cities were as conservative as their Republican colleagues, and some of the more liberal coalitions that took control of city councils demonstrated distinctly limited commitment to minority concerns.

Still, all the successful challenges by liberal coalitions were led by liberal Democrats, and all received significant electoral support from minority groups. They differed in the timing of coalition formation in relation to the development of minority political effort, and in the extent of minority participation.

Liberal Support for Minority Interests

Just as a Democratic majority in a city's electorate was a necessary condition for a new Democratic majority on city council, so too some degree of support for the interests of minority groups by liberal whites was a prerequisite for the formation of coalitions with explicit minority participation.

We found that city votes on a 1964 statewide ballot proposition, Proposition 14, provided a revealing and useful measure of electoral support for antidiscriminatory policies and other programs intended to benefit the black minority. Proposition 14, which passed statewide, was an initiative that amended the state constitution to repeal the Rumford Act, which had prohibited racial discrimination in housing built with public assistance, and to prevent the state or any locality from adopting fair housing legislation.[6]

Proposition 14 was widely understood to be antiblack. We take the percentage voting no on Proposition 14 in a city to be an indicator of electoral support for black interests. The cities varied widely on opposition to Proposition 14, from 27 percent in Hayward to 65 percent in Berkeley. From this figure we also estimate the support of white liberals for black interests: the percent voting no on Proposition 14 minus the percent black of the total voting-age population in the city in 1964.[7] There was wide variation on this measure of white support as well—from 19 percent in Vallejo to 57 percent in Berkeley, taken as percentages of the white adult population, or 16 and 46 percent of total adult population.

The Replacement of Conservative Coalitions

To sum up the evidence to this point, this was how things stood in 1960:

[6]Wolfinger and Greenstein (1968). Proposition 14 was subsequently declared unconstitutional by the U.S. Supreme Court. Unfortunately, we have no parallel measure of attitudes toward Hispanics. Proposition 14 was not seen as aimed at Hispanics, nor do the city votes on it show any substantial statistical association with Hispanic mobilization.

[7]The percent voting no on Proposition 14 has two components: black votes and nonblack votes. We take the percentage of blacks in the total voting-age population in a city (a linear interpolation between 1960 and 1970) as an indicator of the size of the black vote against Proposition 14. Subtracting that percentage from the total "no" vote yields the estimate of white opposition to Proposition 14, that is, of white support for black interests. The accuracy of the estimate rests on the assumption that blacks who cast ballots voted virtually 100 percent against Proposition 14 (not an unreasonable assumption, see Wolfinger and Greenstein, 1968) and that they turned out at about the same rate as whites on this issue. However, even if these assumptions are not fully met, the estimates probably still reflect reasonably well the differences between the cities in levels of white support for black interests. Strictly speaking, what for convenience we call "white support" is a measure of support by nonblacks, including Hispanics, Asians, Filipinos, and other groups. See also appendix C-5.

- substantial minority populations in every city but wide variation in their size and makeup;
- on minority-group issues, conservative coalitions in dominant positions in every city, and no minority representation in city government;
- Democratic majorities among registered voters in every city, but Republican majorities on councils in five cities;
- a continuing movement to elect Democratic majorities to city councils;
- substantial support for minority concerns among whites in some cities, much less in others.

And from across the land, a rising ferment—protest against injustice and a demand for political equality. As the civil rights movement gained momentum and spread to the ten cities, its progress was shaped by these conditions and the forces they represented.

The political incorporation of blacks and Hispanics was closely linked to the replacement of conservative coalitions by liberal challenging coalitions.[8] In which cities were conservative coalitions replaced first, and what explains why they were replaced much earlier in some cities than in others? Figure 5 shows the relationship between year of replacement of conservative coalitions and one of the factors at work: the degree of support for the interests of blacks reflected in the percentage of "no" votes on Proposition 14 in 1964. Figure 5 reads chronologically from bottom to top. In 1961 Berkeley became the first city in which a conservative Republican coalition was replaced. Conservative coalitions were not replaced in Vallejo, Daly City, and Stockton between 1960 and 1980, though Democrats achieved council majorities in all three cities.[9]

Overall the relationship between year of replacement and

---

[8]Many studies of minority politics emphasize the importance of coalitions. See Carmichael and Hamilton (1967).

[9]The placement of San Jose in figure 5 is ambiguous because a moderately liberal but very loose coalition held office for only four years, 1971–75, before succumbing to a concerted conservative effort to regain control (see chapter 2). Because San Jose's minority population is predominantly Hispanic, the "no" vote on Proposition 14 is not directly relevant in any case.

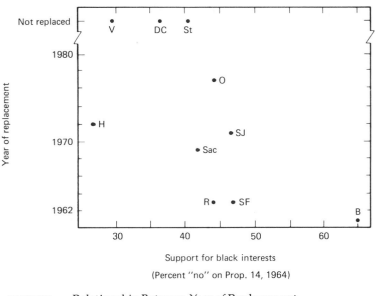

FIGURE 5   Relationship Between Year of Replacement
of Conservative Coalitions and Support for
Black Interests

(B = Berkeley; DC = Daly City; H = Hayward; O = Oakland; R = Richmond;
Sac = Sacramento; SF = San Francisco; SJ = San Jose; St = Stockton; V = Vallejo)

support for black interests is moderately strong. On the average, cities less supportive of the black position on Proposition
14 tended to replace conservative coalitions later or not at all.
Votes on Proposition 14 apparently did tap a dimension of lib-
eralism that was significant for the demise of conservative regimes during this period.

But support for the interests of blacks was not so critical for
some challenging coalitions as it was for others. In San Francisco, Richmond, and Hayward successful challenges were
mounted by coalitions that had no explicit minority participation in the sense of minority candidates on a coalition slate.
These were Democratic challenges led by whites and supported
by minority voters, but they were not explicitly biracial or multiethnic coalitions. In contrast, of the four other cities in which
conservative coalitions were replaced, three saw the formation
of coalitions in which minority candidates ran on coalition slates
from the outset: Berkeley, Sacramento, and Oakland.

What San Francisco, Richmond, and Hayward had in common was that formation of liberal challenging coalitions preceded (in San Francisco and Richmond) or avoided (Hayward) the wave of minority protest that swept through cities nationwide in the 1960s. The first concerted protest campaign in San Francisco—picketing against discrimination in private employment—began in early 1964, soon after Democratic Congressman John Shelley won election as mayor in 1963 (Wirt, 1974, p. 256); Richmond had had no protest. Neither Hayward's tiny (and relatively well-off) black population nor its Hispanic group had produced discernible protest at the time of the liberal challenge in 1972. In these cities, the demands of minority groups were still relatively muted when liberals challenged conservative dominance.

As protest and electoral mobilization by blacks spread in the sixties, it was highly likely that liberal challenges would be explicitly biracial or multiethnic from the start, and this was the case in Sacramento, Oakland, and Stockton. Minority protest, demands for representation, and electoral mobilization in these cities led to the formation of challenging coalitions with explicit minority participation. Minority leaders were no longer content simply to support liberal white candidates. Liberal whites had to have minority support to win, and given that minority populations, though growing, did not constitute majorities in any of the ten cities, they too had to enter into coalitions with liberal Democrats.

The rise of two distinct types of challenging coalitions suggests the importance of two dimensions of latent electoral support: for black interests and for Democrats. Taking the percent voting no on Proposition 14 in 1964 and the percent Democratic registration in 1962 as measures of these dimensions, a regression analysis shows that they had substantial and about equal impact on the replacement of conservative coalitions. On the average, cities higher by ten percentage points on either dimension replaced conservative coalitions six to seven years earlier.[10]

These attitudes and loyalties of local electorates that were already apparent early in this period explain rather well, then, why challenging coalitions formed when they did and why they were successful. Sufficient underlying electoral support for replacement was present early on in the cities where replacement occurred. This in turn suggests that replacement during the sixties and early seventies resulted primarily from the rapid development of the sense that conservative coalitions could be replaced in cities where latent support was already present, rather than from growth in latent support. Democratic coalitions capitalized on Democratic registration already in place, and minority-oriented coalitions arose most quickly and easily in cities where electoral support was already most clearly favorable and opposition least imposing. Substantial levels of minority population and support and of Democratic registration were more important than the relatively modest changes in these characteristics.

For the political incorporation of blacks and Hispanics, replacement of conservative coalitions was a pivotal event, and vice versa. To demonstrate this, figure 6 shows the relationship of minority incorporation in 1978 with the year in which conservative coalitions were replaced. Clearly year of replacement and the level of minority incorporation in 1978 were closely related.

[10]Considering only the seven cities in which conservative coalitions were actually replaced, $R^2 = .59$:

	b	t	$b\overline{X}$	beta
Percent no on 14 (1964)	$-.57$	-2.39	-25.6	-1.07
Percent Dem. registration (1962)	$-.70$	-1.67	-42.9	$-.75$
Constant	136.5	4.01		

The lower t and beta values for Democratic registration are the consequence of the smaller variance of that variable in this group of cities. See Achen (1982) on $b\overline{X}$, a measure of level-importance, and beta, the standardized regression coefficient, a measure of dispersion-importance of the independent variables. The independent variables are negatively related ($r = -.70$), apparently a consequence of the fact that cities with large white blue-collar populations tended to be high in Democratic registration but also not supportive of Proposition 14.

Oakland is a deviant case, replacing a conservative coalition eight years later than estimated by this equation; estimates for the other cities are all within four years of actual replacement; three are within one year.

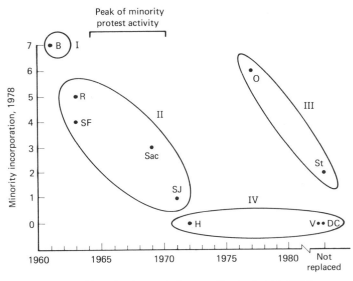

FIGURE 6   Minority Incorporation and Replacement of
Conservative Coalitions

(B = Berkeley; DC = Daly City; H = Hayward; O = Oakland; R = Richmond;
Sac = Sacramento; SF = San Francisco; SJ = San Jose; St = Stockton; V = Vallejo)

There are three implications of figure 6 (setting aside for the moment the indicated groupings, which form the basis for the discussion of evolutionary patterns in chapter 2). First, replacement of conservative coalitions was a necessary condition for *any* political incorporation of blacks and Hispanics in 1978, except in Stockton, where minorities achieved substantial representation but did not register a clear-cut overthrow of the conservative coalition. Second, replacement was followed by *some* sustained minority incorporation in every city except Hayward, where a Hispanic councilmember had left for a seat on the county board of supervisors, and Hispanics were unable to elect another member of their group. Finally, the earlier a coalition was replaced, the stronger minority incorporation was in 1978. Oakland obviously deviates from this pattern—strong incorporation by 1978 in spite of the fact that a conservative coalition hung on through most of the 1970s.

The implication is not that replacement of conservative coalitions explains the strength of minority incorporation in any simple cause-and-effect way; it is more accurate to see replacement and incorporation as related results of many of the same causal factors, as consequences of the unfolding of the same political forces. Furthermore, in the short run replacement and incorporation were themselves causally linked in both directions. Often minority participation in challenging coalitions was a prerequisite to replacement; in other cases, replacement led to minority incorporation, as liberal coalitions sought to co-opt minority groups in response to protest.

Whatever the linkage in different cities, figure 6 suggests that overall the structure of the forces connecting replacement and incorporation was quite stable over a decade or more, except for Oakland; incorporation in 1978 and the replacement of conservative coalitions, mostly much earlier, could not be so closely related otherwise.[11] This finding reinforces our judgment that differences between cities in the politically relevant characteristics of their populations were more important for replacement and incorporation than the amount of change in those dimensions.

Summary

Both blacks and Hispanics were totally excluded from representation on these ten city councils in 1960, but from 1961 on, their numbers among councilmembers increased rapidly. Blacks achieved considerably greater representation than Hispanics. Mere representation was not enough, however, and we have argued in this chapter that the political strength of minority groups is better indicated by their political incorporation—measured by the extent to which they participate in the dominant coalition in the city and by their ability to secure policy responsiveness to minority interests. For blacks and Hispanics

[11]For the cities in figure 6 where conservative coalitions were replaced, the linear correlation is −.38 including Oakland, −.95 excluding Oakland.

trends in political incorporation were very different. Black incorporation increased steadily; incorporation of Hispanics began later, never became as strong, and appeared to be receding as this period drew to a close.

The replacement of conservative coalitions by strong challenging liberal coalitions was a necessary condition for the strongest kinds of minority influence or incorporation in city government. Replacement in turn depended on Democratic initiatives in the presence of large Democratic electoral majorities, on the size of minority populations, and on the magnitude of white support for minority interests. The minority mobilization movement built upon decades of growth in minority populations—first blacks, then Hispanics—which continued to grow rapidly overall during the sixties and seventies (though black populations in several cities reached a plateau). Blacks were more concentrated in a few cities, Hispanics more widely dispersed. The mobilization of black people, then of Hispanics, arose in the midst of Democratic efforts already under way in local politics. Democrats had a majority of voter registration in every city, and Democratic politicians were attempting to replace Republican leadership in several cities even before the peak period of minority mobilization. Their efforts over the two decades were extremely successful. Whereas in 1962 Democrats had majorities on only five of the city councils, by the late seventies there were Democratic majorities on all the councils.

The magnitude of white support for minority interests was the third factor influencing the replacement of conservative coalitions. Cities less supportive of blacks tended to replace conservative coalitions later or not at all, but support for black interests was not important for all challenging coalitions. Early Democratic efforts in San Francisco and Richmond, for example, did not explicitly include minority leaders or minority candidates, nor did they make explicit policy commitments to minorities. Later liberal challenges were more likely to be explicitly biracial or multiethnic from the start—as in Sacramento, Oakland, and Stockton—and support for black interests was important to the outcomes.

There was also a close relationship between the year when conservative coalitions were replaced and the level of minority incorporation achieved. The earlier a coalition was replaced, the stronger minority incorporation was by the end of the period under study. Replacement and incorporation were the related results of the same political forces and were causally linked. Mobilization, replacement, and incorporation unfolded in diverse ways in the different cities.

There were several roads to minority incorporation, and some cities never reached that goal at all. In chapter 2 we will see that the ways in which minority mobilization and incorporation unfolded were critically shaped by the evolving strategies and relationships of minority and white leaders and by the rapidly changing temper of the times.

2

Processes of Incorporation, Co-optation, and Exclusion

The preceding chapter demonstrated the dramatic increases in minority representation and incorporation in liberal coalitions that occurred in the ten cities. It laid out the factors contributing to variations in the processes of mobilization and incorporation and gave particular attention to the replacement of conservative coalitions because that was the critical political development for minority incorporation.

In this chapter we look more closely at the historical processes associated with changes in incorporation as these processes unfolded in particular cities. The differences among the cities are as significant as the overall trends for an understanding of the struggle for political equality and the dynamics of urban policy and politics. Four different patterns of mobilization and incorporation are identified. Profiles of four cities are presented to illustrate these patterns. In recounting the stories of how incorporation was or was not accomplished, we specify when, how, and under what conditions minorities gained influence in local politics. We illustrate the way the factors introduced in the preceding chapter were operating in the flow of events, laying the basis for the statistical analysis of these factors and events in subsequent chapters.

Evolutionary Patterns of Mobilization and Incorporation

In chapter 1, figure 6 showed the relationship of minority incorporation to the replacement of conservative coalitions. The cities indicated in that figure fall into four groupings or types that display distinctive patterns of mobilization, participation in challenging and dominant coalitions, and levels of incorporation. Each pattern results from a dynamic interaction between the mobilization strategies of minorities and their allies and the responses of dominant coalitions to these strategies—the actions of outsiders and the reactions of insiders. Results achieved depend on both the initiatives taken by minorities and the responses of white supporters and opponents. The patterns identify the consequences of minority demand-protest and electoral strategies in various situations.

The types are:

1. *Biracial electoral alliance.* A liberal electoral coalition with strong minority participation is formed prior to the period of peak minority demand-protest 1965–72 and results in strong incorporation (Berkeley).

2. *Co-optation.* Electoral coalition led by whites with minorities in subordinate roles is formed prior to or during peak minority demand-protest. The resulting liberal dominant coalition is characterized by co-optative strategies and partial incorporation (San Francisco, Richmond, Sacramento, and San Jose, temporarily).

3. *Protest and exclusion.* Strong demand-protest is met by a tenacious, resistant dominant coalition. Prolonged intense conflict leads to varying electoral strategies and exclusion from dominant coalitions for some time. Replacement of a conservative dominant coalition was delayed in Oakland and prevented in Stockton, and only temporary in San Jose. Results for incorporation were varied.

4. *Weak minority mobilization.* Little or no concerted demand-protest activity and fragmented electoral effort is met by a resistant dominant coalition. Failure to achieve incorporation (Vallejo, Daly City, and Hayward).

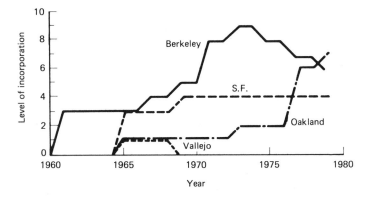

FIGURE 7   Patterns of Minority Incorporation in Four Cities,
1960–79

In the following sections we describe one city in each type in
some detail, the others more briefly. Figure 7 traces changes in
incorporation over time in the four cities whose patterns of mobilization and incorporation will be discussed in detail.

Biracial Electoral Alliance: Berkeley

Berkeley established a model for the peaceful and strong incorporation of blacks into city government—a model that was not
to be followed in other cities. As shown in figure 7, Berkeley
was characterized by a long series of cumulative increases in
the incorporation of blacks, beginning in the year when a liberal coalition simultaneously elected its minority candidate
and won a majority on the city council. A long-established alliance between liberal whites and blacks continued to produce
gains in incorporation throughout the sixties and early seventies. By the late seventies, though still strong, black incorporation had somewhat declined as black representation retreated
to levels approximating parity.

Consistent with Berkeley's international image as a city at
the "cutting edge of local policy and civic response to student
protest, national concerns about war and peace, civil rights, the

environment, and changes in lifestyles and political mores" (Nathan and Scott, 1978, p. xxi), stronger minority incorporation was achieved in Berkeley than in any other of these cities. Although the Free Speech Movement and People's Park are etched into the national memory as symbols of the sixties, less is known about the gradual incorporation of blacks into Berkeley city politics. And many do not realize that Berkeley has not always been dominated by liberal and progressive politics.

Berkeley has a substantial minority population—20.1 percent black but only 5.1 percent Hispanic of a total population of 103,328 in 1980. The socioeconomic characteristics of blacks are well above the mean of our ten cities. Although Berkeley's black population does have problems of low income and unemployment, it also has a long-standing middle-class base, and an unusually large professional and managerial stratum that in 1970 comprised 17.5 percent of the minority labor force.

Berkeley politics prior to the 1960s was neither liberal nor radical. For more than half a century prior to 1961 the city's politics was "dominated by a tightly knit Republican group, mostly downtown businessmen" (Gordon, 1978, p. 272; Kent, 1978, p. 73). During the twenties and thirties Berkeley was predominantly white middle class with a small but growing black minority.

The first efforts at black political organizing began in the 1930s—unusually early. A compilation of firsthand descriptions of Berkeley politics, *Experiment and Change in Berkeley* (Nathan and Scott, 1978), gives fascinating accounts of early black mobilization. Electoral efforts in the mid-thirties focused on increasing black voter turnout to demonstrate opposition to discrimination in public accommodation and employment. Picketing to "put economic pressure on the owners of stores" came together with unsuccessful efforts to elect blacks to the city council (Nathan and Scott, p. 10).

In the forties and fifties black political leaders centered their efforts on electoral mobilization. Blacks became active in the state Democratic party and were instrumental in selecting black delegates to the 1948 Democratic convention. In that year W. Byron Rumford became the first black elected to the California Assembly; he represented a district of predominantly black neighborhoods in north Oakland and south Berkeley. In 1948 also the first Black Caucus was formed in Berkeley, and black candidates for city offices were carefully screened. Rumford, a central figure in the effort, recalls

> We were able to establish the agreement that if one black candidate was selected by the caucus, the others would not run, since there would be white candidates in the field. More than one black candidate would practically insure the election of no black candidates. (Nathan and Scott, 1978, p. 133)

Such organizing by black Democrats formed a strong base for subsequent electoral success in the Berkeley-Oakland area, including the election of Ron Dellums to the Berkeley City Council in 1967 and to the U.S. Congress in 1970.

The ability to control black candidacies along with the recognition of the need to work with white liberals were two central elements that led to formulation of the biracial liberal coalition that ended Republican control of the city council in 1961. A third key element was the unusually strong support for minority concerns among the white electorate. Berkeley's population was very liberal on minority issues, as suggested by the fact that 65 percent of Berkeley voters opposed Proposition 14 in 1964; no other city registered as much as 50 percent in opposition to the measure. Thus when white Democrats in Berkeley began to organize to contest local elections in the 1950s, they were an unusually liberal group, eager for the political incorporation of blacks on grounds of principle. It may also have been fortunate for the cause of a biracial coalition that the Democratic edge in voter registration was very small in Berkeley. To achieve victory, a Democratic challenge absolutely had to have the enthusiastic participation of blacks.

The earlier alliance between blacks and whites grew out of Berkeley's long history of active political parties (Hawley, 1973). The surge of activism by Berkeley Democrats in the fifties stemmed in part from Adlai Stevenson's presidential campaign in 1952. Stevenson's campaign captured the imagination of liberals in the rapidly growing university community. One participant recalled "the feeling of hope and creativity that Adlai Stevenson inspired in me and millions of others in 1952. The Stevenson campaign created almost overnight a grassroots political movement" (Nathan and Scott, 1978, pp. 79–80). By

1955 the biracial Berkeley Democratic Caucus had been established. It too controlled and screened candidacies. "Caucus leaders were committed to the ideal of racial integration" (p. 82), and white and black leaders agreed to accept each other's candidates for a common slate. Although blacks on the liberal slate lost in 1955, 1957, and 1959, in 1961 the coalition both captured a majority of seats and elected the first black councilmember in Berkeley's history—Wilmont Sweeney—and the first in any of these ten cities.

Berkeley City Council in the sixties was dominated by this liberal Democratic majority. It appointed blacks to all boards and commissions and attempted to reduce residential racial segregation by initiating a fair housing ordinance (Nathan and Scott, 1978, pp. 90–92).[1] By 1969 three blacks were serving on the nine-member council.

By the mid-sixties city politics, both black and white, were affected by the confluence of events surrounding student protest, civil rights, and the war in Vietnam. The liberal coalition began to rupture. More radical coalitions were organized and fielded candidates opposed to the liberal Democratic caucus. Political leadership in the black community split over issues of black power. The issue had electoral and organizational ramifications because the forging of an alliance with white liberals or radicals was viewed by some black militants as inconsistent with black interests (Nathan and Scott, 1978, p. 121). Some, like Ronald Dellums, who was first elected with the support of both the liberal and the radical caucuses, represented a view that the issues of the war and civil rights were class rather than race issues. Others, though nominally willing to use the white, leftist coalition to get elected, were not willing to work with it once in office. The splits between and within the "moderate" and "progressive" factions, the Berkeley Democratic Club and Berkeley Citizens Action, characterized coalitional development in Berkeley during the seventies.

For a brief period in the early seventies, blacks held a majority of the council positions, including the office of mayor. The extremely conflictual rhetoric of one of the black councilmen,

---

[1]That ordinance was subsequently narrowly defeated by a referendum vote in the city, but the pro-black position on Proposition 14 was strongly supported in Berkeley (see chap. 1).

however, resulted in his recall. Subsequently, both electoral coalitions retreated to an equilibrium in which one of the four
council candidates on each slate in each election was black, and
slate candidates for mayor were also black. The effect was
gradually to reduce black representation from five to two out of
the nine seats—almost exactly the proportion black of the population—but including the position of mayor. (Although black
representation seemed to have reached a plateau at two out of
nine for some years, this was not a carefully controlled figure.
The election of November 1982 saw two new black councilmembers added to two black holdovers.)

The support by the majority of Berkeley residents for black
candidates and the deeply felt commitment to minority interests on the part of both moderate and more radical leadership
have resulted in a city government more responsive to programs for minorities than any other city in our study. By 1980
Berkeley had not only a black mayor but a black city manager
and the highest proportion of black department heads in our
ten cities.

The story of Berkeley is one of organized electoral response
to potential support for black incorporation within the wider
electorate. In sum, the distinguishing characteristics of the
evolution of mobilization and incorporation in Berkeley were
unusually strong support in the electorate; an unusually clear
ideological commitment to black participation by liberal white
leaders; effective and well-organized leadership in both
groups; a liberal electoral alliance that achieved strong incorporation at a much earlier date than in other cities; and sustained competition for the black vote by lasting coalitions func-
tioning like parties.

The early integration of blacks into Berkeley city government meant that they were already part of the power structure
when the wave of black protest spread across the country in the
second half of the 1960s. Perhaps partly as a result, protest by
blacks in Berkeley did not come so close to the edge of violence
as it did in other cities. Demands were insistently articulated
and pressure to achieve them vigorously mobilized throughout
the period, but racial violence and the threat of violence that
arose in other cities were avoided in Berkeley.

The electoral victories of a biracial coalition in Berkeley were preceded by years of careful, principled, determined leadership and organization. The effort had achieved solid results by the time the pressures of the mid-sixties emerged.

Co-optation: San Francisco

The level and pattern of minority incorporation into the politics of San Francisco have been distinctly different from Berkeley's. Though both blacks and Hispanics have achieved moderate levels of inclusion, neither group in San Francisco has been as successful as blacks in Berkeley. As shown in figure 7, by the end of the seventies minorities had achieved only moderate levels of incorporation. As in Berkeley, a liberal Democratic coalition won council control early (1963). Although minority support was important to the liberal challenge, the challenging coalition did not organize minority candidacies. It was primarily a white effort, far short of the biracial coalition formed in Berkeley. In 1965 a black and in 1968 a Hispanic were appointed to the council and played minor roles in the dominant coalition, but this level of incorporation represented a plateau. The initial steps were not followed by further strengthening of the minority position. In 1979 the Hispanic lost his seat and Hispanic incorporation dropped to zero.

The moderate level of incorporation is a reflection of the relative diversity of San Francisco's population and the complexity of its political processes, within the minority groups and in the wider community. Both minority groups have achieved notable successes over the past twenty years, but neither has been able to forge with whites the sort of cohesive coalition that would be necessary for the highest levels of incorporation.

San Francisco, the largest of our cities with a population in 1980 of 678,974 (a 5 percent loss since 1970), is best known as a beautiful, picturesque, almost European city that is a mighty tourist attraction. It is also a city of minorities, not only blacks and Hispanics (in San Francisco an unusually diverse mix of people of Central and South American origin as well as Mexican Americans), but also Chinese, Japanese, Filipinos, Pacific Islanders, and Vietnamese (Wirt, 1974, chap. 10). Although the combined black and Hispanic populations of Berkeley and San Francisco constituted about the same percentages of each city's population in 1980, blacks were by far the largest group in Berkeley (and in Oakland), whereas black and Hispanic groups in San Francisco were about equal in size. Among our cities only San Jose had more Hispanics, and San Francisco had more than twice as many Hispanics as any of our other eight cities. In 1980 there were 86,000 blacks, constituting 12.7 percent of the population. In the same year there were 83,000 Hispanics, 12.3 percent. So unlike Berkeley and Oakland, blacks are not a clearly dominant minority in San Francisco. The poverty level and occupational profile of blacks and Hispanics in San Francisco are about the same as in Berkeley and Oakland.

The diversity of San Francisco's population is matched by the complexity of its political processes. Wirt has described San Francisco's politics as "hyperpluralist" with active ethnic, labor, and neighborhood groups and political parties with an overlay of "government dominated by clerks" (Wirt, 1974, p. 99; and 1971).

Formally the powers of the mayor are strictly limited, particularly compared to the strong mayoral systems in many of the older eastern cities such as Detroit and Pittsburgh. However, the mayor of San Francisco has more power than mayors in our other cities. The resources available to the mayor result from the prestige of the office, which often attracts statewide and national visibility, budgetary control over those department heads responsible to the mayor, and patronage power developed as a consequence of federal program jobs located in the mayor's office. In San Francisco the mayor is most often the central figure in dominant coalitions vis-à-vis minorities. Mayor Reading of Oakland oversaw a staff of one administrative assistant and three secretaries, whereas Mayor Alioto had 144 staff positions, most of which were federally funded. The prestige of the office was exemplified by Mayor Alioto's ability to secure a Model Cities program for San Francisco by interceding directly with Vice President Humphrey to gain approval of the Model Cities application.

Because of the diversity and size of minority groups and complexity of political processes, black and Hispanic incorporation developed in the context of mayors seeking to gain support for electoral victories and programs. The key features affecting minorities were the relatively early rise of liberal white leaders compared to most of our other cities, and the co-optive way in which mayors brought blacks and Hispanics into their base of support.

In 1963 the Republican bias of the nonpartisan electoral system in San Francisco shifted with the election of the first liberal Democratic mayor, John Shelley. The mayor was more supportive of blacks and Hispanics than his Republican counterpart in Oakland and had a larger proportion of liberals and Democrats on the board of supervisors (the counterpart of city councils in other cities). Like Mayor Reading in Oakland, he was faced with increasingly militant minority mobilization.

Blacks organized marches and boycotts in the early sixties to demand an end to discrimination in private and public sector employment.[2] Leaders from the predominantly black areas of the city, Hunters Point and the Western Addition, and from the Hispanic area, the Mission District, attempted to wrest control of the poverty program away from city hall and succeeded earlier than in Oakland (Kramer, 1969, p. 55). Both blacks and Hispanics also organized to protest urban renewal proposals. Hunters Point experienced a riot. Willie Brown, a black lawyer, won election to the California Assembly in 1964 from a San Francisco district. These mobilization activities greatly increased the political visibility of minority groups, and in 1965 Shelley appointed the first black to the board of supervisors, Terry Francois, who became part of the dominant liberal coalition (Fisher, 1978).

With an eye on Mayor Shelley's problems with minority groups, his successor, Joseph Alioto, won election in 1967 by assembling a diverse coalition of minorities, labor, and business. (He defeated both a Republican opponent and a more liberal Democrat.) In an effort to convert some of the demands emanating from the highly factionalized black and Hispanic leadership into electoral support, Alioto promised jobs and programs in both Hispanic and black areas of the city (Kramer, 1969, pp. 251 – 52). He also appointed the first Hispanic, Robert

---

[2]For an analysis of early black organizing in San Francisco, see Broussard (1981 and 1983).

Gonzales, to the board of supervisors. Mayor Alioto's strategy was remarkably similar to those of other mayors—Daley in Chicago, Tate in Philadelphia, and Wagner in New York, described by Greenstone and Peterson as "liberal pragmatist" (1973, chap. 4). Unlike his eastern counterparts, Alioto pursued his strategy within the context of reform institutions, with resources and patronage provided by federal monies, rather than in the framework of traditional, partisan control of city government by a political machine. Federal programs were central to this strategy because a vigorous mayor had much more influence over federal funds and programs than over regular city appropriations and departments. For instance:

> From 1964 to the end of 1971, $8.6 million in poverty funds entered Hunters Point, of which $6 million paid the salaries for 770 jobs. With top positions for themselves and the authority to distribute many more, the poverty workers became the only black leaders in the city with prompt, supportive access to the mayor's office. (Wirt, 1974, p. 266—67)

Federal funds and access to the mayor's office did not lead to full minority incorporation into the city bureaucracy. The programs were established separately from the regular departments of city government, serving often to insulate departments from minority demands rather than to institutionalize minority interests. Although some major programs with substantial collective impact were carried out, in particular the redevelopment of Hunters Point, the benefits distributed were often privatistic, better suited to reward and co-opt supporters and split the opposition than to achieve lasting collective benefits. The mayor also used federal programs, appointments, contracts, and other benefits to keep blacks and Hispanics competing with each other. The Mission Coalition, at its zenith, and the Hunters Point Model Cities group directed at least as much energy toward fighting each other as they did toward fighting city hall. Whereas by the mid-sixties minority leaders, though often in disagreement, had achieved some political cohesion in their opposition to city hall, Alioto's co-optive strategy induced many minority leaders to involve themselves in program administration and in competition for funds rather than in the building of challenging coalitions.

(Some leaders welcomed this role under the banner of "community control.") This contributed to the loss of cohesion among both black and Hispanic leaders (Rosenbloom, 1976).

After his reelection in 1971 with minority support, there was a noticeable decrease in Alioto's responsiveness to minority demands. Blacks and Hispanics talked openly about their resentment at being co-opted by Alioto when he needed them and being cut adrift when he did not need them any longer. But the two groups continued to constitute components of the coalition of Alioto's successor, George Moscone.

By the early seventies federal monies that provided opportunities for patronage had declined, and Moscone often sought to build alliances with minority leaders who were newer to the scene than Alioto's supporters. Because Moscone was seen as more concerned with cutting program costs than providing jobs, traditional alliances in minority neighborhoods were weakened. During this period many neighborhood groups who were important supporters of Moscone led the move to institute district elections and eliminate at-large elections. Minorities went along with this reform but were not its primary leaders. Moscone referred often to his record of appointing more minorities to commissions than any previous mayor, but even these appointments aroused minority opposition because they were frequently professionals who were not linked to traditional minority leadership.

Incorporation had reached a plateau. Blacks and Hispanics were not achieving major increases or breakthroughs; they were still in largely subordinate positions in city hall and in Mayor Moscone's coalition. Access to top officials was a growing problem because of competition from increasingly powerful white, left-liberal, gay and women's interests. The proportion of minorities on the board of supervisors has stayed stable since 1969—two seats out of eleven. After district elections were instituted, Gonzales lost his seat and Francois did not run, but two blacks gained seats.

The traumatic assassination of Mayor Moscone in 1978 and the catapulting of Dianne Feinstein into the mayoral position along with the rise of gay politics, the continued growth of radical and neighborhood groups, and the fiscal pressures that arose in the late seventies all served to interfere with the building of a stronger minority base in city politics. Neither blacks nor Hispanics were seen as prominent parts of Mayor Feinstein's electoral coalition, which was built from an alliance of groups in favor of economic development and newer neighborhood groups that united to oppose a more conservative candidate than Feinstein. At times minorities found themselves aligned with those advocating economic growth rather than with groups that were more liberal on social issues generally but advocated measures to restrict economic growth (development in particular).

In sum, blacks and Hispanics are just two of many groups contending for influence over city policy. Blacks and Hispanics are no longer totally excluded; they are acting politically and professionally within city hall rather than outside it. As one respondent said, minorities "are now off the streets and into the chamber." But with dwindling federal program monies, reduced demand-protest activity, the split between blacks and Hispanics, and fragmented minority leadership, minorities have remained on the periphery of San Francisco's dominant coalition, which has been in any case a much looser network of allies than the minority-oriented dominant coalitions in Berkeley and Oakland. Consequently minority issues have been less prominent in San Francisco than in Oakland and Berkeley.

Willie Brown's repeated reelection to the California Assembly (and to the office of speaker in 1980) has been a significant advantage for blacks in San Francisco (and for the city generally vis-à-vis state government during the period of fiscal stringency beginning in 1978). Brown was a close associate of Congressmen Phillip and John Burton and what was referred to as the "Burton machine." The Burton group was the most influential continuing political network in San Francisco. Alioto, the maverick, was not closely tied to the group, but Moscone was and Feinstein became more identified with it. Phillip Burton did not make the effort to recruit new black leaders that Dellums did in the East Bay. And Brown did not play the kind of integrative leadership role in San Francisco that W. Byron Rumford and others played in Berkeley in the late 1940s and 1950s, or that Dellums played in East Bay politics after his election to the U.S. Congress. (Commentators refer to the "Dellums machine.") Brown's own ambitions in the 1970s focused on his position in the assembly, and, of course, the relative size of the black population in San Francisco made it a much less promising resource than the black populations of Oakland and Berkeley. Nevertheless, blacks in San Francisco did considerably better than Hispanics in the competition for the distributable benefits of city government.

Structural reforms to reduce the power of the city manager (chief administrative officer) and to institute district elections were pursued, but minorities were not in the forefront of those efforts and their interests were not a primary concern. The board of supervisors did move perceptibly to the left with the district elections of 1977 and 1979, and black representation on it increased and was more autonomous and more liberal (Kleinwaks, 1982). Some of the issues with which the new board grappled were important for minority groups, but minority issues did not occupy the central place on the agenda of city politics that they did in Oakland. With the repeal of district elections in 1981, the future of minority representation is again in doubt.

The two other cities that fit clearly into the group with San Francisco as examples of partial incorporation with co-optation are Richmond and Sacramento. In both, minorities played significant but lesser roles in liberal coalitions led by whites, which responded to minority demands enough to reduce demands.

In Richmond a primarily white Democratic coalition won control of the council in 1963. As in San Francisco, this early replacement of a conservative coalition was carried out by a coalition that had minority support but no minorities on its slate and that did not stress minority issues in the campaign. Support for black interests as measured by opposition to Proposition 14 was less than 50 percent, but Democratic registration was high (71 percent). Richmond has a very large minority population (46 percent in 1970), and blacks are a much bigger proportion than Hispanics. As the civil rights movement spread and demand-protest activity increased in Richmond between 1965 and 1972, the liberal-to-moderate majority on the council, which by then included blacks, was receptive to some black demands. Under the leadership of a liberal city manager appointed by the liberal coalition, the Model Cities program was used to provide some redistributive programs responsive to black interests. However, these programs also had a co-optive effect in that they probably decreased black demand-protest and electoral efforts (see chapter 6).

In Sacramento a liberal electoral challenge under white leadership was organized later than it was in San Francisco and Richmond. It was taking shape in the period after 1965 simultaneously with peak minority demand-protest. Blacks and Hispanics constituted a small proportion of Sacramento's population and the two groups were roughly equal in size. They conducted well-organized and determined but still fairly moderate demand-protest. The coalition led by white Democrats included minority leaders and made explicit commitments to minority interests. The slate included one black and one Hispanic candidate. Blacks and Hispanics translated some of their mobilizing into electoral efforts, supporting this multiethnic coalition. Taking advantage of a substantial Democratic edge in registration (about 64 percent), the coalition was successful in replacing the conservative dominant coalition in 1969. The coalition endured and minorities continued to be included in it, though not as equal partners. The coalition successfully instituted district elections to secure its position. It also brought about the hiring of a liberal personnel director, who was given a mandate to transform the minority composition of city employees and who proceeded to move forcefully in that direction. But the level of responsiveness was still limited.

San Jose also exhibits the pattern of co-optation following protest but for a shorter period of time than San Francisco, Richmond, and Sacramento. San Jose's relatively small minority population is almost exclusively Hispanic. Hispanic protest centered on Model Cities issues in the late 1960s. In 1971 a loosely structured liberal coalition led by mayoral candidate Norman Mineta, including primarily slow-growth groups but also Hispanics, won control of city council. Mineta then appointed a losing Hispanic council candidate to fill a vacancy on the council, and the council also took some other steps to meet Hispanic demands and reduce unrest (Betsalel, 1983; Trounstine and Christensen, 1982, p. 102). When Mineta won a congressional seat in 1974, a less liberal coalition gained ascendancy, and Hispanics were not part of it. San Jose returned to the pattern of protest and exclusion from the same dominant coalition that had existed before Mineta. This pattern is described next using Oakland and Stockton as examples. In San Jose, however, protest and exclusion did not eventually lead to replacement and strong minority incorporation as they did in Oakland. And in view of the small size of the minority population in San Jose and Mineta's departure for higher office, it may be more accurate to attribute the failure to sustain minority incorporation in San Jose to the weaknesses of the liberal coalition—weaknesses both of leadership and of basic support in the population—rather than to the intensity of conflict or to the strength of the conservative coalition.

In sum, the evolution of minority politics in San Francisco, Richmond, Sacramento, and San Jose exhibited a common pattern of partial incorporation and the use of co-optive strategies. In two of the cities moderate-sized minority populations were split fairly evenly between blacks and Hispanics (San Francisco and Sacramento); in San Jose the minority population was small overall and primarily Hispanic. In San Francisco and Richmond loose white liberal electoral coalitions won office prior to peak minority mobilization and demand-protest. In Sacramento minorities had a more stable role in a more cohesive coalition probably because it formed after several years of significant minority protest, thus establishing the political capabilities of the minority groups and making their support more desirable. In San Jose Hispanic protest also produced inclusion in a liberal coalition, but that coalition was unable to sustain itself given the very small total minority population. In all the cities of this type, partial incorporation was followed by executive use of co-optive strategies to reduce pressures from minorities.

Protest and Exclusion: Oakland

Blacks in Oakland, as in Berkeley, had achieved high levels of incorporation by 1978, but the socioeconomic environment and political processes leading to this result were very different. As shown in figure 7 the replacement of a conservative coalition came sixteen years later in Oakland than in Berkeley, after years of protest and exclusion for Oakland's large black population. In terms of the basic resources of support for black interests and Democratic registration, Oakland was quite similar to San Francisco, where a Republican coalition was replaced in 1963. Yet it was years before Democrats and minority people in Oakland would be able to capitalize effectively on the Democratic edge and the large and growing black population.

Oakland is an industrial city, three times the size of Berkeley, with a 1980 population of 339,288. Like many central cities with industries moving to the suburbs, Oakland is becoming a distribution and service center. It has experienced severe fiscal strain and a declining economy. Though total population has declined since 1970, Oakland's minority population is growing in numbers and as a percentage of the total population; blacks increased from 34.5 to 46.9 percent, and Hispanics from 6.7 to 9.6 percent from 1970 to 1980. Whereas the percentage of black residents in Berkeley declined by 3 percentage points between 1970 and 1980, Oakland's black population increased 12.4 points. Oakland's blacks are also poorer than Berkeley's—21.8 percent of black families were below the poverty line in 1970 (ranking it with the cities having the largest proportions of blacks at the poverty level—only Stockton and Sacramento had more). Like some eastern cities, Oakland will soon have a black majority. As described by Pressman, "Oakland is the kind of city that has been discussed at length in the news media as an example of the urban crisis. It is characterized by an increasingly large minority population, geographical separation and emotional tension between races, and a high unemployment rate" (1975, p. 27).

Since World War II when blacks migrated from the South and Southwest to pursue employment opportunities in shipbuilding, food processing, and auxiliary industries, Oakland has served as a point of entry for minority employment (May, 1973, p. 81). Gradually, a black middle class developed: 10.8 percent of the black civilian labor force were professionals and managers in 1970. Although this is a lower percentage than Berkeley's, the actual number of persons comprises, next to San Francisco, the largest group of black professionals in any of our ten cities.

If Berkeley has received publicity for its radical politics,

Oakland is known for its sports teams, booming port, and its inferiority complex vis-à-vis San Francisco. In the literature of social science Oakland is often cited as one of the largest cities that has retained a reformed political system with a weak mayor, a strong city manager, and at-large elections.[3] This system dates back to the 1930s when reformers promised to remove control of policy from elected officials and vest it in a professional manager, and pursued a successful initiative campaign that voted in a council-manager government (May, 1973, p. 75). From the 1930s to the 1970s the council-manager system reinforced the policy-making role of city managers, traditionally committed to "efficiency, cost-cutting and lower taxes" (Pressman, 1975, p. 35), and the nonpartisan ballot had the consequence of enhancing the electoral potential of Republican city councilmen and mayors who most often shared these goals. Within the clear parameters of this conservative system, in which the major issues of the role of government and the role of elected officials in particular had already been decided, politics in Oakland revolved around shifting alliances attached to personalities rather than organized party activities (Hawley, 1973; Pressman, 1975).

Behind the formally nonpartisan politics of Oakland stood a powerful combination of corporate interests, Republican party leadership, and control over local media.[4] The financial and organizational strength of this coalition and its repeated ability to control the issues and win elections probably significantly delayed the formation of a successful challenging coalition in a city that had a majority of registered Democrats and a growing minority population.

Other conditions were also inauspicious for the sort of biracial coalition that developed in Berkeley in the 1950s. In the 1960s Oakland's black population (22.8 percent) was only

[3]Before 1980 Oakland was one of the few large American cities that used a district-at-large electoral system wherein most nominations for the council were made by district, but all nominees were elected at large.

[4]In its original form the nucleus of this coalition consisted of Henry J. Kaiser and Kaiser Industries, Senator William Knowland, and the *Oakland Tribune* of which Knowland was the publisher. The *Tribune* also owned a television station (Hayes, 1972). This sort of corporate structure and dominance was simply not present in Berkeley.

slightly larger than Berkeley's (19.6 percent), but it faced a much less sympathetic white population. Oakland was an industrial city, not a university town. We estimate that only about 30 percent of Oakland's nonblacks voted against Proposition 14 in 1964, compared to 57 percent in Berkeley. Given the much smaller probable support for a biracial coalition in Oakland and the much stronger conservative coalition, it is not surprising that no biracial challenging coalition developed in Oakland.

Although predominantly Democratic in registration, Oakland's electorate continued to choose Republican, business-oriented councilmembers and mayors during the 1960s. Efforts by liberal Democrats to win elections were usually unsuccessful. Mayor Reading's coalition of businesses, Republicans, and whites never included blacks. Reading was both ideologically and temperamentally opposed to a strategy of the inclusion of blacks in a wider coalition (Pressman, 1972). Although the first black councilmember, Joshua Rose, was appointed in 1964 in an effort to reduce pressure from blacks, he was not part of the dominant coalition (Fisher, 1978).

Black leadership in the early 1960s focused mainly on mobilizing to gain control of federal programs (see chapter 6) and develop an independent base of power outside city hall, rather than on winning elections (May, 1973; Pressman, 1975; Viorst, 1977). In 1967, as a result of discussions held at the National CORE Convention in Oakland, an insurgent black leadership formed the Black Caucus. The caucus developed a strategy, in the words of one of its leaders, "to coordinate the activities of various black groups that worked to create a stir and get attention. The Black Caucus was a launching pad for attacks on an agency, starting affirmative action law suits and organizing an economic boycott" (confidential interview by the authors). Through a separate organization, the Muleskinners Democratic Club, the same group of black leaders supported an unsuccessful candidate for mayor in 1969 and for city council (longtime activist Paul Cobb) in 1971. Conflicts between middle-class black professionals administering the programs and insurgent community leaders who sought to gain control of programs often escalated the conflict with the city council, agencies, the city manager, and the mayor. At the violent edge of racial conflict there were shoot-outs between Oakland police and members of the Black Panther Party. The sixties, then, were years of repeated and sometimes violent confrontations between an unyielding city hall and protesting minority groups (May, 1973; Pressman, 1975; Warren, Rose, and Bergunder, 1974). The result was conflict and polarization, a long series of discontinuous developments, with concessions made and then withdrawn.

On the strength of Democratic registration alone we might have expected a Democratic victory by 1968 or 1969, when about 65 percent of Oakland's voters were registered Democrats. But by that time racial politics in Oakland had become far too bitter and confrontational. The rhetoric of protest was too strong and the conflict too sharp for moderate leaders, black or white, to develop support for an effective biracial electoral coalition.

Although Joshua Rose regularly won reelection after his appointment in 1964, no other blacks won council seats until 1977. Only in the 1970s did minorities begin to forge political efforts that won sizeable votes. With their most provocative leaders dead or in hiding, the Black Panthers turned increasingly toward electoral politics, organizing a large voter registration drive and running strong but losing races with Elaine Brown for council in 1971 and Bobby Seale for mayor in 1973. A liberal coalition of whites and minorities was successful in electing the first Hispanic councilmember, Joe Coto, in 1973. So prior to 1977 minorities had gained only two of the nine council seats (22 percent), even though they constituted over 40 percent of the adult population; and the one black councilmember was the choice of the dominant conservative group.

Knowing this much of the story, analysts often conclude from the Oakland case that intense conflict precludes strong political incorporation. Yet in 1977 Oakland began a dramatic political turnaround with the election of a black mayor, Lionel Wilson, and a black councilmember to replace Rose, who chose not to run. Wilson, a moderate judge who had been the chairman of the city's first antipoverty board, was able to forge an uneasy alliance between black militants and moderates as well as white liberals. Wilson had been approached to run for mayor in the two previous elections by prominent white Democratic leaders as well as by the city's black leadership, but by 1977

Wilson felt the timing was opportune. By then conflict over federal programs had receded, the Black Panther Party had turned to a coalition strategy under the leadership of Elaine Brown, and the potential black electorate had grown to a size rivaling the white adult population.[5] In addition Wilson's own financial situation was secure. Furthermore, the corporate foundation of the conservative coalition had disintegrated. One of its leaders, *Oakland Tribune* publisher William Knowland, died in 1974, and the *Tribune* was eventually sold to an out-of-state newspaper chain. Henry J. Kaiser, another leader, had died in 1967, Kaiser Industries was split into many parts, and control passed into the hands of stockholders and executives for whom the maintenance of political hegemony was not a high priority.

Black electoral mobilization continued in 1979 with the election of an additional black councilmember, Wilson Riles, Jr., for a total of three black representatives for the first time in Oakland's history. Wilson won a second term in 1981 with a wider electoral base and the support, for the first time, of large financial contributions by middle-class blacks both locally and nationally. Combined with the growth of the black population, this development has led some observers to conclude that a black candidate for mayor in Oakland no longer needs white liberal support.

The victory of the liberal coalition led to a series of stunning changes in city hall. Appointees to top commissions now include many minority representatives. For example, a second black was added to the port commission and in due course became chair of the commission; another black became chair of the civil service commission. The first black city manager in Oakland's history was appointed. Independently, a black was named editor of the *Tribune*, the Oakland Symphony selected a black conductor, and the Oakland Museum chose a black director.

Although Mayor Wilson was criticized by militant blacks for selling out to whites, his priorities differed sharply from those of his opponent, a registered Republican, but also from those

[5]Projecting support for black interests (the "no" vote on Proposition 14) forward from 1964 and taking into account the increase in the black population of Oakland, we estimate that support reached about 59 percent by 1977.

of his liberal white allies. Wilson shifted the programmatic agenda, stressing minority employment rather than environmental concerns important to his white allies. Wilson also pushed for structural changes similar to those pursued in Berkeley, changes that would contribute to the decline of reform structures. He pushed successfully for a change from at-large to district elections in order to ensure greater minority representation on the council. (In the first district election of 1981, the number of minorities on the council did not change, but by 1983 five of nine members were black.) And he recommended a strong mayoral form of government that would give him veto power and reduce the power of the city manager.

Stockton is the other city that fits clearly into the group with Oakland (and on some dimensions San Jose fits as well). These cities have three characteristics in common: substantial minority protest and conflict with city government in the late sixties and seventies, tenacious conservative coalitions dominating the city council and excluding minorities, and a long delay in the achievement of minority incorporation. They are also different in important ways. Oakland's large minority population is mostly black, Stockton's smaller minority group is mixed, and San Jose's relatively small minority population is almost exclusively Hispanic. These and other factors produced very different strategies and outcomes.

In Stockton, as in Oakland, an entrenched conservative coalition dominated city hall. Demand-protest activity began to build in the late 1960s centering partly on poverty programs but also on educational issues in the minority part of town. As in Oakland the resistance encountered in city hall intensified the conflict. A coalition of blacks, Hispanics, and white liberals came together over educational issues and was not linked to Democratic party activists. White ministers played an active role in this nonparty coalition, which chose an interesting strategy. Rather than directly trying to build a stronger liberal electoral coalition by running slates of candidates, it mounted a subtly quiet campaign for district elections in which the advantages to minorities and minority representation were carefully kept from view. The campaign was engineered by a white with community-organizing experience and a single-minded focus on this structural change strategy. District elections were narrowly approved in 1971.

Before district elections there were no blacks or Hispanics on the Stockton council. After district elections two blacks were elected immediately and several years later a Hispanic was elected, but this increase in representation did not lead to the replacement of the conservative dominant coalition. Whereas protest and exclusion in Oakland led to incorporation of minorities after a long delay, in Stockton replacement of the conservative coalition was prevented.

Stockton is the only one of the ten cities where district elections were instituted as a strategy to benefit minorities before the rise of a liberal dominant coalition. In Sacramento, San Francisco, and Oakland, district elections were adopted after a liberal coalition was in city hall, and the new electoral system did not immediately increase minority representation. (San Jose switched to district elections as the result of efforts by a diverse coalition of minority, feminist, labor, neighborhood, and homeowner groups, all of which felt underrepresented [Trounstine and Christensen, 1982, p. 105].)

The fact that a party-based, liberal, multiethnic coalition sufficient to take over city government did not form in Stockton is probably due to the leadership structure and strategy. The institution of district elections virtually guaranteed minority representation but may also have reduced the incentive for minority participation in such a coalition. After 1970 minority candidates elected from districts could win on the basis of neighborhood support; participation in a broad liberal coalition was not necessary. District elections may also have reduced the chance that liberal whites could win in mostly white districts, because it isolated liberal white candidates from minority support that would be available in an at-large system.

With hindsight, one might argue that it would have been better from the standpoint of replacement of the conservative coalition to have pursued a coalitional strategy in city council elections rather than to have gained district elections and minority representation first. On the other hand, Stockton's minorities did face an intensely conservative and cohesive dominant coalition, and perhaps minority representation achieved as a result of district elections brought about changes in city government policies sooner than would have been possible in any other way. Minority representation may also have reduced the intensity of racial conflict in Stockton during the seventies. In any case, a multiethnic coalition might still be possible, given appropriate leadership.

The evolution of minority politics was obviously different in Oakland with its bitter and prolonged conflict and the fragmentation of minority leadership, and in Stockton with the early decision to follow the structural strategy of district elections. But there were important similarities as well. In both cities minority mobilization occurred in the face of strong and cohesive conservative coalitions; both the bitterness of racial conflict in Oakland and the choice of the structural strategy in Stockton were conditioned by that fact. And in both cities the combination of conservative dominance and minority-group strategies delayed the replacement of conservative coalitions, hence delayed the achievement of the strongest forms of minority incorporation.

Weak Minority Mobilization: Vallejo

The fourth pattern of weak minority mobilization is illustrated by Vallejo. Weak mobilization and strong resistance by a conservative coalition has meant that absolutely no incorporation has been achieved. Figure 7 shows that Vallejo like Oakland had no incorporation at all in the middle sixties. Then in 1965 one black was elected to the council, giving Vallejo representation without incorporation in a liberal dominant coalition, which was what Oakland had at the time. But in Vallejo minorities did not increase their strength on the council, and the sole black councilman was defeated in his bid for reelection, so even representation was lost.

Vallejo is one of the smallest of our cities (80,188 in 1980) along with Daly City, Richmond, and Hayward. The largest city in Solano County, to the north of San Francisco, it is on the rural fringe of the Bay Area and includes a major U.S. military installation, Mare Island Naval Base.

Vallejo has a smaller proportion of families below the poverty line than the other three cities we have been describing, and a higher median income as well (though the white median family income in Vallejo is lower than in Berkeley or San Francisco). Vallejo has a slightly smaller proportion of minorities than San Francisco (20.8 percent in 1970), the smallest minority population of the four cities described in this chapter, and the proportion of minorities has been relatively stable. Blacks are the main minority group, making up 16.6 percent of the population in 1970 (thus a larger proportion of the population than they are in San Francisco), whereas only 4.2 percent of the population are Hispanic. In Vallejo, as in Berkeley, blacks are relatively well off compared to blacks in other cities. White opposition to minority interests was more intense in Vallejo than the other nine cities (about 80 percent of Vallejo's whites voted for Proposition 14), and the level of support for black interests was the lowest of all cities except Hayward.

Vallejo politics both formally and informally fit the reform pattern much more closely than the politics of Berkeley, Oakland, and San Francisco. Its politics were repeatedly described by respondents as extremely conservative. Republicans made up a larger proportion of the council for a longer period of time than in the other three cities. It has a "friends and neighbors" style of electoral politics that inhibits partylike behavior and coalitions (Lee, 1960). A colorful symbol of Vallejo politics is its longtime mayor, Florence Douglas. She was first elected in 1963, when she was in her mid-sixties, having moved to Vallejo after retiring from a civil service career in San Francisco. She relied on friends to run her campaigns, distributing packets of marigold seeds bearing her name. She refused to speak at any political gatherings or to be even remotely associated with any other council candidates. A conservative Democrat, Douglas was critical of what she saw as federal efforts to force unwanted redistributive policies on local governments (for example, grants intended to favor the poor and minorities).

White liberals who might have challenged her and other members of the council were not organized, and minority groups have been quite unable to form any sustained coalition behind potential minority leaders. They were described by whites and minorities alike as extremely fragmented. In 1965 Vallejo was one of the first cities to elect a black councilmember, but since he was defeated at the end of his first term, no black or Hispanic candidate has won election. Black and Hispanic candidates ran for the council and were endorsed by minority groups, but no sustained electoral efforts emerged. White groups convinced blacks and Hispanics to run against each other as "ringers" to split the vote. Various demand-protest activities also occurred sporadically, focusing on federal programs, employment, education, and incidents with the police. Delegations went to city hall, complaints were filed, and letters written, but the actions did not cumulate into strong mobilization. City hall used "divide and conquer" tactics to increase the fragmentation among the various minority organizations.

The absence of minority incorporation in Vallejo is associated with many policies that are unresponsive to minorities. Vallejo has few minority commission members and low levels of minority employment in city hall. There was a minority director of human relations who was sometimes referred to as a token. Minorities were virtually excluded from the political system. Although minority respondents were quick to point this out, white respondents typically insisted that minorities were treated well in Vallejo. At least lip service appears to have been paid to minority interests. As one white interviewee admitted, "It is difficult to say how much city councilmembers resist minority-related programs, because openly they profess great interest in the welfare of minorities but they seem unable to pass or fund any proposals."

Daly City and Hayward also illustrate the pattern of weak minority mobilization and failed incorporation. They too were small cities with small minority populations characterized by the lack of sustained demand-protest activity and extremely conservative coalitions. Daly City has been dominated from 1960 to 1980 by conservative coalitions that resisted minority participation and minority-oriented programs in a city where the minority population is primarily Hispanic. Hayward too has a largely Hispanic minority population that did not organize significant demand-protest activity. But in Hayward, unlike Vallejo and Daly City, a white liberal coalition centered around the mayor and city manager did come into power in 1972. Yet this coalition did not include Hispanics, and even though it did move ahead with some social programs for low income Hispanics, Hispanics did not achieve any incorporation.

Summary

Behind the rise of minority mobilization and increasingly strong minority incorporation in city government lies a diverse reality: vigorous and successful demand-protest and electoral campaigns for political position in some cities, weak and abortive efforts in others. The timing of the struggle for political equality varied and was not equally forceful nor equally fruitful from city to city.

Four evolutionary patterns of mobilization and incorporation characterized the ten cities. The patterns are distinguished by the way in which mobilization and conflict unfolded, by characteristics of coalition formation and the nature of the dominant and challenging coalitions, and by the consequences of these developments for the degree of incorporation achieved. In these cities the evolution of minority mobilization and incorporation followed one of the four patterns:

1. *Biracial electoral alliance.* Strong support for minorities in the electorate, clear commitment by liberal white leaders to the incorporation of blacks, effective and well-organized leadership by both whites and blacks, sustained and effective demand effort, and formation of a strong electoral coalition led to strong early incorporation.

2. *Co-optation.* When minorities had less autonomy and less control over issues and candidates in liberal electoral coalitions led by whites and formed prior to or during periods of demand-protest, the results were partial incorporation and the use of co-optative strategies.

3. *Protest and exclusion.* A long period of intense mobilization, protest, and conflict resulted in some representation but delay in the formation of a sufficiently broad challenging coalition and delay in the replacement of the resistant dominant coalitions necessary for higher levels of incorporation.

4. *Weak minority mobilization.* Stubborn resistance by the dominant coalition and the failure of mobilization efforts meant that no incorporation was achieved.

These processes of incorporation, co-optation, and exclusion illustrated in the city profiles show the evolution of minority politics over time and the effects of minority demand-protest and electoral strategies at different points in time in different environmental contexts. High levels of protest in some cities resulted in increased electoral mobilization and inclusion in liberal challenging coalitions, which, once successful, used co-optative strategies to manage future minority mobilization. The strongest instances of incorporation occurred when minorities formed electoral coalitions in which they played a major role and that had major commitments to minority interests. Sometimes this occurred prior to demand-protest and sometimes simultaneously or subsequently. But demand-protest and electoral mobilization both play prominent and even necessary roles in the movement toward incorporation. Protest in all the cities except Berkeley appears to have been a necessary but not sufficient condition for electoral mobilization and subsequent incorporation.

The four patterns recounted in this chapter highlight the distinctive roles of particular leaders and groups of activists in each city. Without the astonishing energy of their efforts, there would have been nothing. Mobilization burst forth in the actions of local leaders and was defined by what they did, by the degree of their skill and persistence in organizing the resources available to them, by the strength of their commitment, and by their ability to withstand attack. Their actions and motivations are key to understanding the flow of events in each city—of protest and response, of organization and transition, and of conflict and coalition.

In a sense it is enough to know that without their work there would have been no progress toward political equality in these cities. The paramount fact is that it did happen, and they made it happen. But beyond the fact that they were indispensable, beyond the fact of their great diversity, we need to know whether their actions were shaped by common forces, whether the diversity of local beliefs and personal styles was ruled by the diversity of the constraints they worked within: the structure imposed by the power of the national movement and by the opportunities and limitations inherent in local political conditions. It is to that question that we now turn.

3

Mobilization and Incorporation: Why More Was Achieved in Some Cities Than in Others

The struggle for political incorporation varied greatly from city to city, and distinctive patterns of political development over the twenty-year period evolved from particular circumstances and strategies in each city. This chapter stands back from the historical account to assess alternative explanations for the considerable differences between cities in the levels of political mobilization generated and incorporation achieved.

As we saw in chapters 1 and 2, the story of minority incorporation began with conservative coalitions that controlled city governments and were unresponsive to minority concerns. As minority groups mobilized, challenges to those coalitions were mounted in many of the cities, and the strongest incorporation of minorities was achieved where resistant dominant coalitions were replaced by liberal groups in which minorities played significant roles.

In this chapter we shift from close attention to flow of events to a more general level of analysis, assessing statistically a variety of hypotheses about the relationships between resources and results across the cities as a group. We have seen that minority mobilization occurred at different times in different cities. Can we nevertheless generalize about the forces that produced varying degrees of minority mobilization? From the diverse patterns observed in chapter 2, we abstract two measures of minority mobilization—measures of demand-protest and of electoral mobilization—and seek to explain why minority groups mobilized so much more vigorously in some cities than in others.

We know from chapter 2 that minority mobilization occurred in some cities after the replacement of conservative coalitions, in other cities before, with various consequences for minority incorporation. To assess the results of mobilization, we examine the relationship between mobilization and our measure of incorporation. Here we are able to show that stronger political incorporation was indeed achieved only where minority mobilization was intense and that minority population alone does not explain minority incorporation very well. We are able further to assess the relative contributions of demand-protest and electoral mobilization to the levels of incorporation achieved. This analysis shows clearly that protest alone was not enough to produce lasting incorporation.

The simple structure of the analysis mirrors the simple structure of intention and expectation for any group mobilization movement. Mobilization builds on a rising wave of demand and is fueled by local resources and limited by local constraints. If successful, mobilization produces the political incorporation of the group. The analysis of this chapter evaluates the factors that generated local mobilization and the ability of local minority groups to obtain incorporation through mobilization.

For the most part these analyses are conducted with aggregate measures over the whole twenty-year period under study. Although this is consistent with our intention to carry out an overall assessment of the mobilization effort, the data themselves suggested that aggregation over many years was appropriate.

Minority incorporation, the dependent variable of primary interest, produces virtually identical measures averaged over the entire period as it does for shorter periods. Figure 8 shows the relationship between the twenty-year average for incorporation and the value for 1978. The relationship is extremely close, with Oakland being the single deviant case. (Including Oakland, $r = .89$; excluding Oakland, $r = .99$.)

The reason for this relationship is to be found in the common pattern of development of minority incorporation. Typically there was a rapid rise from no incorporation to a level that

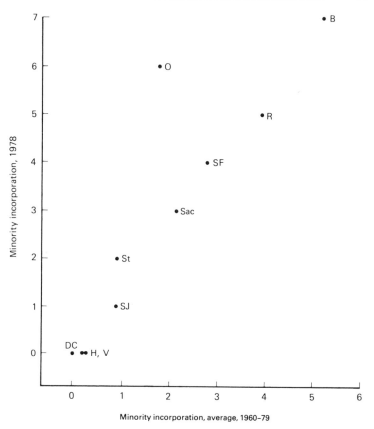

FIGURE 8   Relationship Between Minority Incorporation in 1978
and the Average for 1960–79

(B = Berkeley; DC = Daly City; H = Hayward; O = Oakland; R = Richmond;
Sac = Sacramento; SF = San Francisco; SJ = San Jose; St = Stockton; V = Vallejo)

was maintained with a high degree of stability over the rest of
the period. Oakland was the only case where the average level
of incorporation was held relatively low for most of the period,
then rose rapidly. In no city did minority incorporation stay
strong for most of the period and then plummet at the end.
This is certainly true for the incorporation of blacks, which
dominates the minority incorporation measure; it is less true
for Hispanic incorporation, which has been less stable. All in
all, these findings tend to support the use of twenty-year averages for this analysis.

Mobilization: Measurement and Trends

Minority *electoral mobilization* consisted of efforts to elect minority candidates to city council and mayoral positions, and in some cities, slates that included minority candidates. Many kinds of activity may contribute to such efforts. Increased minority turnout, although clearly a form of mobilization and probably necessary at least for the initial election of minority candidates, seemed inadequate as a measure of sustained mobilization. Our previous research had shown that turnout peaked at times of major challenges to conservative coalitions and then fell, even though minority candidates continued to win elections (Browning, Marshall, and Tabb, 1979b, table 1). Peak turnout seemed necessary to successful challenges but not necessary for sustained incorporation. It was as if the issue had been settled, minority representation was accepted, and peak effort to turn out the vote was no longer needed.

Instead of turnout, we use the degree to which minority groups organized and controlled minority candidacies and campaign efforts. Our historical studies (chapter 2) had suggested that the extent to which minority groups organized to control candidacies was extremely important for minority electoral success and for the autonomy of minority officeholders. The electoral mobilization scale ranges from zero—no apparent activity of any kind—through eight, for the case in which a minority organization chooses the minority candidates for a slate and is able to prevent other minority candidates from running. (See appendix C-4 for more information.)

Minority *demand-protest* refers to a wide range of other mobilization efforts including violent and nonviolent protest (sit-ins, boycotts, picketing, demonstrations, riots), and more traditional demand-articulation tactics such as mass turnouts at city meetings, press conferences, neighborhood meetings, petitions, and formal and informal exchanges with city officials. Scores for each city in each year are based on ratings by interview respondents on an eight-point scale, and on other information. The highest possible values were assigned for three years in San Francisco in the mid-sixties, which included a riot and considerable other vigorous protest activity, and in Oakland for three years in the late sixties, which included shoot-outs between police and Black Panthers and numerous demon-strations. (See appendix C-3.)

Both of these variables are measured as averages over some years: sometimes the entire twenty years, sometimes shorter periods to examine the possibility that different factors might explain levels of mobilization at particular points in time. Be-cause levels of all of these mobilization and incorporation vari-ables were close to zero in the period before 1960 (except for Berkeley in the late 1950s), the twenty-year averages are also measures of change from the preceding period.

From low levels of demand activity in the early 1960s, aver-age demand-protest in these cities increased rapidly and peaked in the late 1960s, then dropped off sharply. Neverthe-less, at the end of this period it was still well above the levels of 1960–64.[1] (See figure 9.) First blacks and then Hispanics artic-ulated demands both through the more traditional political channels and through protest. The movement spread to city after city, generating incidents of disruption and violence in some of them. Black demand-protest started sooner, peaked earlier, and was sustained at high levels for a longer period of time than Hispanic demand-protest. During the 1970s mean levels of black and Hispanic demand-protest effort have been roughly the same in these cities.

During this period minority groups also mobilized in the electoral arena. Trends for blacks and for Hispanics were signi-ficantly different. Black electoral mobilization started earlier and reached much higher levels; Hispanics in the 1970s finally reached levels that blacks had achieved eight to ten years earlier.

Alternative Hypotheses

Any attempt to explain minority mobilization in these cities must be set in the context of the national minority mobilization movement. The early focus on voting rights in the South and in

[1]The trend of black demand-protest parallels closely the national trend during the late sixties and early seventies for race-related riots, which fell from a high of 1,976 in 1967 to 46 in 1971 (Baskin, 1971, cited in Button, 1978, p. 101). The most intense riot years were 1967 and 1968 (Button, p. 15).

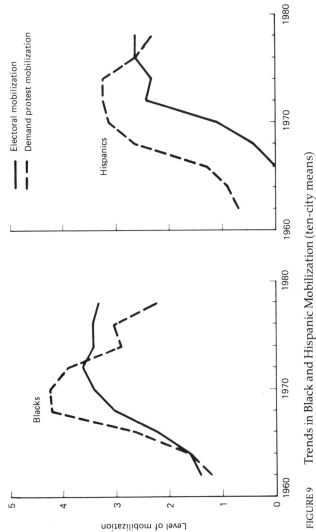

FIGURE 9   Trends in Black and Hispanic Mobilization (ten-city means)

national legislation became a nationwide effort to mobilize blacks in the electoral process, and Hispanic groups took up the effort too, though later. Similarly, a wave of protests against discrimination, urban renewal, police behavior, and other problems swept the country in 1960s. In large part an explanation of the initiation and early growth of minority political activity in these ten cities must be a theory of local participation in national movements and national programs.

Behind the averages of figure 9 the cities varied greatly. Why did minority populations in some cities mobilize early and strongly whereas in others they mobilized weakly, late, or not at all? The question should be approached from the perspectives of the relevant actors: local minority leaders and their potential followers, for whom local needs and resources would be important, and the leadership of national organizations (CORE, NAACP, SNCC, Urban League), for whom mobilization in some cities had higher priority than in others. For all these actors considerations of resources and opportunity were likely to be significant.[2]

We posit nine factors of resources, opportunity, and incentive that might explain levels of local mobilization.

1. *Size of minority population.* This is the most obvious group political resource influencing expectations of success and, therefore, the utility and likelihood of a mobilization effort. It is probably also correlated with other minority group characteristics that may be regarded as resources, such as length of residence (associated with political participation), the development of social networks and organizations, and the growth of skills and financial resources.

2. *Socioeconomic resources of the minority population.* We posit a curvilinear relationship between mobilization and socioeconomic resources, here measured as median family income.[3] The poorest minority populations might have the incentive but lack socioeconomic resources necessary for sustained mobili-

[2]Tilly's analysis of mobilization (1978) is couched in similar terms and has helped us organize our thinking.

[3]Lieske (1978, p. 1335) finds such a relationship between incidents of racial violence in a sample of American cities, 1967–69, and a measure of black social class.

zation, whereas groups that are relatively well off have the resources but may lack the incentive. Groups with middling income levels, by this reasoning, should show the most vigorous mobilization effort.

3. *Political resources outside the group itself.* Several kinds of resources might be relevant. The total size of the minority population, including both blacks and Hispanics, might influence calculations of opportunity of forming a coalition. As indicated in chapter 1, underlying support in the electorate was closely related to replacement of conservative coalitions, to which minority electoral mobilization should also be closely related if it was an important factor in replacement. Not only the size of the minority group but also the size of the nonminority segment of the electorate that is willing to support it is relevant. Chances of winning office through electoral mobilization are a direct function of underlying electoral support, so support should stimulate electoral mobilization and might stimulate demand-protest as well, if the latter tends to respond more to a supportive atmosphere with some potential for success than to steadfast opposition from city hall.

Other relevant outside political resources include the national civil rights movement and federal social programs. The national movement as a stimulus to local action is central to the explanation of minority mobilization developed in this chapter. The effects of federal programs on mobilization are examined closely in chapter 6. There we argue that the programs generally provided a focus and resources for demand-protest mobilizing, but that their specific effects on mobilization and on the degree of incorporation subsequently depended on a complex political dynamic that unfolded from the interplay of local implementation, political structure, leadership, and strategies. Though we do not have a direct measure of programs as such for use in the statistical analyses of the present chapter, local minority demand-protest, which is measured, in fact often reflected conflict over program implementation. As we shall see, much of the difference between cities in levels of mobilization and incorporation can be explained without reference to idiosyncrasies of program development. The implementation of federal social programs of special interest to minorities was by and large shaped by the same local political forces that affected the evolution of minority incorporation generally.

4. *Organizational development through demand-protest.* A typical (though not universal) pattern saw the development of organizations that mobilized first around issues (demand-protest), and later became active in elections. Prior levels of demand-protest in a city may explain subsequent electoral mobilization.

5. *Group competition and modeling.* Typically blacks mobilized first, Hispanics second. Was Hispanic mobilization stimulated by the earlier effort of blacks? Did Hispanics mobilize to a greater extent where blacks were most active?

6. *Resistance of the dominant coalition.* Faced with a dominant coalition that strongly resists the political incorporation of minority groups, a group may mobilize more intensively so as to overcome the greater obstacle. On the other hand, resistance of a dominant coalition may simply reduce expectations of success and therefore of the utility of mobilization effort. Although the historical data suggest that sustained resistance by a dominant coalition delayed minority incorporation, its effects on mobilization are unclear.

7. *Size of city.* Characteristics associated with total size of city might be relevant both to opportunity and to the value of the gains to be achieved through mobilization—for local activists as well as for national organizations seeking to stimulate mobilization. Events in larger cities receive more media attention as a matter of course. Larger local governments have greater resources to be influenced or controlled. Winning office in a large city is likely to generate greater chances for higher office than winning the same position in a small city. Large cities were also more likely to be involved in programs such as urban renewal and the war on poverty, which generated issues that were opportunities for mobilization.

8. *Socioeconomic inequality.* Related to minority income levels (2) but different in mechanism and impact is the objective inequality of minority groups relative to the white population: the magnitude of differences in income and in the percent of group population living in dilapidated housing or working in low status occupations. Hypothetically, the greater the objective inequality between groups in a city, the higher the grievance level and the greater the receptiveness of the minority group to the perception of injustice and the call for action (Morgan and Clark, 1973).

9. *Structure of government.* Local governmental structure may also affect opportunities for mobilization (for example, mayoral vs. city manager forms, and district vs. at-large election of councilmembers [Eisinger, 1973; Karnig and Welch, 1980]). However, for the most part, these cities have reform structures, and there is not enough variance for statistical analysis.

In addition to the possible effects of each of these factors individually, we often need to consider the possibility that factors interact with each other in their effects on mobilization. For instance, the extent to which black mobilization stimulated Hispanic mobilization may well depend on the size of the Hispanic population. Where there are very few Hispanics, even very strong black mobilization is not likely to stimulate much Hispanic activity.

Demand-Protest

Table 5 shows the relationships between demand-protest activity and selected measures of the possible explanations set forth in the preceding section. For both blacks and Hispanics demand-protest was very closely related to the absolute size of the minority group. Correlations between demand-protest and the measures of socioeconomic inequality (8) were virtually zero (not shown in table 5).

The relationship is curvilinear for blacks, hence the logarithmic transformation of size fits the data better: cities with the largest black population did not generate proportionately more demand-protest (see figure 10).[4] This result corroborates for our measure of demand-protest the correlations between

[4]Or perhaps the measure of demand-protest does not capture the full scope of such activity in the cities with the largest black populations. The log transform also has the advantage of eliminating skewness in the distribution of size of black population.

The relationships reported in this book have been examined for linearity, outliers, interaction, and the possibility that correlations might be the result of just one or two extreme observations. These problems usually do not arise in connection with the best-fitting models reported here. Where they do arise, we show that they are not anomalous but have instead clear political interpretations.

TABLE 5   Correlations of Demand-Protest Activity (mean, 1960–79) with Possible Explanatory Factors

Factor and measure	Blacks	Hispanics
1. Size of group		
No. of persons	.84[a]	.87[a]
No. of persons (log)	.96[a]	.88[a]
Relative size (percent)	.59[b]	.28
2. SES resources of group		
Median family income	− .62[b]	− .26
3. Potential political support		
Combined size of black		
and Hispanic populations	.61[b]	.22
Support for black interests		
("no" vote on Prop. 14, 1964)	.68[b]	n.a.
4. Group competition and modeling		
Black demand-protest	n.a.	.64[b]
5. Resistance of dominant coalition	− .17	− .34
6. Size of city (total pop'n)	.67[b]	.90[a]

NOTE: Full regression statistics for this and other tables and figures may be obtained by writing Rufus Browning, Dept. of Political Science, San Francisco State University, San Francisco, CA 94132.

All of the population characteristics in this table are from the 1970 census. The mobilization variables are expressed as means for 1960–79, for which 1970 is the midpoint. The relative positions of the cities do not change much on these variables in any case, and using 1960 or 1980 data does not alter the correlations significantly.

[a]One-tailed $p \leqslant .01$.
[b]One-tailed $p \leqslant .05$.

log of size of minority population and frequency of racial disorders found by Spilerman (1970, 1971, 1976) and Lieske (1978).[5] A rating of protest activity only (excluding more traditional and less disruptive methods) also yielded correlations of .80 to .90. The magnitude of the correlations supports the reasoning that factors associated with size of the minority population were a primary resource for demand-protest activity in this period; it suggests also that demand-protest mobilization had

[5]But Eisinger (1973) reports a correlation of only .14 between protest incidents and size of black population.

diffused pervasively and thoroughly over these cities by the end of the seventies, so that total activity reflected closely the available resources.

Hispanic demand-protest activity appears to be closely correlated with total size of city, but total size is closely correlated with size of Hispanic population ($r = .93$). Black demand-protest is so much more closely related to black population than to total population that we take the size of the minority group to be the key variable for both groups and omit size of city from the analysis that follows.[6]

The high correlation of Hispanic demand-protest with black demand-protest in the sixties is consistent with the hypothesis that high levels of activity by blacks stimulated activity by Hispanics. Overall most of the correlations in table 5 are consistent with some effect of the factors listed, and in the predicted direction. A multivariate analysis is necessary to assess which variables, if any, affected demand-protest independently of the basic population resource—the number of people in the group.

Black Demand-Protest

Our strategy is to take the absolute size of the group as the major explanatory variable (in the form of its logarithm) and to try each other variable in a multiple regression: demand-protest as a function of population and of the other variable. Table 6 summarizes the results for black demand-protest activity.[7]

[6]The relationship of demand-protest to population for Hispanics is not curvilinear, probably because the range of Hispanic demand-protest scores is much smaller, about three-fifths that of black demand-protest scores. Over that range, the relationship for blacks is not curvilinear, either. In subsequent analyses of demand-protest, we use the log transform of population for both black and Hispanic activity.

[7]All of the models presented in this book have been checked for multicollinearity; we routinely give the simple correlations between explanatory variables. The ten cities are not a random sample of any population, but the regression coefficients reported in table 6 and subsequent tables are subject to random measurement error and to random effects of omitted variables. Therefore, we provide the ratios of partial regression coefficients to their standard errors (t with 7 or 8 df). Regression equations with three describing variables were tried but always yielded very small t ratios for one or more regression coefficients and unstable and anomalous values for the coefficients them-

TABLE 6   Black Demand-Protest Activity (mean, 1960–79) as a Function of Size of Black Population and Other Factors

		Standardized regression coefficients						
Model	Explanatory variables	(1) Black pop'n, log of no. of persons 1970	(2) SES black median family income 1970	(3a) Combined size (%) of black and Hisp. pop'n 1970	(3b) White support for black interests Prop. 14 1964	(6) Resistance of dominant coalition 1960–79	Adj. R^2	r of explanatory variables
1	1	.94 (7.62)					.86	—
2	1, 2	.96 (5.59)	.03 (.00)				.85	−.64
3	1, 3a	.94 (5.31)		−.00 (−.13)			.84	.68
4	1, 3b	.93 (9.67)			.24 (2.52)		.92	.02
5	1, 6	.93 (8.12)				−.18 (−1.54)	.88	−.06

NOTE: The table gives the results of regression analysis of five different models—possible explanation of differences among the ten cities in levels of black demand-protest. Variable numbers are keyed to the text. Variables 4 and 5, discussed in the text, are omitted because they are not applicable to demand-protest and to black demand-protest, respectively. Variable 3b is estimated support by whites only, to avoid double counting of black population. The rightmost column shows the correlation between the two explanatory variables in each model. Numbers in parentheses are ratios of unstandardized partial regression coefficients to their standard errors.

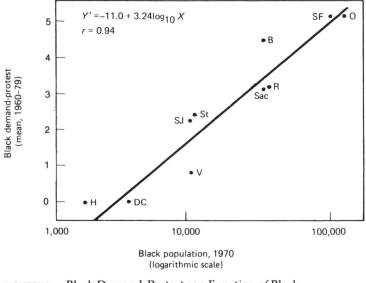

(B = Berkeley; DC = Daly City; H = Hayward; O = Oakland; R = Richmond;
Sac = Sacramento; SF = San Francisco; SJ = San Jose; St = Stockton; V = Vallejo)

Table 6 suggests that several hypotheses about black demand-protest can be rejected. Black median family income (model 2) and the combined size of black and Hispanic populations (model 3) do not appear to have had any appreciable effect on level of demand-protest activity in these cities, independent of size of black population (low t_b). Resistance of the dominant coalition (model 5) may have depressed demand-protest slightly, but the effect was minuscule, if there was any at all.[8] Possibly the difference between blacks and whites in low status occupations (not shown in table 6) had some impact — but in the reverse direction from the hypothesis. Instead of being positively associated with demand-protest — on the

---

selves; therefore, no such equations are reported in this book. Some describing variables may have effects that are not confirmed with this method because of the small number of cases.

[8]The four cities with resistant coalitions for all or almost all of the period were Oakland, Daly City, Stockton, and Vallejo.

grounds that the greater the difference, the greater the grievance and protest—it is negatively associated. Analysis of residuals indicates that this effect was due primarily to one city, Vallejo, with much the largest black-white difference on this measure (26.2 percent), and the lowest level of demand-protest given the size of its black population. As Vallejo is probably the most closed and resistant of these cities toward its black population, this suggests a pattern of consistent exclusion across economic and political spheres, as Morgan and Clark suggest (1973); that is, exclusion underlies the observed negative relationship, rather than the grievance-level response consistent with a positive relationship.[9]

White support for black interests (model 4) is shown to have a modest effect on demand-protest—blacks tended to generate slightly higher levels of demand-protest where whites were supportive than where they were not. Because support for black interests in the electorate and the resistance of the dominant coalition were understandably related (negatively), models 4 and 5 both suggest that blacks were somewhat more active in pressing demands in potentially responsive settings. The impact of white support on demand-protest was relatively small compared to that of black population, but still significant, as we see readily in figure 10. The strong relationship with size of black population is obvious, but the cities with relatively low demand-protest at each population level—Vallejo, Sacramento and Richmond, Oakland—are those in which whites showed relatively little support for black interests, compared with the other cities at the same black population level. Clearly blacks generated demand-protest at levels closely determined by factors associated with population; the absence of white support for black interests probably dampened demand-protest slightly.

Very large differences in demand-protest mounted by blacks in different cities are registered in figure 10. In San Fran-

[9]The other racial difference variable, difference in percent living in dilapidated housing, is not correlated with difference in low-status occupations ($r = .08$), shows virtually zero impact on demand-protest, and does not vary much in this group of cities (differences smaller than 5 percent in every city but one).

cisco and Oakland blacks not only generated very determined, sustained, and well-organized demand activity; they also engaged for many years in numerous protest actions—some planned, some unplanned—and these became violent more than a few times. The next three cities, with black populations around 25,000, saw sustained, organized demand and some vigorous but relatively peaceful protest with little violence. In the next group of three, with black populations slightly over 10,000, demand-protest was sometimes intense but more sporadic, or sustained over a shorter period of time.

Hispanic Demand-Protest

Hispanic activity typically started two or three years after black demand-protest in the same city and reached its peak overall several years later than for blacks, suggesting the possibility that the level of black mobilization in a city might have affected subsequent levels of Hispanic mobilization. Model 4 in table 7 supports the proposition that the stimulus of black demand-protest substantially increased Hispanic activity of the same sort.

Model 4 reflects in part the absolute size of the black population, because black demand-protest is so strongly related to black population. Model 3, which is also plausible on t_b and R^2 criteria, contains a large component of the relative size (percent) of black populations in the term (variable 3a) for the combined size of black and Hispanic groups in which black populations account for most of the variation. Possibly combined size of minority populations generated a supportive environment that played for Hispanic demand-protest the same encouraging role that white support (the pro-black vote on Proposition 14) played for black demand-protest: demand-protest stronger where political support in the electorate was greater. Together, models 3 and 4 suggest some impact of the size and political activity of black populations on the development of Hispanic demand-protest.

Neither Hispanic median family income nor resistance of the dominant coalition appears to have had any effect on demand-protest. The partial regression coefficients are far short of statistical significance.

TABLE 7   Hispanic Demand-Protest Activity (mean, 1970–79) as a Function of Size of Hispanic Population and Other Factors

Model	Explanatory variables	Standardized regression coefficients					Adj. R²	r of explanatory variables
		(1) Hisp. pop'n, log of no. of persons 1970	(2) SES Hisp. median family income 1970	(3a) Combined size (%) of black and Hisp. pop'n 1970	(5) Group modeling: black demand-protest 1960–79	(6) Resistance of dominant coalition 1960–79		
1	1	.88 (5.15)					.74	—
2	1, 2	.90 (4.65)	.07 (0.36)				.71	−.37
3	1, 3a	.91 (6.65)		.32 (2.34)			.83	−.12
4	1, 5	.74 (4.91)			.35 (2.07)		.81	.39
5	1, 6	.85 (4.53)				−.08 (−0.45)	.71	−.30

NOTE: Variable numbers are keyed to the text. Numbers in parentheses are ratios of unstandardized partial regression coefficients to their standard errors (t values). Variable 4, omitted, is inapplicable to demand-protest.

Population Thresholds for Demand-Protest

An examination of the cities with the smallest minority populations shows that even quite small minority groups could and did generate demand-protest. Hispanics in every city did so; the smallest Hispanic group in 1970 was in Vallejo (6,200). Blacks in eight of the ten cities produced demand-protest measurable on our scale; black populations of 3,600 (Daly City) and 1,700 (Hayward) did not.

The Meaning of Group Size for Demand-Protest

Minority-group size—number of people—as a resource for demand-protest is undoubtedly a significant factor. If only 5 percent of a minority group participate in demand-protest during a period of mobilization, this is still 5,000 people in a population of 100,000, and more than 1,000 in a population of 25,000. Whether the group constitutes a large percentage of the city's population may be immaterial, so long as total numbers are adequate to assemble large, vociferous crowds again and again. Though blacks were only 10 percent of San Francisco's population in 1960, this amounted to more than 70,000 people, quite enough to mount impressive displays of strength, anger, and determination.

But group size is probably a surrogate for many other factors as well, beyond the simple conception of numbers of people as a resource. Group size was closely associated with city size, and larger cities are more attractive targets for mobilization, because a high proportion of minority group members live in large cities, and because demand-protest there is likely to receive much broader press coverage than similar events in small cities. Oakland and San Francisco, especially, were the focus of national attention in the media and of deliberate and concentrated effort by national minority-group organizations and by Alinsky-style professional organizers.

As we pointed out earlier, group size is also related to other characteristics that undoubtedly facilitated group organization for demand-protest. In the cities with the oldest minority (black) populations of significant size—Oakland, San Francisco, and Berkeley—blacks had developed the nucleus of an educated middle class, social and political organizations, churches, and some political experience even prior to World War II. Such groups were surely in a better position to participate in the civil rights movement than were groups more recently arrived. Group size, in short, is merely the measurement tip of a much larger set of historical and demographic factors.

Demand-Protest: Summary

Black and Hispanic demand-protest are well accounted for by the strongest models of tables 6 and 7, with R^2 of .955 and .87, respectively. For blacks, by far the most important factor was size of black population (logarithm of the number of persons); and blacks were somewhat more active in cities where the white population was relatively supportive and the dominant coalition not strongly resistant. Hispanic demand-protest was not so closely tied to the basic population resource, and the regression results suggest that the hypothesis of group competition and modeling applies to the Hispanic case or that sizeable black populations facilitated Hispanic demand-protest. For blacks these results are consistent with the hypothesis that factors associated with group size determined the level of demand-protest mobilization in response to the national movement, with white support providing additional impetus. For Hispanics the results indicate clearly that the number of blacks and their mobilization in a given city stimulated similar activity in Hispanics, in addition to the size of the Hispanic community.

It is well to keep in mind that these results involve variables that measure the cumulative behavior of blacks and Hispanics over a twenty-year period. Replicating these models for shorter periods (four and ten years) confirms the twenty-year models, however, producing substantially the same structure but with lower R^2 values, typically in the range .60 to .80. Random measurement error or differences between cities of several years in the appearance of measurable demand-protest activity affect the closeness of relationships in a given short period but tend to be swamped in the data for the whole twenty years.

Because all forms of mobilization were close to zero prior to 1960, these equations describe the cumulative change from 1960 as well as the total amount of activity over the twenty-year period.

The closeness of the relationship in these equations is astonishing. It is surprising that events that were often so chaotic, so laden with emotion, were so closely determined in the aggregate by the size of the group in the city. Why should this be so? A fundamental reason, for blacks especially, was the strength of the national mobilization movement. The movement was so strong that minority groups of similar size in otherwise diverse cities responded to it with much the same level of local demand-protest activity in the aggregate. Although demand-protest patterns differed qualitatively from city to city, there is little evidence in this aggregate analysis for the effect of variation in local minority leadership. What variation may have existed prior to the movement was apparently swept away by its force. There was enormous competition and turnover among leaders, and leaders in different cities tended to be held to the same high standards of activism and public leadership. In the larger cities dozens of major leaders and hundreds of significant activists were involved; these were not situations that could be easily dominated by a single leader, hence responsive to idiosyncratic inclinations.

A surprising finding is that objective differences between white and black populations in quality of housing and in occupational status were not related to demand-protest in ways consistent with the hypothesis that higher levels of grievance would lead to greater protest. Instead it appeared that black groups with relatively low status tended to mobilize for demand-protest somewhat less than we might have expected on the basis of group size. This finding also supports our conclusion about the strength of the national movement. Differences from city to city in level of grievance (at least on these dimensions) made little difference in demand-protest. The movement defined the intensity of the grievance, and local variations were immaterial. On the other hand, the negative impact of low occupational status on black demand-protest is consistent with a resource hypothesis: low status minority groups may be more difficult to mobilize.

The strength of the national movement cannot explain why the relationships between size of group, on the one hand, and demand-protest or protest alone, on the other, in this study are so much closer than the same relationship in other studies of 1960s protest referred to earlier. Proximity surely had a great deal to do with it. Because these ten cities are in the same region of a single state, because they are close to each other, and because communication between them is high, these cities should be much more alike in their response to the national movement than ten cities not so selected. Major protest events in one city tended to be reported in the mass media in the others. Political leaders, both minority and white, were in communication with each other; minority leaders in particular directly promoted diffusion of the movement from cities with the largest and most active minority populations to smaller cities where the movement had not yet taken hold. Surely this accounts for a large part of the closeness of the relationships reported. Finally, other studies have used shorter periods of observation of protest variables—from one to nine years in the 1960s. Aggregation over the twenty years 1960–1979 smooths out that part of the variation between cities observed in other studies that was the result of differences of a year or several years in the time at which demand-protest arose. Extending the period of observation reduces the observed differences between cities in which black demand-protest began early in the sixties and those in which it began later.

The Hispanic response to the demand-protest movement was also strongly determined by size of population, but perhaps not so strongly as the black response. Comparison of unstandardized partial regression coefficients for the models in tables 6 and 7 shows that the effect of group size was about 10 percent less for Hispanic demand-protest than for black in these cities. The suggestion is that the Hispanic movement was somewhat weaker, hence more subject to the idiosyncrasies of leadership and other local factors, including black mobilization. Hispanic demand-protest was also weaker for a given population. For group size of 100,000, for example, Hispanic demand-protest is estimated at 4.3 on the average, black demand-protest at 5.2. However, this difference is attributable to the later start and, therefore, shorter duration of the Hispanic movement in this period rather than to weakness of demand-protest when it did occur.

Electoral Mobilization

We should expect the significance of group size for electoral mobilization to be different from its significance for demand-protest. The fundamental resource in elections is not the number of people in the group but the proportion of the total electorate that the group constitutes.

Electoral mobilization by blacks—control of candidacies and campaign efforts—fits this expectation (table 8): it is most closely related to percent black of the adult population. It is also closely related to our estimate of support for black interests (the Proposition 14 vote in 1964), suggesting that the votes of supportive whites stimulated electoral mobilization by creating opportunities for electoral success.

For Hispanics, electoral mobilization was only weakly related to the percent Hispanic in the population, suggesting that the movement for mobilization of Hispanic populations was much less consistent from city to city, given the size of the fundamental population resources, than it was for blacks. Hispanic electoral mobilization was most strongly associated with prior demand-protest by Hispanics, raising the possibility that it was fueled more by the development of organizational resources via demand-protest work than by consistent development of population (relative size) as a resource.

Black Electoral Mobilization

Minority electoral mobilization is a key factor in our conception of how conservative dominant coalitions were replaced by liberal ones in which minorities played significant roles. We saw that the replacement of conservative coalitions was closely associated with the level of electoral support for blacks recorded in the vote on Proposition 14 in 1964. If strong electoral mobilization by blacks was an important factor in the replacement of conservative coalitions, we should find that black electoral mobilization was also closely associated with 1964 levels of support and with levels of political incorporation achieved by blacks.

Again our strategy for the multivariate analysis is to take as the major explanatory variable the factor that had the highest bivariate correlation in table 8—the percent black of the adult

TABLE 8   Correlations of Electoral Mobilization (mean, 1960–79) with Possible Explanatory Factors

Factor and measure	*Blacks*	*Hispanics*
1. Size of group		
No. of persons	.42	.59[a]
No. of persons (log)	.67[a]	.69[a]
Relative size (percent)	.83[b]	.33
2. SES resources of group		
Median family income	− .45	− .42
3. Potential political support		
Combined size of black and Hispanic populations	.66[a]	.57
Support for black interests ("no" vote on Prop. 14, 1964)	.79[b]	n.a.
4. Organizational development		
Prior demand-protest (1960–79)	.59[a]	.75[b]
5. Group competition and modeling		
Electoral mobilization of the other group	.66[a, c]	.66[a, c]
6. Resistance of dominant coalition	− .19	− .42
7. Size of city (total pop'n)	.00	.54

NOTE: Population characteristics are for 1970 except for percent black, which is the percent black of the adult population in 1964.

[a]One-tailed $p \leq .05$.
[b]One-tailed $p \leq .01$.
[c]Excluding Berkeley, a deviant case. Including Berkeley, $r = .13$.

population—and to estimate the effects, if any, of each other variable in a multiple regression with it. The results are presented in table 9. They establish clearly that black population and white support for the policy interests of blacks were the key determinants of variations in level of black electoral mobilization in this group of cities. Of models 1 – 7, model 4 yields by far the highest R^2 of .89. The variables in the model are simply the components of such electoral support: the relative size of the black population and the estimated size of the white group that supported black interests. White support should not stimulate black mobilization where the black population is very small, however; nor should blacks mobilize with the same vigor where white support is very low, because then the expectation of forming a successful liberal challenging coalition is reduced, given that neither blacks nor liberal whites constituted majorities in any of these cities. To express the way the two factors might interact with each other, black electoral mobilization was taken as a function of the product of percent black population and percent white support (model 8 and figure 11). It is clear that black electoral mobilization is best viewed as a function of the interaction of black population and white support.

Of other models in table 9, model 7 suggests possibly a modest effect of resistance by dominant coalitions, dampening (rather than stimulating) electoral mobilization. Prior demand-protest may have facilitated electoral mobilization, but the effect was very slight, if there was any at all. The socioeconomic inequality measures (not shown in table 9) proved to have virtually no effect on electoral mobilization.

How black population and white support interacted can be seen by examining particular cities. Very small black populations in San Jose, Hayward, and Daly City—three cities where less than 6 percent of the adult population was black in 1964—did not develop any significant organization of candidate recruitment and selection, regardless of the level of liberal support by whites indicated by the Proposition 14 vote. Below a threshold level, between 6 and 10 percent in these cities, black populations generated negligible activity of this kind. Above that threshold the level of sustained organization of candidate

TABLE 9   Black Electoral Mobilization (mean, 1960–79) as a Function of Black Population and Other Variables, Ten Cities

Model	Explanatory variables	(1) Black pop'n, percent black of adult pop'n 1964	(2) SES black median family income 1970	(3a) Combined size (%) of black and Hisp. pop'n 1970	(3b) White support for black interests Prop.14 1964	(4) Organizational development: black demand-protest 1960s	(5) Group competition and modeling: Hisp. electoral mobiliz'n 1960–79	(6) Resistance of dominant coalition 1960–79	Adj. R^2	r of explanatory variables
1	1	.83 (4.27)							.66	—
2	1, 2	.78 (3.48)	.12 (0.51)						.62	−.43
3	1, 3a	.98 (2.52)		−.18 (−0.45)					.62	.85
4	1, 3b	1.01 (8.48)			.50 (4.13)				.89	−.36
5	1, 4	.70 (3.50)				.32 (1.57)			.71	.44
6	1, 5	.83 (3.98)					.00 (0.10)		.61	.13
7	1, 6	.87 (4.85)						−.30 (−1.66)	.72	.12
8	1 × 3b (interaction)	⌐—→ .985 (8.09) ←—⌐ (interaction of columns (1) and (3b))							.97	−.36

NOTE: Variable numbers are keyed to the text. Numbers in parentheses are ratios of unstandardized partial coefficients to their standard errors (t values).

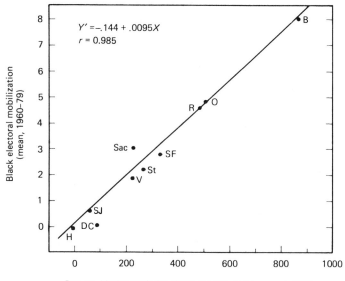

FIGURE 11   Black Electoral Mobilization as a Function of Black Population and White Support

(B = Berkeley; DC = Daly City; H = Hayward; O = Oakland; R = Richmond;
Sac = Sacramento; SF = San Francisco; SJ = San Jose; St = Stockton; V = Vallejo)

recruitment and selection that blacks entered into can be regarded almost entirely as a response to factors of expected levels of support in the electorate.

Where whites were sufficiently supportive, as in Berkeley, a black group of modest size generated very strong and sustained electoral mobilization early on. At the other extreme, in Vallejo, where few whites supported the black position on Proposition 14, black mobilization efforts remained weak and intermittent. Sacramento, San Francisco, and Stockton, which had smaller black populations than Vallejo, generated greater electoral activity; the difference was in the level of support to be expected from nonblacks.

But black population was a more critical resource for electoral mobilization than white support was. The sum of black population and white support, which is just the total vote no on

Proposition 14, was about the same in Sacramento, Stockton, and San Francisco as it was in Oakland and Richmond, which produced much more electoral mobilization. The difference lay in the fact that blacks constituted 22–23 percent of the adult population in the latter two cities in 1964, but only 7–9 percent in the former group. White support, although necessary to sustain a liberal coalition with some chance of success, was simply not an equivalent resource.[10]

Thus the interaction of black population and white support was a much more potent force than either the simple sum or the additive combination of these factors. Nevertheless, the sum of black population and white support is a key variable, because successful challenges by well-defined liberal coalitions depended on a figure exceeding 50 percent. In figure 11 an interaction term of 400 on the horizontal axis signifies sums of black population and white support in the range of approximately 40–53 percent. $(20 + 20 = 40, 9 + 44 = 53$, both pairs of numbers multiply to about 400.) Similarly, an interaction term of 500 signifies sums in the range 45–57 percent, and 600 is associated with sums in the range 49–60 percent. Therefore, the interval 400–600 of the interaction term encompasses what should be the critical step from electoral minority to electoral majority. In figure 11 Richmond, Oakland, and Berkeley were within or above this interval in 1964. Black electoral mobilization in these cities in the sixties and early seventies was qualitatively different. Only in these three cities did blacks frequently take the long

---

[10]The greater importance of black population can be demonstrated also by comparing the regression slopes for the two variables in the interaction model. By substituting the extreme values of one variable in the interaction term, we can estimate the range of the slope of the other variable. The slope for percent black population ranges from .15 to .44 and is .31 at the average white support level; the slope for percent white support ranges from .003 to .21 and is .10 at the mean size of black population. One percent difference in white support generated on the average about one-third as much mobilization as 1 percent difference in black population. Both factors were necessary, but it was black population that was in short supply, hence more critical to black electoral mobilization. (Black population in 1964 ranged from 0.3 to 23 percent of adult population, whereas white support ranged from 16 to 46 percent.) It is likely also that the relative size of the black population was a more important consideration in the calculations of black leaders who organized electoral mobilization.

step from the recruitment and endorsement of black candidates to negotiations over the formation of biracial coalition slates or to centralized control over serious black candidacies on coalition slates. (These conditions correspond to values of 4, 6, and 8 on the mobilization scale, respectively.) In short, the interval from 400 to 600 in figure 11—that is, the interval corresponding to potential majority status for a coalition of blacks and supportive whites—is also the interval at which we begin to find frequent efforts by blacks to develop coalition slates. Black electoral mobilization generally was driven by the interaction of black population and white support, but the transition from candidate recruitment to slate formation in particular was driven by the prospect of electoral majority.

The closeness of the relationship in model 8 and figure 11 testifies to the strength and pervasiveness of the national movement, as well as to the impact of local resources on local mobilization. The strong observed effect of support on mobilization should be seen as the result of the strength of the national movement and of its implementation in this region. The relationship in figure 11 is evidence also of the consistent political rationality of black mobilization in these cities. If the movement were the sole determining factor and generated an impulse to mobilize regardless of the likelihood of local success, mobilization would have occurred to the same extent in all cities. Obviously this was not the case. The movement was realized locally in direct and close proportion to the available local electoral resources, hence in close relation to the likelihood of local success. The consistency of the relationship suggests the consistent diffusion in this region of a common calculus of support and opportunity.

Taking into account cumulative effort over the entire two decades, we can attribute little of the variation in levels of mobilization achieved by black populations to local differences in leadership or other organizational factors. Figure 11 yields only spotty evidence of the impact of strong leaders or of especially facilitative strategies in particular cities. On the one hand, the relatively strong electoral mobilization of blacks in Sacramento is consistent with the stimulus of the coalition-oriented leadership and therefore the coalition opportunity that arose there but not in Vallejo or Stockton, which were similar on the population-support factor. On the other hand, although the leadership and strategy of the biracial liberal coalition in Berkeley were years ahead of their time, this does not show up in figure 11, where Berkeley's actual mobilization is almost exactly equal to the estimated level, given the magnitude of white support and black population. (Possibly we underestimate the electoral mobilization of blacks in Berkeley, however, because they were strongly mobilized for several years prior to 1960, which our measure does not pick up.)

For the most part, where conditions were right, leadership emerged and responded in strength. Where prospects were less promising, the response was much weaker. With a less vigorous national movement we would have found more variation from city to city in the response to local resources; the magnitude of mobilization would have depended more on local variations in leadership, strategy, and the like.

It would be a mistake to conclude from the close association between black mobilization and the size of the black population that population "explains" most of the variance in mobilization and that "political" factors are secondary in their impact. At least in the area of minority mobilization and incorporation, it does not make sense to pit "population" and "political" factors against each other; the perceived dichotomy between demographic and political explanations that underlies much of the policy-determinants literature is simply misleading here.[11] In the present analysis we are not examining the "effect" of population on mobilization; instead, we are studying the effects of the national movement on the relationship of minority political mobilization to the components of electoral support for black interests. In particular, we are observing the movement's intensity as black populations and black leaders in every city were galvanized by their participation in the movement to levels of effort that drew upon and corresponded closely to the available resources of electoral support from both blacks and whites. The correlation of mobilization with population size and white support measures the consistency of the response from city to city and, therefore,

[11]Peterson (1981) makes the same point.

the strength of the political movement. In 1950 there was virtually no electoral activity among blacks in any of these cities and, hence, no variation for differences in size of black population to "explain." It was the movement that transformed black population and white support from statistics to political resources, and it was the local mobilization effort that sought to transform the potential support of both blacks and whites into control over city government.

Furthermore, the initial stages of black electoral mobilization were largely autonomous efforts to test the possibilities of electoral support, not just responses to the efforts of liberal Democratic politicians to form challenging coalitions. Although strengthened mobilization often accompanied the sustained and sometimes successful drive to organize biracial and multiethnic coalitions, it preceded coalition formation in several cities—by some years in two instances. It was local mobilization, including control over minority candidacies, that made coalition formation an attractive possibility; further strengthening of candidate recruitment and selection was a natural outcome of the commitment to coalition.

White Support for Black Policy Interests

Because the level of white support for black interests was so important to black electoral mobilization and coalition formation, we must ask why white populations were so much more supportive in some cities than in others. Table 10 shows that the differences between cities in estimated white support were great.

We cannot use our aggregate data to disentangle the factors that might explain differences from city to city in level of white support. However, Wolfinger and Greenstein (1968) analyzed survey data from the California Poll conducted by the Field Research Corporation. These and other data they set forth show that vote intentions on Proposition 14 were associated with respondents' education and with minority-group status. Blacks, Jews, Asian Americans, and Mexican Americans all intended to vote no on 14, in support of the black position, at rates 20–50 percent higher than the white population as a whole (pp. 757,

TABLE 10   White Support for Black Policy Interests

| City | Estimated nonblack vote "no" on Prop. 14, 1964 | |
	Percent of nonblack adult population	Percent of total adult population
Berkeley	57	46
San Jose	46	46
San Francisco	42	38
Sacramento	38	36
Stockton	36	33
Daly City	35	34
Oakland	30	23
Richmond	28	22
Hayward	27	27
Vallejo	19	16

SOURCE: See appendix C-5.

759). Better educated people were also more likely to vote no on 14. Among white gentiles, the difference in percent intending to vote no, for those with less than high school education compared to those with more than two years of college, was 23 percent for Republicans, 35 percent for Democrats (Wolfinger and Greenstein, 1968, table 8, p. 760).

Wolfinger and Greenstein showed also that opposition to Proposition 14 was associated with respondents' general political orientation, that is, with their party identification. Among white gentiles, Democrats were two to three times as likely to intend to vote no on Proposition 14 as Republicans at the same levels of education (19–32 percentage points difference) (Wolfinger and Greenstein, 1968, table 8).

In short, beyond the effects of education and of minority-group status, people's positions on Proposition 14 followed from broader political commitments. White electorates differed in their political orientations toward the interests of minority groups in ways that are partly but not wholly explained by education and other socioeconomic characteristics.

Researchers in other settings may have difficulty finding a measure of white support for black interests as direct and timely as the "no" vote on Proposition 14. It may be possible to tap survey data in some cases. Votes in other elections may also be useful. For example, the citywide percent Democratic in the 1966 California gubernatorial election is correlated with the 1964 Proposition 14 vote in these cities: $r = .66$, $b = .48$, $a = 34.1$. In that election Edmund G. "Pat" Brown defeated Richard M. Nixon. On the other hand, the Proposition 14 vote was only weakly associated with the 1962 gubernatorial election ($r = -.32$, $b = -.15$; a negative relationship) and with the 1964 presidential vote ($r = .42$, $b = .14$). Because different races engage different issues, there is no reason to assume a priori that a given election will tap the dimension of support for black interests.

Hispanic Electoral Mobilization

The bivariate correlations of table 8 suggested that the pattern of factors shaping the mobilization of Hispanics was different from that of blacks. Group size (percent) was practically unrelated to Hispanic mobilization, but Hispanic demand-protest was closely associated, supporting the hypothesis that Hispanics tended to mobilize in proportion to their organizational development versus the hypothesis that they mobilized in proportion to their basic population resource. The relationship of Hispanic electoral mobilization to demand-protest is given as model 1 of table 11. Models 2 and 3 add potentially relevant population variables: Hispanic population and the size of the black and Hispanic groups combined, respectively. We argued in chapter 1 that because of the way black and Hispanic populations were distributed, some black population was a necessary condition for Hispanic participation in successful challenging coalitions. Model 3 supports this view. The relative size of the Hispanic population alone (model 2) adds nothing to the explanation of electoral mobilization, whereas the relevant resource for coalition formation, combined black and Hispanic population (model 3), adds substantially to it. The combined minority population variable plays somewhat the same role for Hispanic mobilization as black population and white support play for black mobilization. Where conditions of potential electoral support were propitious for the formation of multiethnic coalitions, Hispanics tended to mobilize more strongly in the electoral arena.

It is somewhat more plausible to think of demand-protest and potential electoral support as interacting with each other in their effects on Hispanic electoral mobilization. If combined minority population was large enough to support a multiethnic coalition, then prior demand-protest led to electoral mobilization; if there had been prior demand-protest, then substantial minority populations tended to stimulate stronger Hispanic electoral mobilization. This equation is set forth in model 4, and models 5 – 8 present the results of adding each of four other variables to the interaction term formed by the product of prior demand-protest and percent minority population. The strongest of these is model 5, which registers a modest effect of percent Hispanic population. Once we have accounted for the crucial role of organizational and leadership development through prior demand-protest (contingent on size of minority population), then the basic population resource, the percent Hispanic of the population, is associated with stronger electoral mobilization, as we should expect.

Economic Status and Group Mobilization

A surprising finding in the analysis of demand-protest is that objective differences between white and black populations in quality of housing and in occupational status were not related to demand-protest in ways consistent with the hypothesis that higher levels of grievance would lead to greater protest. Instead it appeared that black groups with relatively low status tended to mobilize for demand-protest somewhat less than we might have expected on the basis of group size. This finding also supports our conclusion about the strength of the national movement. Differences from city to city in level of grievance (at least on these dimensions) made little difference in demand-protest. The movement defined the intensity of the grievance, and local variations were immaterial. On the other hand, the modest negative impact of low occupational status on black

TABLE 11 Hispanic Electoral Mobilization (mean, 1960–79) as a Function of Hispanic Demand-Protest and Other Variables

| | Standardized regression coefficients | | | | | | | |
| | (4) Organiz'l dev'ment: mean Hisp. demand-protest 1960–79 | (1) Hispanic pop'n percent of total pop'n 1970 | (2) SES Hisp. median family income 1970 | (3a) Combined size (%) of black and Hisp. pop'n 1970 | (5) Group comp. and modeling: black electoral mobiliz'n 1960–79 | (6) Resistance of dominant coalition 1960–79 | Adj. R² | r of explana-tory variables |
Model / Explana-tory variables								
1 4	.75 (3.61)						.57	—
2 4, 1	.74 (2.73)	.10 (0.38)					.57	.10
3 4, 3a	.65 (3.59)			.41 (1.80)			.67	.25
	Interaction, (4) and (3a)							
4 4 × 3a	.85 (4.63)						.69	.10
5 4 × 3a, 1	.84 (5.06)	.28 (1.71)					.75	.05[a]

6	4 × 3a, 2	.80 (4.21)	−.20 (1.06)			.69	− .27[a]
7	4 × 3a, 5	.86 (4.29)		(−.04) (−0.18)		.65	.20[a]
8	4 × 3a, 6	.83 (4.46)			(−.18) (−0.94)	.69	−.11[a]

NOTE: Variable numbers are keyed to the text. Numbers in parentheses are ratios of unstandardized partial regression coefficients to their standard errors (*t* values).

[a]These are correlations between the interaction term and the other variable in the equation.

demand-protest is consistent with a resource hypothesis: low status groups are difficult to mobilize.

Efforts to ascertain the effects of group median family income on mobilization of both kinds did not establish that income had any effect on mobilization independent of the effects associated with population. Nevertheless, behind the obviously very strong relationships with group size, relative size, and white support are relationships with median income that are suggestive even if not conclusive. For blacks and Hispanics electoral mobilization is related to income in a way that supports Lieske's (1978) hypothesis of a curvilinear relationship between mobilization and income. (Lieske finds evidence to confirm the hypothesis for the case of racial violence in the sixties and seventies.)

Figure 12 summarizes with regression lines the relationships for blacks and Hispanics separately, for different but corresponding periods. For blacks figure 12 gives the relationship between average electoral mobilization in the 1960s and non-

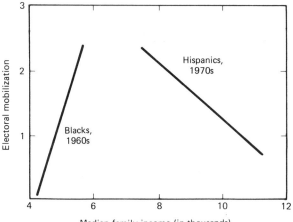

FIGURE 12   Electoral Mobilization as a Function of Median Group Income

NOTE: Lines are regression lines. For blacks, mean 1960s electoral mobilization as a function of 1960 nonwhite median family income, $r = .56$, $N = 7$. For Hispanics, mean 1970s electoral mobilization as a function of 1970 Hispanic median family income, $r = -.55$, $N = 9$. See text.

white median family income in 1960; for Hispanics, between electoral mobilization in the 1970s (when almost all of it occurred) and Hispanic income in 1970. Each regression line extends over the ranges of the two variables involved. In order to remove the most obvious effects of group size, the cities with the smallest minority populations have been omitted: for blacks, Daly City, Hayward, and San Jose; for Hispanics, Berkeley.

The pattern clearly confirms the curvilinear hypothesis. For blacks in the early years, groups that were relatively poor mobilized least. For Hispanics in their early years, groups that were relatively well off mobilized least. But the ranges of median group income were quite different. Hispanic income in 1970 was virtually equal to white median income in several cities at the high end of the scale. In those cities Hispanics had little reason to mobilize, at least as far as local economic status was concerned. The lower the income of Hispanic groups, the more likely they were to mobilize.

The upper end of black median income in 1960 was about equivalent to the lower end of Hispanic income in 1970—substantially below the median income of whites, but well above the poverty level and with a high proportion of steadily employed people. Like Hispanics at this income level, blacks in these cities mobilized strongly in the 1960s. But electoral mobilization was much weaker (almost zero) among the poorest black populations.

The pattern revealed in figure 12 suggests the combined effects of resources and incentives on mobilization. Both factors affected group capacity for mobilization. Where incentives for mobilization were high—that is, where group status was significantly lower than that of whites—mobilization was positively related to resources. The stronger the economic position of the group—with all that implies for education, leadership, organizational ability, and political awareness—the more strongly and quickly mobilization occurred. And where group resources were sufficient, mobilization was inversely related to objective deprivation; the smaller the difference between minority and white incomes, the less mobilization occurred.

Maximum mobilization was achieved where the sense of grievance was high, fueled by substantial objective disadvantages compared to whites, but where the group still had substantial resources of income and of other factors related to income.

The positive relationship between the income and mobilization of blacks disappeared in the 1970s ($r = -.03$). By that time the political aspirations and strategies of the movement had spread even to cities with relatively low resource black populations. The obstacle of low resources was only temporary, and for the twenty years as a whole, as we have seen, black electoral mobilization reflected closely the size of the black and supportive white groups.

Demand-Protest and Electoral Mobilization: Reinforcing or Conflicting Efforts?

The relationship between demand-protest and electoral mobilization is a point of contention in the literature. One hypothesis is that electoral mobilization and demand-protest are mutually reinforcing.[12] In the competing hypothesis demand-protest interferes with electoral mobilization by diverting energies that might otherwise be devoted to winning elections.[13]

Table 8 showed that electoral mobilization was correlated positively with prior demand-protest for both blacks ($r = .59$) and Hispanics ($r = .75$), which suggests that demand-protest at least did not sharply interfere with electoral mobilization. For Hispanics it is clear that the intensity of demand-protest consid-

[12]For Piven and Cloward, electoral strategies are a poor second choice to protest in terms of their political impact (1979, pp. 15, 256, 358), but the effects of disruptive protest depend nevertheless on the electoral vulnerability of elites (p. 31). Thus political impact is generated by mass protest in the presence of electoral instability. Electoral mobilization of minorities may increase the vulnerability of elites; therefore, electoral mobilization may enhance the political impact of demand-protest. Piven and Cloward place more faith in the efficacy of demand-protest. Our analysis stresses the effects of demand-protest on electoral mobilization and the levels of minority incorporation achieved via the electoral route. Button (1978) shows the effect of local protest activity on national policy.

[13]Hamilton (1978) and Pressman (1975) discuss the difficulty of translating program-related activity, including demand-protest arising from citizen participation in programs, into electoral mobilization. Others like Greenstone and Peterson (1973) see citizen participation and related demand-protest mobilization as promoting the institutionalization of minority interests.

erably enhanced the electoral mobilization achieved subsequently. Although differences from city to city in levels of black demand-protest cannot be shown to have produced variation between the cities in subsequent electoral mobilization by blacks, the historical evidence is that in most cases demand-protest did reinforce or facilitate electoral mobilization. In several cities blacks engaged in demand-protest activity first, and electoral mobilization grew out of the leadership and organization established during demand-protest efforts. The connection was often very direct and deliberate. An organization would demand and eventually receive funding to operate programs; then the newly obtained resources would facilitate more demand activity and electoral efforts such as voter canvassing and turnout campaigns. At the extreme such organizations operated like minimachines, distributing program benefits systematically on the basis of participation in political work.

In Oakland a small group of black leaders was successful in pyramiding scarce political resources provided by the poverty and Model Cities programs. They were able to use a "no compromise" position on program issues against a resistant city hall to build support within the black community and translate resources generated partly from control of and conflict over federal programs into the electoral coalition that eventually overturned Oakland's conservative administration. Demand-protest usually centered on federal program issues, secured media attention, made minority leaders public figures, increased communication among leaders and activists, and created organizational structures that were applied also to electoral objectives, thus enhancing electoral mobilization. It was common to conduct both demand-protest and electoral activity, usually with the same organizations and leaders participating in both. Demand-protest drew attention to issues and galvanized electoral support, and electoral mobilization enhanced the impact of demand-protest.

Although in Oakland, as in other cities, organizations and leaders typically carried out demand-protest and electoral effort in mutually supportive ways, the unusual intensity of protest in Oakland, and in particular the extreme militancy of the Black Panther Party, did disrupt and postpone the kind of unity among blacks and between blacks and supportive whites that would have been necessary for a successful challenge to the conservative dominant coalition, as we noted in chapter 2. For example, in 1973 this situation produced two black mayoral candidates, who split the black vote. Although their combined total was greater than 50 percent, the leading black candidate, Black Panther Bobby Seale, was unable to draw upon all of that total and lost in the runoff to the white candidate, the incumbent Mayor Reading.

In San Francisco demand-protest activity interfered more clearly with electoral mobilization. For both black and Hispanic electoral mobilization, San Francisco is on the low side; minority groups in San Francisco produced lower levels of electoral mobilization than we would predict from the best models of tables 9 and 11.

In order to assay more precisely the impact of black protest in the turbulent 1960s, we replicated model 4 of table 9 with average black electoral mobilization in the 1960s only, as a function of the interaction of black population and white support, and of black protest. To do this, we developed a measure of black protest alone, focusing on the most intense and violent forms of protest, as distinguished from the more inclusive measure. Study of this model indicates clearly that in cities where black protest (X_2) was most intense and frequent—San Francisco and Oakland—black electoral mobilization (Y) was somewhat weaker than expected, given the size of the black population and of the supportive white group (X_1):

$$Y' = -.331 + .010X_1 - 1.24X_2 \qquad \text{Adj. } R^2 = .93$$
$$ (-0.90) \quad (10.0) \quad (-3.65)$$

When intense protest was at its peak, these results imply, it interfered rather strongly with electoral mobilization, at least with the aspect of electoral mobilization measured here. For the twenty-year period as a whole, however, the intensity of black protest had no discernible independent effect. The delay and diminution of electoral mobilization as a result of protest in the late sixties were reversed when protest waned in the seventies.

In contrast, Sacramento shows much higher than predicted electoral mobilization for both blacks and Hispanics. The comparison of Sacramento and San Francisco vividly illustrates how minority demand-protest, leadership, and coalition strategies can interact, producing long-term effects on electoral mobilization.

Blacks and Hispanics in Sacramento conducted well-organized and determined but still fairly moderate demand-protest, translated early on into formation of a cooperative, cohesive, and mutually supportive electoral coalition that successfully challenged a dominant conservative group. San Francisco presents a contrast on all of these points. Minority demand-protest was more disruptive and more radical, its target was usually a Democratic administration already in office, neither blacks nor Hispanics were subsequently strongly incorporated into the Democratic coalition, and they both mobilized for elections at a lower rate than in Sacramento. Minority groups in San Francisco were faced with a Democratic mayor already in power, one temperamentally inclined to play the classic San Francisco divide-and-conquer strategy. Mayor Alioto used federal programs, Model Cities and urban renewal in particular, to meet some demands and to build his electoral support in minority neighborhoods. With a relatively conservative dominant coalition at the time cities made application for Model Cities grants, Sacramento did not apply, but San Francisco did. To satisfy the demands of potential minority supporters, Alioto established two Model Cities programs and organizational structures for separate black and Hispanic neighborhoods, the only such arrangement in the country and quite contrary to the objectives and regulations of the program, and he acceded to demands for community control, also contrary to program standards. Hispanic groups in the Mission District had briefly united to stop urban renewal and to obtain Model Cities funding; the result of community control was to pit them against each other in a struggle for control over funds and programs. Within two years Hispanic leadership was hopelessly fragmented. Subsequently, Hispanic candidates were unable to win election in the supervisorial district that included the Mission, and the one Hispanic seat on the board of supervisors was lost two years later.

The pattern was similar for blacks. Rather than try to unite blacks in a stable coalition, Alioto used Model Cities funds to play one group of black leaders against the other. In the predominantly black Bayview-Hunters Point Model Cities neighborhood, community control and the lack of close supervision of allocations and operations permitted widely publicized scandals that discredited the entire effort. For the period as a whole, black electoral mobilization in San Francisco was lower than in Sacramento and lower than we would estimate based on the size of its black population and the level of support for black policy interests among whites. (However, black electoral mobilization in San Francisco revived during the city's brief experience with district elections. With the advent of the new system in 1977, the first black appointee to the board of supervisors, Terry Francois—from 1965 to 1977 the only black supervisor—declined to run for reelection. District elections meant that blacks could be elected from districts in which blacks were a plurality of the electorate, and candidates no longer needed to appeal to the predominantly white electorate citywide. By 1980 two new black representatives, both of them women considerably more liberal than Francois, had won seats on the board.)

The problem was not with demand-protest as such nor with minority group participation in federal programs. The problem lay in the combination of several factors: the availability of a federal program, Model Cities, that could be stretched to serve a divisive political strategy; a too-willing mayor; and minority groups unable to resist the lure of community control. With a stronger position in a more receptive dominant coalition in Sacramento, Hispanic organizations like Concilio have managed to operate social programs and play a potent role in elections without the problems that beset minority-run programs in San Francisco. In Oakland Mayor Reading's administration established programs with black participation, but city hall continued to be an obviously hostile political force. Mayor Reading was conservative, cautious, electorally secure in the short run, and not ambitious for higher office. He lacked the incentive to try for a strong co-optative effort that might have sustained the fragmentation of black leadership in Oakland (Pressman, 1972). The running conflict between city hall and black leaders helped to keep black mobilization alive. But in San Francisco, where the mayor needed minority support to win elections and could as a Democrat bid for it without alienating his electoral base, the co-optative effort was vigorous and successful in conciliating and diverting minority organizations and in disrupting minority mobilization in both the electoral and protest arenas. The experience in San Francisco was consistent with Piven and Cloward's thesis that efforts by government to conciliate protestors with programs "usually led to the demise of the protest movement" (1971, p. 32).

But San Francisco was the exception. Overall, demand-protest and electoral strategies did not interfere with each other and were often used effectively together. The bulk of our evidence supports Mollenkopf's view that minority groups used a wide repertoire of militant and traditional tactics constructively (1973, 1983). Vigorous demand-protest activity often supported other efforts to negotiate, reconcile, compromise, and implement (Steedley and Foley, 1979), and helped to stimulate mobilization in the electoral arena.

Political Incorporation

If minority mobilization was closely linked to resources of population and support that imply political strength, did mobilization in fact propel blacks and Hispanics into positions of power? We saw in chapter 2 that minority groups gained access to city government in diverse ways. Strong, unified electoral mobilization led to a biracial coalition and strong incorporation in Berkeley. In other cities minority protest led to their inclusion in existing or forming coalitions. Oakland's large black population eventually overcame the fragmentation of intense conflict and extreme militancy to win control of city government. Summarizing the aggregate impact of twenty years of minority politics, the cross-sectional analysis of this chapter cuts across the diversity of these patterns of development. Was it primarily demand-protest or mainly electoral mobilization that led to incorporation? Was mobilization necessary for the achievement of incorporation?

Black Incorporation

Levels of incorporation achieved by blacks followed closely the levels of electoral mobilization they generated. However, because black electoral mobilization was so closely determined by potential electoral support, we must interpret incorporation as the result of the combination of mobilization and potential support. In the cities where black organizations developed, recruited, and screened candidates most vigorously, they were also tapping stronger basic support in the electorate than black groups that were less thoroughly mobilized in other cities. When we calculate the regression of incorporation as a function of electoral mobilization, we are not suggesting that mobilization alone can produce incorporation; rather, the mobilization variable includes the factors that shape it. For blacks the electoral mobilization that was generated by strong political support was also applied to that support. Elections were won and political incorporation achieved because mobilization effort was applied in the presence of strong underlying support.

The relationship of black incorporation to electoral mobilization is given in figure 13, where data for each city and the best-fitting (regression) line are plotted. Average levels of incorporation over the twenty-year period were very closely related to average electoral mobilization.[14]

Incorporation lower than expected in Oakland and Vallejo is readily explainable by the presence of resistant dominant coalitions—delaying and limiting black representation and reducing the influence of blacks who did achieve office—and by the delayed formation of a unified challenging coalition in Oakland. Resistant dominant coalitions had little effect on electoral mobilization, but they did reduce the incorporation achieved as a result of mobilization. The incorporation of blacks in Stockton was only slightly lower than we would expect, given the electoral mobilization there. Stockton's district election system ensured black representation in spite of the dominant position of a resistant coalition.

The positions of San Francisco and Richmond, somewhat above the estimated incorporation for the levels of electoral mobilization, reflect the co-optation of blacks in both of these

[14]For this equation, $Y' = -.25 + .66X$, $r^2 = .86$, s.e. of slope $= .095$, s.e. of intercept $= .346$. Zero is the lower bound of the incorporation measure, and the intercept should not be and is not significantly lower than zero. We do not include resistance of dominant coalition in a multiple regression here because the measure of resistance and the measure of incorporation are connected. Resistance is not really an independent causal factor. Sustained resistance is in part just the failure of mobilization to achieve the replacement of the dominant coalition.

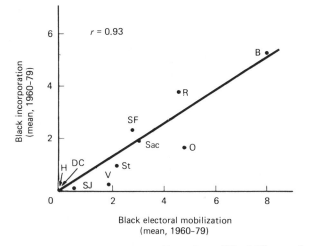

FIGURE 13   Black Incorporation as a Function of Black Electoral
Mobilization

(B = Berkeley; DC = Daly City; H = Hayward; O = Oakland; R = Richmond;
Sac = Sacramento; SF = San Francisco; SJ = San Jose; St = Stockton; V = Vallejo)

cities by liberal coalitions already in power. In San Francisco
this took the form of the appointment of a black to the board of
supervisors and the preemption of more autonomous black
electoral efforts until the advent of district elections. In Richmond incorporation resulted from the ability of blacks to win
elections for council and access via Model Cities and its inclusion in city government, even without a cohesive electoral coalition. Demand-protest and co-optation in San Francisco both
limited the opportunity for electoral mobilization and produced more incorporation than otherwise, albeit in a relatively
diffuse and not strongly minority-oriented coalition. In Richmond the access to city government produced by the Model
Cities co-optation, following protest, reduced the incentive for
electoral mobilization, which seemed unnecessary with a
dominant coalition so yielding.

Did demand-protest generate black incorporation independently of electoral mobilization? Oakland and San Francisco,
with much the largest black populations in absolute terms, experienced far more demand-protest than any of these cities,
but the consequences were quite different, as described in

chapter 2 and demonstrated in figure 13: lower incorporation relative to electoral mobilization in Oakland in this period, higher incorporation relatively speaking in San Francisco. Thus the effect of intense demand-protest was contingent on the nature of the dominant coalition at the time—pragmatically liberal in San Francisco and determinedly resistant in Oakland—and their different responses to protest. The average effect of demand-protest on black incorporation, independent of electoral mobilization, was nil; the effects, positive or negative, in particular cities that experienced the most demand-protest were contingent on the reactive strategies of dominant coalitions.[15]

We noted earlier that the especially intense protest experienced in San Francisco and Oakland dampened black electoral mobilization; now we see that intense protest interacted with the response of the dominant coalition to generate greater incorporation from limited electoral mobilization in San Francisco, but less incorporation from already constrained mobilization in Oakland. In a sense the co-optative response in San Francisco made up for the protest-limited electoral mobilization in that city, at least in terms of level of incorporation. Qualitatively, to be sure, we might expect co-optative incorporation to be less fruitful for minority interests than the same level of incorporation achieved with a more autonomous minority effort. But in Oakland extreme protest reduced incorporation at both stages of the process—both by upsetting the conditions on which electoral mobilization depended and by delaying the successful translation of electoral effort into strong incorporation.

Hispanic Incorporation

The Hispanic case is somewhat more complicated. We know that more of the Hispanic officeholders attained their positions

[15]Because of the contingent effects of intense demand-protest in these cities, a multiple regression cannot tap the effects of demand-protest on incorporation. The partial $b = -.02$, $t = -.12$. The causal connection we know to have operated in three cities in which demand-protest led directly to appointments of black councilmembers in the sixties is swamped by the diverse effects of subsequent interaction with dominant coalitions and by the generally greater impact of electoral mobilization over the twenty-year period and over all ten cities.

by appointment following demand-protest, not through prior electoral mobilization, so demand-protest was a major direct influence on Hispanic incorporation. The relationship between these variables is presented in figure 14 and as model 2 of table 12. We have shown already that Hispanic electoral mobilization followed closely from demand-protest, hence part of the relationship in figure 14 stems from that development rather than from demand-protest alone. Nevertheless, we can read the effects of other factors readily from this graph. The three cities with highest demand-protest are at the right side of the graph. In San Francisco (about 10 percent Hispanic) and San Jose (17 percent), liberal dominant coalitions responded to demand-protest by appointing Hispanic councilmembers in 1968 and 1971, respectively. A conservative coalition in Oakland, where there were fewer than 7 percent Hispanics, did not appoint a Hispanic to city council; however, the same coalition did not respond to black demand-protest with appointment of

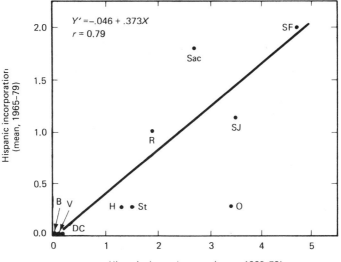

FIGURE 14   Hispanic Incorporation as a Function of Hispanic Demand-Protest

(B = Berkeley; DC = Daly City; H = Hayward; O = Oakland; R = Richmond; Sac = Sacramento; SF = San Francisco; SJ = San Jose; St = Stockton; V = Vallejo)

a black. This suggests an interaction between Hispanic demand-protest and the relative size of the Hispanic population. Where there were enough Hispanics as a percentage of the population to make the dominant coalition potentially vulnerable electorally, demand-protest led directly to appointments to council, hence to incorporation.

In the next four cities, reading left in figure 14, Hispanics gained office through election rather than through appointment; therefore, electoral mobilization rather than demand-protest was the direct cause. In both Hayward and Stockton we find only single-term Hispanic councilmembers, and failure to form liberal coalitions with strong Hispanic participation.

Comparison with Richmond and Sacramento, where Hispanics achieved much greater incorporation, demonstrates the importance of coalitions. In Richmond a Hispanic councilmember benefitted from the biracial liberal coalition already in place. In Sacramento Hispanics participated in the founding of a liberal coalition with whites and blacks and greatly increased their cumulative incorporation over the level they could have expected. These comparisons suggest that the level of incorporation produced by Hispanic electoral mobilization depended on the formation of liberal coalitions that included blacks. If we use black incorporation as a measure of the extent to which this occurred, an interaction term is indicated: the product of Hispanic electoral mobilization and black incorporation.

Table 12 shows the results of regressions with and without the two interaction terms just described. Without the interactions (top half of table 12), we know that both demand-protest and electoral mobilization should account for some of the variance in Hispanic incorporation (model 3), but these two variables are too closely correlated to yield reliable partial coefficients (note the t-values in parentheses). Model 5, with both interaction terms, is clearly much the strongest on all points. Hispanic demand-protest and electoral mobilization did both lead to incorporation, but their effects were conditioned by the size of the Hispanic population and by the formation of liberal coalitions including blacks. The pattern of relationships is plausible, and it fits our understanding of the history of Hispanic political development in these cities.

Although we have used black incorporation as a surrogate

TABLE 12 Hispanic Political Incorporation (mean, 1960–79) as a Function of Mobilization and Other Variables

| Model | Explanatory variables | Standardized regression coefficients | | Adj. R^2 | r of explanatory variables |
		(10) Hispanic demand-protest 1960–79	(11) Hispanic electoral mobiliz'n 1960–79		
1	11	—	.74 (3.06)	.48	—
2	10	.79 (3.69)	—	.58	—
3	10, 11	.54 (1.50)	.32 (0.89)	.57	.79
		Interaction with Hisp. pop'n 1970	Interaction with black incorp'n 1960–79		
4	10 × 1	.82 (3.93)	—	.64	—
5	10 × 1 11 × 9	.67 (4.11)	.43 (2.65)	.79	.36

NOTE: Numbers in parentheses are ratios of partial regression coefficients to their standard errors (t values).

for the presence of liberal coalitions with black participation, it would not be accurate to conclude that blacks generally supported the political aspirations of Hispanics or that black incorporation necessarily facilitated the incorporation of Hispanics. Some black activists regarded Hispanics as whites who were achieving political influence with little effort, that is, on the coattails of the black mobilization movement. Where blacks were able to form successful biracial coalitions without explicit Hispanic participation, they did so, and blacks in such coalitions were not notably receptive to Hispanic interests. The eventual victory of the biracial coalition in Oakland in 1977 actually meant the end of Hispanic representation on city council, when the sole Hispanic councilmember made the mistake of running for mayor against the coalition's candidate.

Even where they supported the same coalition, relationships between the groups sometimes remained highly competitive, as in San Francisco. Only in Sacramento were they clearly cooperative, perhaps in part because blacks comprised the smallest component of the coalition there and could not afford to alienate their partners.

Nevertheless, in spite of the lack of mutual support between the groups, the net effect of the formation of liberal coalitions in which blacks were essential partners was to strengthen the incorporation of Hispanics —often simply because it was better for Hispanics to be represented on a city council dominated by a liberal coalition than on a predominantly conservative council. The benefit was not reciprocal. Black incorporation was typically not strengthened by Hispanic incorporation, because blacks achieved strong incorporation first, except in Sacramento, where both groups participated in the founding of the challenging coalition.

Mobilization and Incorporation: Blacks and Hispanics Compared

In order to bring out the structure of causal factors operating on black and Hispanic political development, we show in figures 15 and 16 the path diagrams for the best-fitting regression equations discussed earlier in this chapter.[16] The figures add some quantitative information, in particular the path coefficients for the U terms, representing other factors and measurement error; the rest of the path coefficients are standardized regression coefficients reported earlier. The major use of the diagrams, however, is to facilitate qualitative comparisons of black and Hispanic political effort.

Black and Hispanic mobilization responded to similar factors. The demand-protest response for both groups was conditioned primarily by the size of the group in absolute numbers. Blacks mobilized slightly more vigorously in cities where whites were relatively supportive; Hispanic demand-protest was stimulated by the intensity of the earlier black demand-protest.

Electoral mobilization by the two groups was also conditioned by similar factors: the size of the group (in relative terms, that is, percentage) and the magnitude of the potential support in the electorate. What is distinctive in the Hispanic case is the critical role played by demand-protest in the development of Hispanic electoral mobilization. Although black electoral mobilization is associated with prior demand-protest ($r = .59$), the latter adds nothing to the explanation afforded by black population and white support. This difference suggests that Hispanic leaders were politicized and brought into the electoral arena by their experience with demand-protest, with the federal programs of the sixties and early seventies, and with the establishment of community-based organizations to influence or to run such programs. It is clear that a very high proportion of the present Hispanic political activists in these cities first achieved prominence in leadership roles with the community-based organizations. Although this was frequently the case for blacks as well, black electoral mobilization was more pervasive from city to city, whether or not there had been major local demand-protest. For blacks the considerably stronger national movement was sufficient to generate electoral mobilization, contingent on the local potential for support. For Hispanics local electoral mobilization depended also on the politicizing experience of prior local demand-protest.

[16]Correlations of variables in figure 15 can be found in tables 5, 6, 8 and 9; for figure 16, in tables 5, 7, 8, 11 and 12. The graphic ⊐↦ is used to indicate interaction between two variables in their effects on a third.

Both black and Hispanic incorporation are seen to be determined primarily by the strength of local mobilization—in conjunction, of course, with the resources of minority group population and of other electoral support that were necessary to the mobilization efforts. The more vigorous electoral mobilization and greater electoral strength and coalition success of blacks are apparent in the fact that black demand-protest had much less effect on incorporation once the effect of electoral mobilization is taken into account.[17] In contrast, Hispanic demand-protest, conditional on the relative size of the Hispanic population, was an important factor in the incorporation of Hispanics because much more of the total time in office by Hispanic councilmembers stemmed from appointments following demand-protest rather than from potentially and typically more autonomous electoral mobilization, in which minority activists were able to have a greater say in the selection of candidates. The subsidence of demand-protest does not bode well for the future political position of Hispanics in cities not already touched by it. (On the other hand, it is possible that electoral mobilization will slowly diffuse on its own without the impetus of a protest movement.)

Hispanic mobilization was clearly stimulated by the wave of mobilization of black populations. Local black demand-protest contributed to the development of local Hispanic demand-protest, which led, in turn, to Hispanic electoral mobilization and to incorporation; and the extent of black incorporation also facilitated Hispanic incorporation directly. There is no evidence, however, that the level of black political effort was much affected by the level of Hispanic mobilization in the same city. The distribution of minority populations was partly responsible for this. Hispanics, somewhat smaller in number in the ten cities as a whole, were also less densely concentrated in a few cities, and

[17]Even taking into account the diverse effects of black demand-protest on black incorporation discussed earlier, it is clear that demand-protest accounted for less of the resultant incorporation for blacks than for Hispanics. Also, the effect of demand-protest for Hispanics was positive on the average, at least during the period under study. Again, however, the adverse effects of co-optation in San Francisco are apparent, as we showed earlier in this chapter. Hispanic unity was lost in the conflict over community control of Model Cities in the Mission District, and the eventual defeat of Alioto's Hispanic appointee to the board of supervisors left a fragmented Hispanic population with no direct representation.

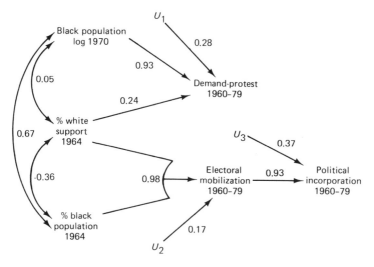

FIGURE 15   Black Mobilization and Political Incorporation—Path
Diagram

this reduced their potential strength; furthermore, moderately large Hispanic populations in three cities were left virtually stranded without black groups sizeable enough to be coalition partners. In addition, the mobilization of blacks occurred first and with greater intensity, and this was bound to affect the subsequent mobilization and incorporation of other groups.

A common element in both the Hispanic and the black experience was the necessity for alliance with other supportive groups of sufficient size. Blacks comprised relatively large proportions of the population in three cities (over 20 percent) and were able to form biracial coalitions there. Where black or Hispanic groups comprised smaller proportions of the total population, from 10 to 20 percent, they had to ally themselves with each other and with supportive whites if successful coalitional challenges were to be mounted. Where whites were sufficiently supportive—for instance, in San Francisco and Sacramento—such coalitions formed; where white opposition was stronger or total black and Hispanic population was too small, they did not.

The models of figures 15 and 16 emphasize again that black mobilization was more consistent in these cities, whereas His-

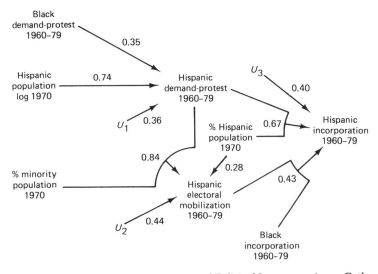

FIGURE 16   Hispanic Mobilization and Political Incorporation—Path
Diagram

panic mobilization was more a series of local efforts significantly influenced by local black demand-protest and facilitated by black electoral mobilization and coalition formation.
We can see this clearly in a comparison of path coefficients in
figures 15 and 16. The more thoroughly and consistently the
national movement diffused to these cities, the more local response should depend on real local resources available for mobilization (that is, minority population). The path coefficients
for black population terms are in fact larger than those for the
Hispanic population variables. Also consistent with the more
idiosyncratic character of the Hispanic movement is the fact
that the coefficients for the U terms, representing the effects of
local factors not explicitly identified in the models, such as particular characteristics of local leadership and political development, are uniformly larger for the Hispanic mobilization and
incorporation measures.[18]

[18]Because of the interaction terms in these models, it is difficult to evaluate
them by comparing actual correlations with predictions from the paths. For
blacks a simpler model without an interaction term performs well: three of the
five nontrivial predicted correlations in that model lie within .01 of the actual

Incorporation and Population

To summarize the cumulative effects of factors that influenced the process of mobilization and incorporation, we lay out in figure 17 the relationship between percentage minority of city population and incorporation for blacks and Hispanics separately. The comparison brings out several aspects of the phenomena and of the differences between black and Hispanic incorporation and can serve as a kind of scorecard. What level of incorporation was achieved by black and Hispanic groups of a given size?

The naive hypothesis about minority population and its effect on local minority politics is that differences between cities in the strength of the minority position depend almost entirely on the relative size of the group, its percentage of the population. The high values for path coefficients of population terms in figures 15 and 16 might lead one similarly to conclude that group size explains virtually all of the difference in group political strength from city to city. Figure 17 dispels this notion. Minority political incorporation and the usual percentage measure of group size are not very closely related.[19] Population does not "explain" political strength, and it is apparent that the other factors that influenced minority mobilization and incorporation made a large difference.

If relative size of minority population does not explain the magnitude of incorporation in general, it is still clear in figure 17 that very small groups—up to 5 or 6 percent—obtained almost no incorporation (and no representation). (Indeed, the two cities with the smallest Hispanic populations appear to account for the relationship in figure 17(b), as there is no clear relationship among the other eight cities.)

---

correlations; the other two, within .05, and the discrepancies appear to be related to the omission of the interaction term. In the Hispanic case, analysis showed that earlier models without interaction terms were not well specified. The model of figure 16 is an improvement on several counts, but because of the interaction terms, we have not carried out the comparison of correlations.

[19]The r^2 values for figures 17(a) and 17(b) are .44 and .12, far below the .86 and .84 values for the best-fitting regression equations for incorporation reported earlier in this chapter. The addition of the absolute size of the group in a multiple regression still falls far short of the explanatory equations developed earlier.

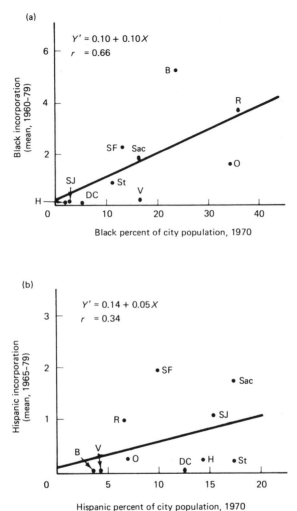

FIGURE 17   Minority Incorporation as a Function of Minority
Population

(B = Berkeley; DC = Daly City; H = Hayward; O = Oakland; R = Richmond;
Sac = Sacramento; SF = San Francisco; SJ = San Jose; St = Stockton; V = Vallejo)

It is easy to read in figure 17 the cumulative effects of the factors other than population that affected incorporation. Of the deviant cities in figure 17(a), Berkeley showed especially strong support among whites for black interests; on the same measure Vallejo showed especially weak support. Vallejo and Oakland were resistant-coalition cities. In the Hispanic case shown in figure 17(b), the two cities far above the regression line are the only cities where multiethnic coalitions formed, and only in these cities (San Francisco and Sacramento) did Hispanic incorporation for a given population approach the average level of black incorporation for the same size of group. Of the cities well below the regression line, Daly City and Hayward had insufficient black populations to support such coalitions. Vallejo, Oakland, Daly City, and Stockton were all dominated by resistant coalitions for most of the period, which sharply limited both black and Hispanic incorporation.

To obtain a fair comparison between the fruits of black and Hispanic mobilization, figure 17(b) shows Hispanic incorporation averaged over a fifteen-year period rather than over the twenty-year period in figure 17(a). The reason for this is that Hispanic mobilization began later and led to representation later—five years later, on the average. The fifteen-year average for Hispanics allows a comparison of the two groups over comparable periods since their respective mobilization efforts got under way.[20]

Note that the scales in figures 17(a) and 17(b) are different. The entire Hispanic graph could fit into the lower left quadrant of the graph for black incorporation and population. The axes of figure 17(a) cover twice the range of the axes of figure 17(b). Because three cities had much higher concentrations of blacks than Hispanics in any city, there is greater variation on both black population and black incorporation.

We may estimate the level of incorporation associated with various population percentages by applying the regression equations given in figure 17; the results are presented in table

[20]The use of twenty-year averages for both groups in earlier analyses in this chapter does not affect results reported there because the variables were standardized in any case.

TABLE 13   Comparison of Estimated Average
Incorporation Levels of Blacks and Hispanics

Group, data base for estimates	Estimated average incorporation level, given group percentage of city population, 1970	
	10%	20%
1. Blacks, 10 cities	1.10	2.10
2. Hispanics, 10 cities	.64	1.14
3. Blacks, 7 cities with fewer than 20% blacks	.86	1.75

NOTE: Cell entries are average incorporation levels estimated from regression equations given in figure 17 for lines 1 and 2. For line 3, $Y' = -.03 + .089X$.

13, lines 1 and 2. By this comparison Hispanic populations generated only slightly more than half as much incorporation as black populations of the same size. But perhaps this is an unfair comparison, and we should remove from the estimates of black incorporation the three cities with the largest black populations; then we would be comparing estimates from black and Hispanic populations in the same size range (less than 20 percent). The resulting estimates of black incorporation are given in line 3; now estimated Hispanic incorporation figures are about 70 percent of black incorporation, still substantially less. All things considered, black populations gained considerably stronger political incorporation than Hispanic populations of the same size. (And as we have shown already, part of the variation in Hispanic mobilization and incorporation was attributable in any case to the presence of strong, local black political efforts.)

Summary

In this chapter we have undertaken a statistical analysis of minority mobilization and incorporation into city government, interpreting both the the main findings and the deviations from them in terms of our historical understanding of the evolution of these processes, as developed in chapter 2. The principal findings of this analysis are as follows.

1. For both blacks and Hispanics, aggregate demand-protest over the period 1960 – 79 was very closely related to the absolute size of the minority groups, where size is a basic resource for demand-protest and an indicator of other significant resources and incentives for political action. Blacks tended to generate slightly higher levels of demand-protest where whites were relatively supportive and the dominant coalition was not strongly resistant to minority initiatives. Hispanic demand-protest began and peaked somewhat later, and was stronger where black demand-protest was strong. Hispanic mobilization was stimulated by the black movement, both overall and in particular cities.

2. Electoral mobilization for both blacks and Hispanics — their control of minority candidacies—depended on the presence of resources for electoral strength. For blacks, especially, the relative size (percent) of the group in the local electorate was critical: larger relative size generated proportionately greater electoral mobilization. For blacks the relative size of the group of supportive whites (including Hispanics, who tended to be more supportive than other whites) was also a critical resource. For Hispanics, however, electoral mobilization was not closely related to percent of the population. Instead Hispanic electoral efforts were much more vigorous where there had been significant Hispanic demand-protest prior to the period of rising electoral effort, probably because demand-protest helped Hispanics generate resources of leadership and organization not already present. Black electoral mobilization did not depend on prior demand-protest, suggesting more consistent diffusion of the movement for black mobilization and less dependence on idiosyncracies of local leadership.

3. For the most part, demand-protest and electoral strategies did not interfere with each other and were often used effectively together. Demand-protest strategies by themselves produced limited results in terms of political incorporation. In

some cities liberal coalitions co-opted minority groups as a result of demand-protest, and even conservative coalitions appointed minorities to city councils. These coalition responses typically increased minority representation in the short run but in several cities may have reduced autonomous electoral mobilization, controlled by the group itself instead of by the white leadership of the coalition. And in Oakland the sustained intensity of demand-protest and extreme militancy of the Black Panthers delayed the unification of electoral forces that might have brought about an earlier effective challenge to the conservative coalition in that city.

4. The factors that produced political incorporation were significantly different for blacks and Hispanics. For blacks electoral mobilization and the resources of electoral support it reflected were by far the most important factors. In spite of the appointment of black councilmembers in some cities as a result of demand-protest, the average net effect of demand-protest on black incorporation was negligible. Hispanic incorporation also depended somewhat on Hispanic electoral mobilization. However, it was also to a significant extent a direct result of co-optation following demand-protest in those cities with substantial Hispanic populations, and even the impact of Hispanic electoral mobilization depended on the presence of black coalition partners. It was not that the Hispanic demand-protest effort was stronger than that of black; rather, the distribution of Hispanic population meant that Hispanic electoral mobilization was significantly weaker, and, consequently, their chances of entering a liberal dominant coalition depended on the presence of substantial, politically active black populations.

5. The cumulative impact of other factors means that the relative size of minority populations does not explain very well their levels of incorporation in the period 1960–79. For both groups, the size of other supportive groups in the electorate, including whites, was critical to the fruitful initiation and continuance of minority electoral mobilization, the formation of biracial and multiethnic coalitions, their victory, and therefore the inclusion of minorities in city governance. Coalition was the key to strong political incorporation, and the combination of minority and white resources was the prerequisite for successful coalition.

Underlying the statistical findings presented in this chapter were streams of action of great intensity sustained over many years. We have pointed out that the motive force for action was common to the broader national movement. The statistical analyses show the pattern of relationships between local actions and local resources that emerged from the working out of local demands and expectations and patterns of action, but the diffusion of these phenomena was part of the national movement—that is, its realization in this region.

Although the call to action was national in scope and brought about widespread awareness of the purpose and possible strategies of mobilization, the dynamic of mobilization, incorporation, and responsiveness was still created locally day by day, year by year, by local people. Where there had been only anger, actions were taken. Where action was inchoate, organizations sprang up. Where leadership was passive, it was replaced. People learned new skills, invented new roles, forged new associations and alliances. Enormous energies flowed into local mobilization efforts, and events ensued in most of the cities that probably forever transformed the political positions of minority populations.

We portrayed in chapter 2 the several paths of mobilization and incorporation that evolved in particular cities. The statistical work of the present chapter makes it clear that even though the dynamics differed sharply and in many ways from city to city, still the cumulative levels of mobilization and incorporation that were achieved were strongly influenced by a few major factors, especially by the size of the minority populations and by the magnitude of white support for minority interests. Although these findings do tell us much of the reason why minorities in some cities mobilized, entered into coalitions, and gained incorporation more strongly than in others, they do not "explain" why minorities mobilized in the first place. That can be understood only by acknowledging the conditions under which blacks and Hispanics lived in this country and the long and gradual rise of their political consciousness and capacity for action.

PART TWO

The Impact of Incorporation on Policy

4

Governmental Responsiveness: Policies and Appointments

Even though minority groups mobilized and gained representation on city councils and in dominant coalitions as analyzed in the preceding chapters, did all of this strenuous activity really produce significant results? The proof, after all, surely is in the benefits of more responsive policies. Did blacks and Hispanics enjoy increased responsiveness from their city governments? Some would answer in the negative, arguing that the protest of the sixties and a few black and Hispanic officeholders in the seventies did not really make much difference in what city governments did. City governments are, after all, severely constrained by economic pressures and by the limits and mandates set by state and federal government (Peterson, 1981). The policies and programs of city governments are also strongly influenced by a formidable array of local forces including the rules and operating procedures established by bureaucrats (Levy, Meltsner, and Wildavsky, 1974; Lineberry, 1977). Under such limitations, how can we expect demonstrations, the efforts of a few minority officeholders, or even a change of dominant coalitions to have much impact?

In this chapter and in the chapter following we show that substantial responsiveness to minority interests was achieved in some cities, but much less in others. The shifts in city policies that took place will not satisfy the sharpest critics of American government, nor did they satisfy many of those who demanded them. Nevertheless, in spite of many failures and setbacks, the policy shifts were not inconsiderable.

If some cities responded much more positively than others to the interests of minority groups, what explains the range of responses? For most of the policy areas examined we demonstrate that minority incorporation in city government, and related minority political activity, explain variation in responsiveness that cannot be fully explained by simple representation as usually defined, or by minority population. In particular policy areas, for reasons having to do with the structure of the policy area, representation and population play a role; overall, incorporation is clearly the best predictor of responsiveness. The analysis confirms that it was minority participation in dominant coalitions, not simple representation or population alone, that brought about most of whatever responsiveness was achieved. Demand-protest also yielded some gains.

In addition, we compare responsiveness to blacks and to Hispanics, finding that black populations in these cities have obtained greater responsiveness than Hispanics and that incorporation explains responsiveness to blacks better than it does responsiveness to Hispanics. That is, the greater gains that blacks achieved depended more on the strength of black incorporation than Hispanic gains did on the strength of Hispanic incorporation.

This chapter first addresses the question of whether a minority presence on councils was important in and of itself apart from any impact on policy responsiveness. Second, we describe the breadth of city government responsiveness, the many ways in which cities with strong incorporation altered policy to meet minority concerns. Then we examine three specific policy areas: handling of the civilian police review board issue, minority appointments to boards and commissions, and minority contracting by city government. An aggregate measure and a rating of overall responsiveness to minorities are also evaluated. Chapter 5 assesses city progress in minority employment, where time series data permit us to trace the evolution of affirmative action and to disentangle the effects of local mobilization and of state and federal pressure, and concludes by discussing the implications of the findings and the decline of reform institutions.

The Significance of a Minority Presence on Councils

A major argument of this book is that minority incorporation is a better predictor of policy responsiveness than simple representation and that higher levels of incorporation have more impact on policy than lower levels. But our evidence suggests that the presence of minorities on councils was important for city politics even if it had not had an impact on policy. Simple representation—that is, descriptive representation (Pitkin, 1967)—is important regardless of its effects on policies and programs.

The mere presence of black and Hispanic councilmembers has increased minority access to councils and changed decision-making processes.[1] We were told repeatedly that minority councilmembers were important in linking minorities to city hall, in providing role models, and in sensitizing white colleagues to minority concerns. Blacks and Hispanics talked about how different it was to be "on the inside," to attend council meetings and see minority representatives sitting on the council, and to be able to call that councilmember on the phone to raise an issue. Even where minorities were not strongly incorporated, councilmembers talked about a new atmosphere and new pressure on the council once minorities were members. One official said, "When minorities talk to the city council now, councilmembers nod their heads rather than yawn." Another official said

City hall is trying more—we are not as afraid as we used to be. We no longer refer to "those people," we know their names. We

---

[1]Here we support Cole (1976, p. 211); Fainstein and Fainstein (1976); Henderson (1978); Keller (1978); Nelson and Meranto (1977, p. 375).

know each other. Minorities know there are human beings in city hall and city hall knows that not everybody out there is a swindle artist.

But in cities without any minority councilmembers, officials made remarks such as the following:

The trouble with most of these Hispanics and blacks is that they only appear before the city council occasionally, don't vote, don't speak for a block of voters when they do appear, and they are totally unwilling to serve on boards or commissions or donate time or energy to the improvement of the city.

Yet a minority leader in the same city reported

I've sort of given up myself. I plan to sell and move out of this city. I've been as active as I know how, but there has been no response from the white majority here.

Minority members made a difference on city councils. They were not the same as whites; they were not Uncle Toms or Tio Tacos. They had different backgrounds and priorities, interests, and ideologies (Aberbach and Walker, 1973; Conyers and Wallace, 1976; Greenstone and Peterson, 1973). Biographical data on the blacks and Hispanics elected to councils show that they were different from white elected officials. The thirty-two blacks and Hispanics who won council races between 1961 and 1977 had been active in minority causes, including minority political clubs or civil rights organizations such as the NAACP and the Urban League. Eleven of them had links with Model Cities, poverty, or Community Development Block Grant (CDBG) programs in our cities. Minority elected officials were generally from more prestigious occupations than the white officeholders. More than 85 percent of them were in professions such as law, education, social services, public administration, and the ministry. In five of the cities the first minority officeholders were lawyers; in two cities, educators; in one, a social service professional. In contrast, white councilmembers included a lower percentage of professionals and a higher proportion of small businessmen. (In some ways, of course, white and minority councilmembers were similar. The proportion of women is the same among minority and white officeholders: 6 percent. Minority incumbents won at approximately the same rate as white incumbents: 80 percent of the time. Length of time in office was also similar for whites and minorities.)

Not only were minority councilmembers different than whites, minority constituents appeared to feel more positive toward them than they would toward white elected officials. Although we do not have systematic evidence to support this point, the notion of trust was expressed frequently to us. Our impression from fieldwork that minorities felt better represented by members of their own group is confirmed by other studies. Keech found that Negro elected officials were expected to articulate the interests of Negroes (1968). Aberbach and Walker found that in response to a question about whether respondents felt they had any public champions, whites selected prominent white officials and blacks mentioned elected black officials and Martin Luther King, Jr. (1973, p. 36). Lamb found that eight out of ten blacks said black officials can generally be trusted (1975, p. 75). Levine (1971, p. 120) and Rossi, Berk, and Eidson (1974) reported that a mayor received high ratings from blacks if he had a strong reputation of being sympathetic to black demands and an additional positive rating if he was black.

The Breadth of the Policy Response

At its strongest the governmental response to minority interests extended across many programs and agencies of city government and permeated routine decision making and service delivery. At its weakest, the response was sporadic, half-hearted, undertaken only under duress, and limited to verbal assurances and an occasional, isolated action. Across a wide range of issues and routine actions that never became issues, the responsive governments were pervasively different.

The incorporation of minorities was typically accompanied by significant changes in the ideology and interests of dominant coalitions, as we noted in chapter 1. Resistant conservative dominant coalitions with no minority representation were replaced by liberal coalitions with minority incorporation. The policy commitments of liberal coalitions, not the mere presence of minorities on them, help explain the responsiveness of city governments. Our research underscores the importance of policymakers' orientations in shaping policy (Crain, 1968; Eulau and Prewitt, 1973; Greenstone and Peterson, 1973).

Berkeley, where by 1980 blacks had been incorporated in liberal dominant coalitions for nineteen years, developed the broadest range of responsive programs and allocated more general fund revenues to minority programs than other cities. Vallejo exemplifies the opposite extreme: steadfast resistance, slow and grudging changes only under great pressure, and then only in particular instances. The comparison of these two cities, with selected examples from the others, will demonstrate the sort of responsiveness that was sometimes achievable, and how different it was from the virtually complete inattention that had gone before.

Berkeley spawned an astonishing array of programs for low income and minority people, and many continuing functions of city government were revamped to meet minority needs. An economic development project was planned and federal funding obtained to beautify and upgrade a rundown business district on Sacramento Street in a predominantly black neighborhood. Two of the three senior centers built with CDBG funds were located in the largely black areas of South and West Berkeley. Minority neighborhoods were conspicuously early beneficiaries of programs for street tree planting, sidewalk repairs, and the undergrounding of utility lines and poles. Significant city-supported health services were located in minority neighborhoods, including the West Berkeley Health Clinic and the Community High Blood Pressure Control Program in South Berkeley.[2] The city operated the South Berkeley Child Care Program.

[2]Berkeley was already unique among these cities in operating its own public health department. Public health is a county function in California, and city residents are taxed by the county for health services. In Berkeley they also pay through the city. Thus the city had already established its willingness to pay extra for special services at the time of minority mobilization in the sixties. Throughout this period Berkeley continued to maintain and improve other city services as well as those specifically responsive to minority interests. Property tax rates stayed at or near the top rate for Bay Area cities. In Berkeley responsiveness to minority interests was consistent with a long-standing and generally supported pattern of a relatively high level of service at additional cost.

By the late sixties and early seventies Berkeley had invested heavily in the development of major parks in South and West Berkeley. Much of the money raised by a special parks bond issue in 1975 has been spent on park facilities in minority neighborhoods. The city blocked off streets in a major black area, so that the neighborhood would not be bisected by high-speed commuter traffic, and landscaped the closures attractively.

The city also supported dozens of community-based organizations that offered employment, health, educational, social, and cultural services to residents; many of these were clearly run by and intended for minority people, such as Adelante, a job-training program for the Spanish speaking; the South Berkeley Welfare Rights Organization; and the Black Repertory Theater. Funding for the human service agencies, including some that served largely nonminority clientele, amounted to $850,000 in 1980–81, both from city funds and from federal and state funds allocated by the city.[3]

With high dropout and unemployment rates among black youths in particular, Berkeley was one of only eight cities in the country selected to implement an experimental Labor Department youth employment program, which guaranteed youths work, income, and job training. The grant was highly competitive and was the result of a major lobbying effort by Mayor Warren Widener (a black lawyer) and other city officials.

Even the city library developed responsive programs. These included not only the usual sorts of library programs and materials on black history and on ethnic heritage generally, but also a tool-lending office located in a trailer behind the South Berkeley Branch, on the edge of the southwest quarter of the city. Residents of low income neighborhoods were able to borrow tools for nothing or at modest cost.

Blacks in Berkeley achieved strong incorporation into the city's system of citizen advisory bodies as well as into elective offices. Minority representatives (mostly blacks) already held

[3]Funding for all of the agencies was cut sharply in 1982 as a result of the fiscal crunch caused by Proposition 13. For January–March 1982, they were funded at a rate less than half that of 1980–81. In March 1982, the city services tax referendum failed to win the required two-thirds approval, several agencies closed, including the South Berkeley Welfare Rights office, and the future funding and existence of many of the agencies were very much in doubt.

11 percent of Berkeley's commission posts in 1962, more minority appointees than any other city in this group at that time, and 46 percent by 1976, nearly twice the percentage of minorities in the city's population.

More than in any other city in this group, the dominant ideology in Berkeley in the seventies stressed a high level of citizen participation. A structure of unusually active boards and commissions held regular meetings, commonly had city staff assistance, and developed proposals and plans with great vigor. In the late seventies, to prevent the mayor or a majority of the city council from controlling appointments to these groups, the council gave each councilmember authority to appoint one member to each board or commission. Although this system was not instituted to protect minority interests in particular, it did ensure that many of the minority appointees would be chosen by elected minority officeholders rather than by white officials who only consulted with minority groups, as in other cities. Although the citizen participation movement in Berkeley was broader than the minority demand for access to city government, it served to support minority participation as well. And even though white activists had their own agenda, the core elements of the minority program, such as strong affirmative action in the appointment of top administrators, continued to receive strong support from whites as well as from blacks. Clearly minority interests as well as minority persons had been brought into the system.

Vallejo offers a sharp contrast on all points. Minority participation increased but was still severely limited. Minority appointees to boards and commissions did grow from 3 to 15 percent of all members from 1962 to 1976, which was somewhat more than half the percent minority of the population. In 1980 the mayor could claim accurately that he had appointed more minority members to boards and commissions than any of his predecessors. Minority respondents we interviewed did acknowledge that he was at least not hostile to minorities—a distinct improvement, in their view. Nevertheless, and in spite of the growth of minority representation on boards and commissions, minority activists felt that minority participation was sharply constrained and a strong minority perspective still largely excluded. In their view, because the dominant coalition in Vallejo was fundamentally opposed to minority interests, the minority people who were appointed were not very responsive to the needs of their groups.

As of the late seventies, for example, Vallejo had appointed no minority representatives to the redevelopment commission, probably the most important commission, and finally did so only when black activists took their complaints to the federal Department of Housing and Urban Development, which told the city it had to do so. Even then the influence of two new minority appointees was diluted because the size of the commission was increased, and they could be and were outvoted.

The contrast with minority participation in Berkeley could hardly be greater. Whereas in Berkeley minority participation was promoted and institutionalized across the board, in Vallejo it was sharply limited, excluded from areas of greatest concern to business interests, and kept ineffectual.

Even in cities where minority incorporation was much weaker than in Berkeley, where the dominant coalition was not strongly minority oriented, and where minority representatives were not clearly partners in it, consultation with minority leaders had become more common. In most of the cities demand-protest in the sixties and seventies, followed by electoral mobilization and representation, had made access to many governmental plans and decisions routine by 1980. In 1960 such access to policy making was not possible even on demand.

With respect to substantive programs, Vallejo scarcely moved a muscle. One could point to the occasional gesture. In 1977, for example, the city had leased a recreation building from the school system and set up a program for youths in the black neighborhood. One could report that two supervisors in the city recreation department were black—at a time when Berkeley's mayor, city manager, police chief, and many other administrators were black. One elected official admitted in 1980 that Vallejo had no minority-oriented programs, but that it would fund a swimming pool and senior center as capital improvements with federal CDBG funds. Minority leaders scoffed, stating that the facilities would be located in middle income neighborhoods and would not serve a low income or minority clientele. At their urging, the local legal services agency filed suit to force the city to build the facilities in locations more convenient to Vallejo's low income population, but the suit was unsuccessful. City officials noted that a park project in the city's black neighborhood was the number one priority when funds became available, but the commitment was made at a time when it was not likely that funds would become available. Federal programs were drying up, and Vallejo, like other California cities, had been hit by the effects of Proposition 13, the property tax limitation measure.

The gap in responsiveness between Berkeley and Vallejo is demonstrated also by the kinds of intervention undertaken by the courts and by federal and state agencies. Whereas black activists tried to use the courts to force Vallejo to allocate more city services to black residents, courts were used to pull the city of Berkeley in the opposite direction. In a suit begun in 1974, Berkeley firefighters eventually won an injunction against Berkeley's quota system for minority hiring. (By the time the decision was handed down, Berkeley had long since abolished the quota system but had found other ways to continue hiring minority personnel at a high rate.) Whereas in Vallejo the authority of HUD was engaged to obtain representation of blacks on city boards, HUD in the late seventies scolded and threatened Berkeley with defunding of several programs, charging that the city gave too much autonomy to citizen boards or was spending more grant funds on social services than regulations permitted. (San Francisco also ran afoul of HUD regulations on the latter issue.) Federal and state agencies and the courts often assisted minority groups in pressuring city governments, but they could also be invoked on the other side if they felt a city had gone too far.

In the bulk of the cities where minority incorporation was neither so strong as in Berkeley nor so lacking as in Vallejo, the extent to which city governments admitted minority interests into the policy-making process and allowed them to alter the delivery of services varied greatly from city to city and from agency to agency within cities. The activities of the San Francisco Redevelopment Agency illustrate a limited shift in responsiveness that could take place in cities that were less strongly incorporated than Berkeley. That agency became more responsive to the interests of a black community in the mid-sixties after the heedless redevelopment of another black neighborhood generated furious protest and after the rise of a liberal dominant coalition with modest minority incorporation.

Black opposition to the redevelopment of San Francisco's Western Addition district was the major focus of mass protest by blacks in the sixties, and the project became notorious nationally as a case study in how not to do redevelopment.[4] The next major housing project the agency wanted to undertake in a predominantly black neighborhood was in the Bayview-Hunters Point district. To be sure, the situation was different to begin with—black leaders there wanted redevelopment—but the agency's approach was very different too. The usual planning effort might have taken six months; instead, an agency planner worked with community representatives during eighteen months of extraordinary conflict and pressure, eventually hammering out a plan that did indeed meet the approval of a loose but sufficient coalition of neighborhood leaders. Whereas agency planners had been accustomed to acting regardless of residents' objections, the new approach required the planners to run a gauntlet of tests of experience simply to win a workable level of trust from the activists. That they were able to do so is striking evidence of their skill, given the tension and mistrust of the times.

The redevelopment agency was far from completely transformed by the success of its new approach in Bayview-Hunters Point. Subsequent projects again brought it into conflict with the expressed interests of leaders and organizations representing blacks, Asians, the aging, and low income residents. Even so, protests and the promise of more of it and the pivotal position of blacks in the city's electorate did transform the redevelopment process at Bayview-Hunters Point.

It was relatively easy to mobilize protest around the perceived massive "collective bads" of redevelopment and thus force some responsiveness. More modest claims on administrative agencies, small improvements much desired by neighborhood organizations but not critically threatening like redevelopment, were often presented to deaf ears in San Francisco. Pathetic tales are told of neighborhood groups striving to orga-

[4]The Western Addition story is told by Mollenkopf (1983).

nize themselves, picking as their first issue some small project such as repair of a park center or the installation of new playground equipment, and experiencing years of frustration in their efforts. One activist in San Francisco, after weeks of fruitless requests to the parks department simply to get it to open a building so that neighborhood people could fix and paint it, borrowed a couple of busloads of children on a warm day, bought them all ice cream cones, and trooped them into the mayor's offices, where, of course, they waited, dripping sweet goo onto the carpet. The building was opened. That was not the end of it—union objections had still to be overcome—but the building was painted eventually, and the group went on subsequently to prevent planned zoning changes that would have radically altered the neighborhood.

Although the picture was very uneven, it is clear that demand-protest and especially incorporation produced some responsiveness. It is also clear that strong incorporation, as in Berkeley, or, later, as in Oakland, could produce across-the-board change in city government and significant changes in the allocation of neighborhood improvements, the prevention of unwanted change in neighborhoods, the provision of new social services, the distribution of traditional city services, and access to decision making.

In one crucial respect the effort to make city governments more responsive failed. Only in Berkeley did substantial social and health services of special concern to minority groups penetrate the general fund budget, and even in that city, it appeared by 1982 that the cutbacks induced by Proposition 13 would decimate the city's allocations to the organizations that delivered those services. Cities were careful to keep minority-oriented social services funded from intergovernmental grants. In the more traditional general fund functions of California city government, some reallocation of funds and services and some restructuring of decision making to meet minority interests was achieved.

Other claimants on city government funds and authority during the sixties and seventies may have done significantly better than minorities. We have not attempted to evaluate the increments gained by other groups—for example, major business interests or city employees. The latter, like workers at other levels of government, enjoyed substantial increases in real income and in retirement and other benefits. Whether they managed to secure a larger share of the increments in city budgets is a question that is difficult to pose in a meaningful way and even more difficult to answer. Certainly there were other claimants on city revenues, and some of them competed for funds vigorously and with success.

Responsiveness: Three Issues Analyzed

The preceding section described the breadth of responsiveness where incorporation was strong and illustrated the range of governmental responses to minority interests in our ten cities. In this section we examine three specific policy issues to show concretely what responsiveness meant for cities with moderately strong incorporation, as well as for cities at the extremes, and to weigh alternative explanations for the wide range of responsiveness observed.

At the end of the period under study, much progress had been made on the average, but some cities were still much less responsive than others. What best explains why some cities were responsive, others less so? With the data presented here and in chapter 5, we can attempt answers to that question in four policy areas: the establishment of civilian police review boards, minority appointments to boards and commissions, city government contracting with minority firms, and (chap. 5) minority employment. Minority leaders put pressure on city governments in all of these areas, and they tap governmental performance with respect to widely held and frequently expressed interests of minority groups (Eisinger, 1980, chap. 7; Jennings and Niemi, 1981, pp. 320–21).[5]

[5]We looked for and attempted to develop comparable measures of responsiveness in many policy areas, including housing, employment and job training, and social services. These efforts did not yield data suitable for comparative analysis. Dates of program initiation and levels of expenditures, frequently used indicators, did not differentiate city treatment of minorities in meaningful ways. Data on the distribution of services to minority neighborhoods are not consistently maintained by the cities and are difficult to

We examine the relationships of responsive behavior in each policy area with each of four measures: minority incorporation, minority representation, minority population, and minority demand-protest. The measures are linked to alternative explanations of responsiveness. One might suppose that responsiveness diffused broadly so that city governments came to respond to the needs of substantial minority populations even if they were not well represented or strongly incorporated, in which case we would expect the strongest relationships between responsiveness and size of minority populations. Or one might hypothesize that city governments responded only if minority populations were represented, and in proportion to their representation; then representation would be most closely correlated with responsiveness. Or, as we have argued already, it might have been that minority participation in dominant coalitions — our measure of incorporation — was significantly more important than mere representation, in which instance responsive behavior should be most closely associated with incorporation. We may also ask whether demand-protest or incorporation better explains variations in responsiveness.

The Civilian Police Review Board Issue

Police treatment of blacks and Hispanics is a perennial issue in cities with substantial minority populations, and these ten cities are no exception. Minority complaints about police brutality figured prominently in protests throughout the sixties and seventies, and minority leaders often advocated the creation of civilian review boards as a means of publicizing and investigating incidents of excessive use of force by police, of disciplining the police officers involved, and of pressuring police departments to adopt more restrictive policies on the use of force, especially the use of guns.

---

reconstruct even in one city for one point in time; the results lack comparability across cities over time. An exception is the data on Community Development Block Grants discussed in chapter 6. Aggregate municipal expenditure data are not easily divisible into geographical areas of the city, and their analysis requires questionable assumptions about which functional areas are beneficial to minorities (Eisinger, 1982).

If feelings ran high on the minority side, the police were also determined to prevent civilian review. To be faced both with a dangerous and difficult job on the street and the possibility of civilian review of police behavior must have seemed a kind of double jeopardy, and departments and police officers' associations typically defended their autonomy with great intensity (Lyford, 1982).

In the 1960s none of the ten cities had police review boards of any type. By the late 1970s two cities had established civilian police review boards, and three cities had considered such boards and rejected them. In the other five cities minority complaints had not been able to place the issue on the agenda for serious city council consideration. (The data are from our 1980 survey. See appendix C-7.)

Table 14 shows that city council action on the police review board issue is perfectly related to the extent of minority incorporation. But as we see from the descriptions of the incorpora-

TABLE 14   Minority Incorporation and the Police Review Board Issue

Action on police review board	Minority incorporation, 1979		
	Weak (0–2)	Moderate (3–5)	Strong (6–7)
Approved			Oakland Berkeley
Considered, not approved		Sacramento San Francisco Richmond	
Not considered	Daly City Hayward San Jose Stockton Vallejo		

Strong: Black mayor leads the dominant coalition; blacks by far the largest minority group.

Moderate: White mayor leads the dominant coalition; minorities weaker in the dominant coalition or unclear coalition structure; minority population split between blacks, Hispanics, and others in Sacramento and San Francisco.

Weak: Minorities lack representation in the dominant coalition. Hispanics the larger minority (Daly City, Hayward, San Jose) or split minority population.

TABLE 15   Correlates of Council Action on the Police Review Board Issue, 1977–80

Characteristic of group	Correlation (r) with black characteristics	Correlation with Hispanic characteristics
Incorporation	.89[a]	−.26
Percent representation on city council	.52	.15
Percent of city population	.49	−.39
Demand-protest	.55	.63

NOTE: For these calculations, categories of city council action in table 14 were coded 0, 1, or 2. Because black and Hispanic characteristics are potentially confounded with each other in their effects on council consideration of the issue, we have omitted from the correlations for each group the three cities with the largest population of the other group. Daly City, San Jose, and Hayward were omitted from correlations with black characteristics. Oakland, Berkeley, and Richmond were omitted from correlations with Hispanic characteristics. This has the disadvantage of reducing the variance on the political and population factors but the more important advantage of removing the most severe potential confounding effects of the size and political position of the other group.

[a]One-tailed $p \le .01$.

tion categories at the bottom of the table, it was the incorporation of blacks that was the effective force. The only cities to establish police review boards as of 1980 were cities where blacks had gained control of independently elected mayoral offices and led the dominant coalition in city council. All three of the cities where blacks comprised the larger minority group had either adopted review boards or considered the issue; the three cities with sizeable Hispanic but small black populations had not even considered it. Only where black incorporation was also relatively strong, in Sacramento and San Francisco, was Hispanic incorporation associated with consideration of the issue. Adoption of civilian review boards apparently required strong minority leadership in the dominant coalition, a position only blacks had achieved in these cities.

City council action on the police review board issue was much more closely related to black incorporation than it was to any other factor (table 15). It is apparent that black incorporation explains virtually all of the difference between cities in their response to the police review board issue and that the other measures of black political and population characteristics do not tap the key factors at work in the politics of this issue. A leading role for blacks in the dominant coalition was the critical factor.[6]

Correlations with the Hispanic factors are so weak and variable that it is difficult to be confident of any Hispanic effect on the issue. Possibly Hispanic demand-protest had some effect, probably only in conjunction with significant black demand-protest and incorporation, as in Sacramento and San Francisco.

The way city governments handled the police review board issue reveals a great deal about the political dynamics of responsiveness. When minority groups raised the issue in cities with little or no incorporation, it never got on the council agenda. In cities with moderate incorporation the issue did reach the council and was handled very gingerly by officials who tried to placate minority concerns about police performance without making the kind of concessions that are unacceptable to police officers. An instructive example of this strategy occurred in San Francisco in 1981 when Mayor Dianne Feinstein first defended the police against charges that citizen complaints were not given a speedy and fair hearing by the police bureau responsible for investigating incidents. Then when internal police reports also indicated that there were problems, the mayor backed modest changes in procedures, changes supported by the police, but stopped short of recommending the addition of civilians to the investigating bureau, a step the police bitterly opposed.

The difference made by higher levels of incorporation is best illustrated by a comparison of Oakland's handling of the police review board issue in the mid-sixties, when there was minority representation on the council but a resistant dominant coali-

[6]Note that reliance on the percent black on the council, the conventional measure of representation, would have led one to the conclusion in this case that black representation had only a modest impact on responsiveness. Taking into account representation on the dominant coalition, as the measure of incorporation does, we see that the impact is much greater.

tion, and in the late seventies, when a liberal coalition led by a black mayor dominated the city council. In the mid-sixties the Oakland poverty agency was involved in a major confrontation with city hall over its proposal to establish a police review board with poverty funds (Kramer, 1969, p. 139). The city refused to make any concessions, and in the ensuing stalemate, the poverty agency actually severed its relationship with city hall. In contrast, a decade later, Mayor Wilson took the lead in supporting minority group demands for the creation of a police review board in the wake of several violent incidents in which blacks were killed by police. He spoke forcefully at large, emotionally charged public meetings on the issue and was instrumental in designing a review board that met the main concerns of minority groups. Some did criticize the new board's lack of power, but the fact remained that a new structure was created to increase the amount of attention given to a problem of great concern to the minority community. Police opposition, which had successfully blocked such an organization in the past, was overcome by the new dominant coalition. As Mayor Wilson put it, "the Police Officers Association came in here and they weren't nasty. They gave up a lot and were willing to agree to it. Now we have a project and it should work and be something that everyone can accept."

Minority Representation on Boards and Commissions

Whereas the police review board issue was a one-time, controversial decision by the city council, minority appointments to city boards and commissions are typically not so controversial and the structure of interests is different. Moreover, we are assessing the cumulative effects of many appointments over a long period of time rather than any single decision. Whereas the dynamics of the review board issue were structured by the sharp conflict between minority groups and police, commission appointments are used for a variety of purposes by mayors, who typically appoint, and by councils, who typically must approve and who may participate in the appointment process. Appointments to commissions enabled elected officials to re-

TABLE 16   Minority Membership on Selected Commissions,
1962 and 1976

City	Minority commission members		Parity ratio	
	1962	1976	1962[a]	1976[b]
Berkeley	11%	46%	.41	1.75
San Francisco	4	30	.17	1.26
San Jose	10	24	.49	1.12
Stockton	3	25	.10	.83
Richmond	0	36	.00	.74
Vallejo	3	15	.11	.64
Sacramento	0	16	.00	.58
Oakland	4	26	.12	.55
Hayward	0	9	.00	.45
Daly City	0	7	.00	.31
Mean	3.5	23.4	.14	.82

[a]Ratio of 1962 percent minority commission members to 1960 percent minority population. The latter are based on the Census Bureau's different definition of "Hispanic" in 1960; this may introduce some modest error into the 1962 parity ratios, for cities with large Hispanic populations. Because parity ratios are zero for all of those cities except San Jose, the error involved might be substantial only in the case of San Jose, perhaps as much as ±.20. See notes to appendix A.

[b]Ratio of 1976 percent minority commission members to 1974 percent minority population.

ward supporters, to give at least symbolic representation to groups, and to give ambitious activists the opportunity to gain visibility for future political candidacies. Some commissions have significant decision-making authority, and appointments to those bodies may also present the opportunity to influence city agencies and programs. Even where some real threat to other interests was involved, however, appointments of minority representatives to commissions could usually be negotiated so as to mollify both sides. Again this contrasts with the police review board issue.

Table 16 shows that minority representation on boards and commissions increased sharply from 1962 to 1976 in every city. Minority people constituted only 3.5 percent of commission members in 1962, on the average, but 23.4 percent in 1976. In spite of increasing minority populations, minority representation on commissions was much closer to parity with minority population. The parity ratio rose from .14 in 1962 to .77 in 1976. Although police review boards were established in only two cities, substantial gains in minority representation on boards and commissions occurred in every city, including some that we know to have been generally unresponsive. As we noted in the preceding section, however, minority activists in those relatively unresponsive cities complained about the quality of minority appointments and about their slim prospects for influence; rising minority representation on commissions in those cities did not signal a proportional impact on programs.

By 1976 eight of the ten cities had a greater proportion of minority representatives on commissions than on councils. Because minority representation on commissions did not typically involve minority control over decision making, it appears that dominant coalitions used commission appointments to provide symbolic representation to minority groups.

Minority representation was also weakened by the fact that it was concentrated in certain commissions and was very sparse in others. Human relations commissions typically had the highest concentration of minority members; in Richmond, 63 percent of all minority commission members in 1976 sat on the human relations commission. Minorities were poorly represented on commissions dealing with economic issues such as redevelopment and ports. For example, in San Francisco white males made up 65 percent of all appointments to all major commissions between 1960 and 1977, but 95 percent of appointments to the five most important commissions—city planning, port, redevelopment, police, and public utilities.

Although minority representation on commissions was diluted by many factors in most cities, commission appointments could be used by liberal dominant coalitions, especially those headed by black mayors, to achieve significant minority interests. The strategic nature of Mayor Wilson's appointments in Oakland was notable. In his first year in office (1977–78), he appointed a second black to the powerful port commission and then a Hispanic, in an effort to make the Port of Oakland more sensitive to affirmative action considerations and to make creation of jobs a higher priority for the port. To the civil service commission, Wilson appointed an aide to Congressman Dellums; the aide had been a key worker in Wilson's mayoral campaign and subsequently became chair of the commission investigating police brutality, which led to the establishment of a police review board in Oakland. Wilson's appointments typically brought strong, active minority representatives into significant commission posts; they were people with long experience, considerable skill, and good standing in the political networks of the city. In Oakland and Berkeley, and to a lesser extent in cities where minority incorporation was weaker, commission appointments often involved more than symbolic representation.

As with city councils, blacks and Hispanics achieved very different levels of representation on city boards and commissions. In 1976, on the average, 16 percent of the commissioners in these cities were black, which is almost equal to the average 18 percent black of city populations. Hispanics, with 14 percent population on the average, held an average of only 7 percent of the commission seats. Blacks had achieved a parity ratio of .88; Hispanics, .53. Blacks achieved commission representation close to parity in most cities, whereas Hispanic representation was generally well below parity.

The correlations presented in table 17 suggest that either incorporation or representation was the key factor in commission appointments for blacks; for Hispanics, representation but not incorporation appears to have been the operant factor. Although effective control of a dominant coalition was essential for establishment of civilian police review boards, the data

TABLE 17   Correlates of Black and Hispanic Representation on City Boards and Commissions, 1976

Characteristic of group	Correlation (r) with group characteristics (N = 10)	
	Black	Hispanic
Incorporation	.90[a]	.34
Percent representation on city council	.85[a]	.87[a]
Percent of city population	.59[b]	.48
Demand-protest	.72[b]	.44

[a]One-tailed $p \leq .01$.
[b]One-tailed $p \leq .05$.

suggest that lesser degrees of incorporation could be translated at least into increases in the number of minority representatives on commissions. Even if not part of the dominant coalition, councilmembers may have been able to influence appointments, and dominant coalitions may have thought it in their interest to appoint minority commissioners as a symbolic gesture or to co-opt minority leaders. Nor were appointing officials simply responding to the size of their minority populations. Note the low correlations of commission representation with black and Hispanic population. In the distribution of what was often symbolic representation on commissions, what was important was actual representation on the council.

Although Hispanic representation on commissions lagged behind that of blacks in relation to their respective populations, this was not because Hispanic representation on city councils was less effective than that of blacks. On the average, both blacks and Hispanics were represented on commissions at parity with their representation on city councils.[7] The shortfall occurred not in the translation of representation on councils into representation on commissions, but at the earlier stage at which representation on councils was generated by electoral mobilization. As we saw in chapter 3, black populations generated stronger incorporation than did Hispanic populations of the same size. The same was true for simple representation. If there was a shortfall in Hispanic representation on boards and commissions, these results suggest that the problem lay in the mobilization of Hispanics and the amount of electoral representation achieved, not in the effectiveness of the representatives who did hold office.

Although numerical representation on commissions followed from numerical representation on city councils, it is clear from the study of the quality of minority appointments and their policy consequences in each city that the strong articulation of minority interests on commissions followed only from strong incorporation of minority leaders in the dominant coalition. No representation or mere representation on city council

[7]Specifically, if we take commission representation as a function of council representation by linear regression, the regression estimates of commission representation are very close to the corresponding council representation figures for both groups.

typically meant largely symbolic representation on commissions. Incorporation into the dominant coalition resulted in a significantly stronger minority voice on commissions, and a leading minority role in the dominant coalition could be used to support moves toward important minority objectives.

Minority Contracting

The shares of city contract funds that go to minority businesses engage a different set of interests than minority appointments or the police review board issue, but city governments have been the target of increasing pressure from minority leaders and businesses in this area as well. We can draw upon measures both of program effort and of output. The measures of effort were obtained from our 1980 survey. One of the measures is a count of the number of elements of a strong minority contracting program mentioned by respondents in each city; the other is the average of respondents' ratings of program aggressiveness. The measure of program output is the percentage of Community Development Block Grant (CDBG) funds that went to minority contractors. (See appendix C-7 for more information.)

Cities varied widely in the vigor and effectiveness of their efforts to develop contracts with minority-owned businesses. Some cities—such as Berkeley, Oakland, and San Francisco—implemented many elements of a strong program: targeting minority entrepreneurs in advertising for bids, giving preference to local or minority contractors even if they were not the lowest bidders, setting aside a percentage of funds for minority firms, requiring firms that bid on contracts to meet affirmative action criteria, and setting goals for minority contracting. Other cities, such as Daly City and Stockton, had few of these program elements. Cities with many elements of a strong program were typically rated as having more aggressive programs, but the correlation was not perfect. Some cities with elements of a strong program on paper did not run aggressive programs, whereas others that lacked some of the elements were nevertheless very strong on implementation.

Surprisingly large shares of CDBG contract funds went to

TABLE 18   Total Dollar Value of CDBG Contract Monies and
             Percentage to Minority Contractors, 1975–78

	Total $ Value (millions)	Percentage to minority contractors
San Francisco	$49.7	59.9
Oakland	10.9	35.7
Berkeley	.5	31.4
Daly City	.7	27.7
San Jose	.1	26.7
Richmond	3.0	5.7
Hayward	1.7	4.6
Vallejo	2.1	4.1
Sacramento	3.5	1.9
Stockton	3.6	0.1

SOURCE: HUD San Francisco Area Office, from Grantee Performance Reports.

TABLE 19   Correlates of City Contracting with Minority-
             Owned Businesses

Characteristic of group	Correlation (r) with black characteristics	Correlation (r) with Hispanic characteristics
Incorporation	.74[a]	.67[a]
Percent representation on city council	.54	.36
Percent of city population	.64	−.13
Demand-protest	.54	.62

NOTE: $N = 7$, see note to table 15. The measure of city contracting with minority businesses is a combination of three measures of program effort and output; see appendix C-7.
[a]One-tailed $p \leq .05$.

minority-owned businesses in San Francisco, where minority contractors received almost 60 percent of the dollar value of CDBG contracts let from 1975 to 1978, and in Oakland, even before Lionel Wilson's coalition took over in 1977. (See table 18.) Five cities awarded only very small shares to minority contractors. Although Berkeley, Daly City, and San Jose awarded substantial shares, the total dollar amounts are so small that the percentages may be quite unreliable indicators of actual program effectiveness.

Because each of the measures of responsiveness in minority contracting has shortcomings, we combined them, giving equal weight to each measure. (See appendix C-7.) We are not able to break down contract amounts by black and Hispanic shares, but we are able to show in table 19 the correlations of the combined measure with black and Hispanic political and population characteristics, omitting in each case the cities with the largest populations of the other group, as in the analysis of the police review board issue.

For both blacks and Hispanics incorporation was most closely correlated with minority contracting. For both groups also, demand-protest was fairly closely correlated, and it is reasonable to suppose that the strength of the minority position in the dominant coalition (incorporation) and the intensity of the minority demand effort were both important and reinforced each other as minority businesses sought larger shares of city contracts.

Interview data confirm the causal connection between incorporation and minority contracting. The liberal dominant coalition in Berkeley established an affirmative action policy for all contracts over $3,000 in the early seventies. The program required that all firms doing business with the city have an affirmative action program, with specific goals, certified by the city. It also provided for penalties for noncompliance, including cancellation of the contract, a monetary penalty, and ineligibility for further city contracts. Berkeley was also one of the first cities to respond to HUD's request that cities do their business with minority banks. The city's entire payroll is handled by a minority bank. Oakland too, since the election of Mayor Wilson, has taken aggressive steps to increase the amount of contracting the city does with minority firms. In 1979, for example, the city set aside funds to allow small minority contractors to be assured of bonding capacity when they bid on jobs. This action doubled the size of construction bonds available to such firms, thus eliminating the problems they had encountered because the bonding industry felt they were too high a risk (*San Francisco Chronicle*, September 8, 1979). Oakland also gave a 5 percent preference rating to local minority firms (*Montclarion*, March 14, 1979).

Minority contracting was not as closely determined by minority political position—incorporation or representation—as minority appointments or as the treatment of the police review board issue. Other factors played a greater role in this area, such as the particulars of bids submitted by minority firms and their performance, or the effectiveness of lobbying by minority businesses in particular cities. Still, minority incorporation was the best predictor of minority contracting, and incorporation made a substantial difference in the flow of large sums of money.

An Aggregate Measure of Policy Responsiveness

In order to clarify further the factors associated with responsiveness, we combined four measures—the three measures analyzed in the preceding sections and percent minority employment in 1978—into one aggregate measure.[8] Cities high on any one measure of responsiveness tended to be high on others as well, though, of course, some cities were strong in some areas but relatively weak in others.[9] Especially in the middle range of minority incorporation, responsiveness was likely to be uneven from area to area in a given city. The effect of combining the separate measures is to eliminate this variation from area to area; the combined measure is an indicator of the average responsiveness of city government.

Table 20 shows the average responsiveness score for each city. Because the score is an average of standard scores, the mean is 0. Thus Berkeley was about 1.5 standard deviations above the mean level of responsiveness in this group of cities, and Daly City was about 1 standard deviation below the mean.

[8]Each of the four original measures was transformed to its standard score; the aggregate measure is the mean of these standard scores. Analysis of all the separate measures revealed no clear evidence of scalar relationships among them, except for minority employment overall and minority employment in professional and administrative positions. All cities with high levels of minority employment in the top positions also had high levels of minority employment overall; the converse was not true.

[9]Between the separate measures of responsiveness, bivariate correlations ranged from .50 to .95. Compare with hypotheses in Kirlin (1973).

TABLE 20   Average Policy Responsiveness, by City

City	Average responsiveness score
Berkeley	1.54
Oakland	1.13
Richmond	.65
San Francisco	.39
Sacramento	−.29
San Jose	−.39
Stockton	−.45
Vallejo	−.87
Hayward	−.90
Daly City	−.97

SOURCE: Average of city government performance in four policy areas of interest to minority groups; see ch. 4 fn. 8, and appendix C-7.

Zero or negative scores on this scale did not mean zero responsiveness; even some of the cities at the bottom of the scale on this measure took steps to change city policies—though often slowly and only under pressure from outside, and limited to one or two areas.

Most of the variation from city to city in average responsiveness is due to variation in responsiveness to blacks. We have seen already that the police review board issue and minority contracting were affected primarily by strong black incorporation. Similarly, blacks achieved greater representation on both city councils and city boards and commissions, for a given population, than did Hispanics. Furthermore, black population itself was more variable from city to city, more concentrated in a few cities. The point is not that there was little responsiveness to Hispanics, but rather that the variation from city to city in average responsiveness scores reflects mainly variation due to black population, the greater intensity of black mobilization in several cities, and the stronger incorporation of black interests in city governments. For this reason it is misleading to correlate average responsiveness scores with Hispanic political and population characteristics, and table 21 shows correlations only with black characteristics.

It is obvious in table 21 that the average responsiveness of city governments was much more closely related to the political incorporation of blacks than to the other indicators of

TABLE 21   Correlates of Average Policy Responsiveness in Ten Cities, Late 1970s

Characteristic of black population	Correlation (r)
Incorporation	.87[a]
Percent representation on city council	.72[a]
Percent of city population	.54
Demand-protest	.71[b]

[a]One-tailed $p \leq .01$.
[b]One-tailed $p \leq .05$.

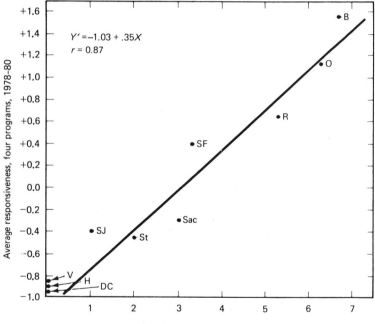

FIGURE 18   Average Responsiveness as a Function of Black Incorporation

(B = Berkeley; DC = Daly City; H = Hayward; O = Oakland; R = Richmond; Sac = Sacramento; SF = San Francisco; SJ = San Jose; St = Stockton; V = Vallejo)

political strength and activity, or of group size.[10] Figure 18 portrays the relationship with incorporation. This is a key relationship, confirming that black incorporation generated responsiveness. The modest deviations of particular cities can be readily explained. San Jose's relatively strong showing is obviously attributable to Hispanic incorporation and demand-protest; blacks comprise a much smaller proportion of the population, and their representation on city council is very recent. Berkeley's strong showing stems from a long history of incorporation, which is not fully captured by the 1977 – 79 incorporation scores graphed in figure 18. The relatively strong responsiveness of San Francisco is striking, especially compared to the much lower position of Sacramento. The cities were very similar in black and Hispanic incorporation. The difference in responsiveness surely lay in the much greater demand-protest produced by San Francisco's much larger black population in the sixties and early seventies (see chapter 3, figure 10). San Francisco's strong showing on responsiveness is not unusual; it is consistent with the different pattern of mobilization produced by a black population of large size. In Richmond, also, a black population of large size produced significant demand-protest but still much less than the absolutely larger groups in Oakland and San Francisco, and therefore less responsiveness in the long run than we would estimate from the level of black incorporation alone.[11]

[10]A reputational measure of overall policy responsiveness produced findings that confirm those obtained with the aggregate measure. The ranking of cities according to their reputation for responsiveness to minorities (see appendix C-7) correlates very closely with the aggregate measure and was also more closely related to political incorporation than to other independent variables. In our 1980 survey respondents also indicated that elected officials were more important in bringing about minority-oriented policies than department heads, providing additional evidence for the hypothesis that political incorporation was key.

[11]In a multiple regression analysis Hispanic incorporation had no detectable association with average responsiveness, independently of black incorporation. Black demand-protest was weakly correlated with average responsiveness, independently of incorporation. However, these models are not well specified, because the dependent variable combines measures that are cumulative over long periods of time (minority employment and representation on boards and commissions) with measures that reflect actions taken in a much

Summary

This chapter has shown that high levels of minority incorporation were associated with important changes in urban policy — the creation of police review boards, the appointments of more minorities to commissions, the increasing use of minority contractors, and a general increase in the number of programs oriented to minorities. Cities with strong minority incorporation were much more likely to be responsive to minority interests. Incorporation is the best predictor of policy responsiveness and is better than simple representation, the size of the minority population, or demand-protest. Of course we should not interpret this as meaning that incorporation was all-important whereas the other factors had no importance. As we saw in chapter 3, population was one of the significant factors in the achievement of strong incorporation, and representation was a prerequisite for incorporation. And demand-protest almost always preceded incorporation and usually accompanied and reinforced it. As we will show in chapter 5, demand-protest had a noticeable effect on employment policy in the sixties and early seventies, independently of incorporation. We also find that blacks have obtained greater responsiveness than Hispanics and that incorporation explains responsiveness to blacks better than responsiveness to Hispanics. Our evidence also shows that simple representation of minorities produces some effects of its own, but it is important regardless of its impact on policies and programs, because it has increased minority access to councils and changed decision-making processes.

Still, the highest levels of responsiveness were attainable only with strong incorporation. Incorporation yielded fruits that could not be reached with large population alone, or with simple representation without access to the dominant coalition, or with demand-protest unsupported by incorporation.

---

shorter time frame (police review board and minority contracting). The analyses of particular policies in this chapter and in chapter 5 relate responsiveness to incorporation for different periods, depending on the time interval relevant to each policy area.

5

Governmental Responsiveness: City Employment

Governmental employment has long been an important goal and point of early access for excluded groups in American society, most recently for blacks and Hispanics. Longitudinal data on city government employment enable us to trace the evolution of responsiveness in this policy area.

Discrimination in employment was one of the prime targets of black protests in the early sixties. Several federal programs included in their stated goals the elimination of discrimination in public employment, or the employment of the poor in general or of minorities in particular. Among these were the poverty program (1964), Model Cities (1967), and Equal Employment Opportunity (1972). At the local level significant minority political activity focused on changing city policy regarding government employment.[1]

The first set of questions to be asked about minority employment in city government has to do with levels of responsive-

---

[1]Government employment policy can be seen as incrementally redistributive if over time a disadvantaged group gets more employment than it had and

ness. Have these cities been responsive to the demand for minority employment? What changes in city personnel policies and programs were undertaken? What levels of minority employment were reached? What patterns of change can be observed, and what do they tell us about the likelihood of future gains? Have these city governments been more responsive to blacks than to Hispanics?

We show that levels of minority employment have, in fact, increased very substantially, but with wide variation from city to city. The second set of questions, then, concerns alternative explanations for the gains achieved and for the variation among cities. Can we attribute increased responsiveness primarily to internal political forces—minority incorporation and demand-protest, especially—or to external forces, in particular the enforcement efforts of state and federal agencies? Do the political factors of minority incorporation and demand-protest explain gains in minority employment that cannot be attributed simply to differences in the size of the minority population? How much difference do they make? Which political factor seems to produce the greatest gains? Do the same factors explain gains in Hispanic and in black employment?

To answer these questions, we rely on historical reconstructions of minority employment efforts, obtained through interviews with city personnel directors and from city documents, and on data prepared by the cities. Beginning in 1974, all cities were required to submit detailed information on minority employment to the U.S. Equal Employment Opportunity Commission (EEOC). We obtained these data from the cities for 1974 and 1978. For 1966 and 1970, minority employment figures are based on city ethnic surveys and on personnel directors' estimates (see appendix C-6 and Browning and Marshall, 1976). (All of these data were checked and rechecked, and many errors in the original sources were corrected.) The modest time series permits some analysis of factors associated with change in minority employment. The data also have the

---

relatively advantaged groups get less. However, Peterson (1981) classified employment policy as allocational rather than as redistributional, narrowly defining redistributional policies as those benefitting low income groups and negatively affecting the local economy.

advantage that benefits to blacks and Hispanics can be separated. This chapter also analyzes the movement of minorities into top administrative positions. It concludes by discussing the implications of the findings on policy responsiveness and the associated decline of reform institutions.

Gains in Minority Employment

More than for any other governmental program, the definition of responsiveness for minority employment in city government is linked to minority population. Population parity—the ratio of percent minority employment in city government to the percent minority of city population—is not the only possible standard but is the one against which minority employment is typically evaluated.[2]

Minority employment in these cities increased rapidly on the average from 1966 to 1978, as shown in figure 19. This parallels the general trend in state and local government employment of minorities.[3] Every one of these cities had increased minority employment overall since 1966 at a faster rate than the increase in minority population. Figure 19 traces average mi-

[2]Federal guidelines also permit cities to use less demanding standards: the percentage of minorities in the civilian labor force (less demanding because minorities, with a higher proportion of children in their populations, typically constitute a smaller percentage of the labor force than of the population as a whole) and the percentage of minorities in the available labor force in relevant occupations (still less demanding because of the underrepresentation of minorities in many of the occupations that city governments employ). In the early seventies the choice of employment targets in some of our cities was a controversial issue. By the end of the 1970s the only cities that were still formally adopting specific minority employment targets were those required to do so by external enforcement efforts—by courts, by the Office of Revenue Sharing, and by the California Fair Employment Practices Commission. Some with vigorous affirmative action efforts dropped specific goals because they were on the verge of exceeding them and did not want them to act as a brake on minority hiring.

[3]See Cayer and Sigelman (1980); Eisinger (1982); Hutchins and Sigelman (1981); Kranz (1976); U.S. Equal Employment Opportunity Commission (1977 and 1980); and Viteritti (1979).

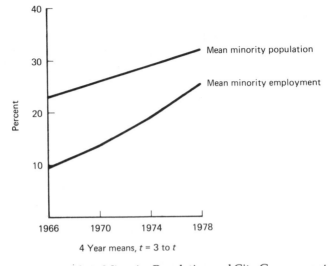

FIGURE 19   Trends in Minority Population and City Government
Employment. (Ten cities, means 1966–78)

nority population and employment percentages since 1966. In
1966 average minority employment in city government in the
ten cities was 9.5 percent, minority population was 23 percent
(parity ratio of .41). By 1978 average minority employment
overall stood at 25.5 percent, minority population at 32.1 percent (parity ratio .79). If the increases registered between 1974
and 1978 were to continue, average minority employment
would equal minority population by about 1985. These averages do not reveal the substantial differences between blacks
and Hispanics. In 1966 average black employment was 6.5 percent, black population was 13.6 percent for a parity ratio of .48.
In contrast the Hispanic parity ratio was .32 (employment at 3
percent and population at about 9.4 percent). By 1978 the black
parity ratio was .90 (with employment at 16.6 percent and population at 18.4 percent), whereas the Hispanic parity level was
.65 (with employment at 8.9 percent and population at 13.6
percent).[4]

[4]A black-Hispanic discrepancy was also found by Dye and Renick (1981),
but parity levels are generally lower in their cities than ours (black parity .44,
Hispanic .33). Welch, Karnig, and Eribes (1983) found a high Hispanic parity
ratio of .97 in 1978 in five southwestern states, an increase from 1973.

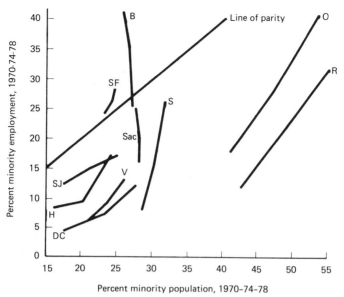

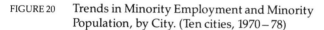

Percent minority population, 1970-74-78

FIGURE 20   Trends in Minority Employment and Minority
Population, by City. (Ten cities, 1970 – 78)

(B = Berkeley; DC = Daly City; H = Hayward; O = Oakland; R = Richmond;
Sac = Sacramento; SF = San Francisco; SJ = San Jose; St = Stockton; V = Vallejo)

Figure 20 shows that all ten cities have increased minority
employment in relation to minority population since 1970, but
some much earlier and much more than others. Three cities
were already close to parity in 1970 (Berkeley, San Francisco,
and Sacramento) and were at or above parity by 1978. Others
started lower, did not experience their greatest gains until the
late seventies, and were still some distance from parity in 1978
(Hayward, Daly City, and Vallejo).

How large are the gains shown in figure 20? How great an
effort had to be made to achieve them? Reliable data on the
percent minority of new hires proved too difficult to obtain,
but a little arithmetic shows that cities had to be hiring substantial percentages of minorities in order to increase their
proportions of minorities in the work force at the rates shown
in figure 20. For example, if we assume no growth in city employment and 10 percent annual turnover affecting whites and
minorities equally, about one-third of new hires would have to

be minorities to increase the overall percent minority from 20 to 24 in four years. To increase from 30 to 38 percent minority in four years—not an uncommon occurrence—minorities would have to make up more than half of the new hires. Although growth in city employment makes it easier to achieve such gains, the cities where the greatest gains have been made have continued to make them even when they were not growing. Clearly, many cities made strenuous efforts to hire minorities.

The Transformation of City Personnel Practices

The evidence from the case studies is conclusive that substantial gains—in some cities, any gains—in minority employment were achieved only after city government hiring practices were completely overhauled with affirmative action as the goal. Every stage of the hiring process was revamped to meet demands for increased minority employment.

Cities developed new recruitment methods to attract more minority applicants. Comprehensive mailing lists, including minority and women's groups, were compiled to advertise openings. But more active methods were developed as well. Oakland instituted a "coaching and schooling committee" headed by the highest ranking black fire department officer. He coordinated the city's equal employment opportunity program, a labor union recruitment program, and a fire department training program. By the spring of 1973, the department's aggressive recruitment and training effort resulted in thirty-two minority persons in the top sixty names of the new hiring lists.

Application forms were revised to eliminate questions that might bias against minority applicants. Preemployment tests were "validated"—revised so as to test actual job-related skills. Many cities changed final selection rules to reduce the weight given to test results and to make it easier for affirmative action objectives to affect the final hiring decision. San Francisco, which had followed a "rule of one" (the highest scoring applicant had to be hired), adopted a rule of three. Two cities (Berkeley and Sacramento) used "selective certification" methods, which resulted in rapid affirmative action progress until courts declared these methods invalid on reverse discrimination grounds. Daly City, under pressure from the California Fair Employment Practices Commission (FEPC), shifted from a rule of three to "multifactor certification" in which affirmative action objectives could play a significant role. Under the new system, the personnel office sent a list of "eligible applicants"—applicants who met minimum qualifications for the jobs—to the hiring department. The department had to interview all the eligibles. The personnel office also sent a note about the status of minority employment in the department and about how that status would change if minority persons were hired. The city manager had to approve the final hiring decision and could raise affirmative action objections before a final hiring decision was made.

The Politics of Affirmative Action

Transformation in city government hiring practices coincided with significant political changes. Different stages in the movement to increase minority employment involved different political factors, shifting as the emphasis in minority politics changed from demand-protest to electoral mobilization and incorporation, and as the machinery of federal and state enforcement was established and set in motion. Demand-protest was especially important in the 1960s; incorporation, cresting later, was important throughout these two decades but especially in the late sixties and early seventies. In the middle and late seventies, federal and state enforcement was a key stimulus. These political changes brought about policy changes that altered hiring procedures and greatly accelerated the hiring of blacks and Hispanics.

The Sixties: Black Demand-Protest

Discrimination in employment generally and in city government in particular was a significant theme of demand-protest activity from the early 1960s onward. Where such activity occurred—in Berkeley, Oakland, and San Francisco—it focused the attention of city officials on minority hiring. The establishment of human relations commissions by city councils was followed by council-mandated ethnic surveys of city government employment—in Berkeley in 1960–61 and in San Francisco in 1964–65. Dominated by a less responsive council coalition, Oakland did not take these steps but still increased minority employment rapidly (Thompson, 1975).

Minority Incorporation

The effects of changes in the incorporation of both blacks and Hispanics can be seen in several ways throughout this period. In addition to human relations commissions and ethnic surveys, city councils passed affirmative action resolutions and plans and moved to require minority hiring reports. Cities with relatively strong minority incorporation in 1970 had adopted two or three of these affirmative action steps; other cities, none or one. In that year the number of affirmative action steps taken was very closely related to the percentage of minorities in city government employment, $r = .92$.[5]

The effects of incorporation can also be seen in the succession of city managers and personnel officers. A typical pattern is the replacement of an older, resistant dominant coalition by one in which minorities are well incorporated; the firing or resignation of the city manager; his or her replacement by one more enthusiastic about affirmative action; and the hiring of a new personnel director to implement affirmative action programs.[6]

That these changes were not mere window dressing is ap-

---

[5]By 1978, however, all cities had taken at least four of these steps, some of them under considerable outside pressure, and the relationship with percent minority employment had evaporated: $r = -.01$. Formal actions of city governments are only sometimes good indicators of policy outcomes.

[6]This sequence even involved the same personnel director in three of these cities. William Danielson developed a reputation for effective affirmative action in Berkeley in the sixties. He was hired by Sacramento following a shift in dominant coalitions in 1969 and implemented affirmative action there. He was later hired by Oakland after the victory of a liberal coalition there in 1977. Thompson (1978) discusses the links between personnel administrators' attitudes toward minorities and affirmative action efforts.

parent in the way that gains in minority employment were linked to changes in minority incorporation. In four of the five cases for which the data permit an evaluation, a spurt in minority employment followed one to three years after a major increase in minority incorporation. This is clearly the case for Sacramento (1966), San Jose (1969), Stockton (1971), and Richmond (1971).

Federal and State Enforcement

By the mid-seventies legal remedies for weak or nonexistent minority hiring programs were available, and federal and state agencies took an increasingly active role in pushing cities to take affirmative action to increase minority employment. Federal policies began to require affirmative action efforts by cities that received federal grants, and the Neighborhood Legal Services Program made it easier for minority groups to challenge city hiring practices and other policies in the courts. In the seventies after Ronald Reagan left the governorship, the California Fair Employment Practices Act was more vigorously enforced resulting in investigations or surveys of hiring practices and employment patterns in many California cities.

Efforts to increase minority employment using these tools reached into cities with little or no minority incorporation or demand-protest. The FEPC undertook investigations of city employment practices in Vallejo (1973) and Daly City (1975), which resulted in stronger affirmative action plans and increased hiring of minorities. An FEPC survey, which investigates employment conditions but does not carry enforcement weight, was done in Stockton in response to minority complaints.

The external enforcement apparatus was invoked also in cities with significant minority incorporation and demand-protest. Thus the U.S. Office of Revenue Sharing threatened San Francisco (1978) and San Jose (1978–79) with loss of General Revenue Sharing funds for failure to adopt an affirmative action plan (San Francisco) and allegedly inadequate hiring of Hispanics (San Jose). The FEPC surveyed police and fire employment in Oakland. Lawsuits in Oakland (1966) and San Francisco (1973) against police and fire department hiring practices led to changes in testing requirements.

Thus several agencies for external enforcement of affirmative action standards complemented local minority incorporation and demand-protest in some cities, partly compensated for the weakness of minority political efforts in other cities, and reached into departments most resistant to minority hiring (police and fire in particular). Demand-protest and incorporation appear to be associated with significant early gains in some cities, whereas external enforcement complemented and extended these gains in the seventies and stimulated minority hiring in cities where minority groups were politically weak. However, the highest levels and most dramatic gains in minority employment were associated with strong minority demand-protest and incorporation (Berkeley, San Francisco, Sacramento, Stockton, and Oakland) rather than with external enforcement in the absence of strong minority political factors (San Jose, Daly City, and Vallejo).

Models of Black and Hispanic Employment

The analysis to this point can be extended and reinforced with a more systematic statistical approach that clarifies and takes into account sharp differences in the dynamics of black and Hispanic employment. It is also necessary to take into account differences between cities in the sizes of their minority populations. We accomplish these tasks in this section and show that simple models of governmental behavior with respect to minority employment can explain a very large part of the difference between cities in minority employment gains.

Figure 21 shows the relationship between employment and population for blacks and Hispanics separately in 1970, 1974, and 1978. The relationships are consistently linear, and the figure shows the relation between percent black or Hispanic population and the percent black or Hispanic employment for the ten cities in each of the three years. The lengths of the lines are determined by the lowest and highest values of percent black and Hispanic population in each year. It is apparent that both groups were advancing toward parity over this period, as

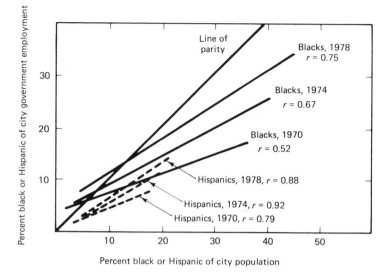

Percent black or Hispanic of city population

FIGURE 21   Relationship of Minority Employment in
City Government to Minority Population.
(Ten cities, 1970 –78)

evidenced by the way the regression lines for both groups approach the line of parity over time. But black employment at the same level of population was already considerably higher than Hispanic employment in 1970 and has advanced more rapidly since then. There may be a time when Hispanic employment catches up with black employment in city governments, but during the 1970s, in spite of improvements in Hispanic employment, the gap between the groups widened somewhat. Hispanic populations in these cities were getting less of the city government employment benefits than blacks were.

For both groups, employment at the end of this period is much more closely related to the size of the groups in the city than it was at the beginning. This is consistent with the fact that hiring practices encouraging minority employment spread from a few cities that hired minority employees in significant numbers in the fifties and early sixties to the bulk of the cities that responded to minority demand-protest and incorporation in the sixties and seventies and/or to external pressure in the seventies.

However, employment is more closely related to population for Hispanics than for blacks in all three years, in spite of the more limited variation of the Hispanic population figures. We shall show that this occurs because the incorporation of blacks in city governments has had a strong and direct effect on black employment, partly independent of the size of the black population in the cities, but that the incorporation of Hispanics has had little or no such effect.

The Dynamics of Minority Hiring

A simple—but in this case inappropriate—conception of the steady increase in minority employment suggests that minority employment may be more or less closely "explained" by minority population and that minority incorporation might explain some additional variance between cities. This is a familiar mode of analysis in political science. In the long run, of course, we might expect minority employment to approach minority population, and figures 19 and 20 show that this was the trend during the 1970s.

For our purposes this model is not adequate. First, we have already shown (chapter 3) that the incorporation of blacks over the period 1960–80 depended not just on the size of the minority population but also on the willingness of white voters to support black interests and on the existence of a dominant coalition that could block or facilitate the incorporation of blacks into city government. Second, because minority population and incorporation are rather closely related, it is not feasible to treat them as independent variables in a statistical analysis of factors affecting minority employment. Third, such a model describes expected relationships at a point in time, whereas we wish to examine the dynamics of gains in minority employment over a period of time: 1966 to 1978 for blacks and 1970 to 1978 for Hispanics (the shorter period for Hispanics because consistent population data on Hispanics are not available before 1970).

Let us look at the minority employment problem from the perspective of the responsible authorities of city government: the city council, city manager, and director of personnel. If they wish to do so, they can take a variety of steps to increase the rate at which minority employees are appointed. There are two main reasons why they might. First, if minority interests are strongly represented through demand-protest or through incorporation, the city has an incentive to commit itself to increased minority employment. Minority demand-protest and incorporation are obvious candidates for causal factors of prime importance.

A second reason for taking steps to increase minority hiring has to do with the magnitude of the problem. If a city's minority employment level falls far short of parity with the size of its minority population, its officials are likely to be under much greater pressure to accelerate minority hiring, both from minority interests within the city and from federal and state agencies, than if the city already employs minorities at a level close to parity. Thus the parity gap—the difference between percent minority of population and percent minority of city government employees—is a measure of the magnitude of the problem and a likely causal factor. Minority population is, of course, an element of parity gap but is not statistically closely related to it because there is so much variation in minority employment unrelated to population. Nevertheless, the parity gap measure captures that part of minority population that might stimulate action—the part by which minority population exceeds minority employment.

From the perspective of city government, therefore, actions taken to increase minority employment over current levels should depend upon the level of minority demand-protest and incorporation and upon the size of the parity gap. [7]

How are gains in minority employment best measured? Affirmative action reports universally refer to percentage point increase, simply the difference between percentages at two

[7] As we noted in footnote 2, some cities defined parity as percent minority of the labor force or as percent minority of the labor force in relevant occupations. To the extent that city governments actually followed these criteria, our measure of parity gap, based on percent minority of city population, will slightly overstate the magnitude of the problem from the city's point of view. The difference is quite small in terms of its effect on our analysis, though it could be important to a city trying to defend itself against accusations of discrimination in hiring and threats of the cutoff of federal aid.

points in time. One could imagine progress measured in other ways; however, analysis of alternative measures of the minority employment responses of city governments confirms the weight of common usage, in that the simple difference-of-percentage measure yields much stronger and more plausible relationships.

Relationship between Political Factors and Parity Gap

To this point, we have proposed that gains in minority employment might be explained as a function of the magnitude of the problem (parity gap) and of minority demand-protest and incorporation. We hypothesize that both variables affect gains in minority employment, but there is a question about the way the two variables operate in relation to each other. In particular, do the minority political factors only increase responsiveness to parity gap, or does a strong minority political position generate employment gains regardless of the size of the parity gap?[8]

Overall, there is clear evidence that minority political factors generated increased minority employment, regardless of parity gap. The primary model is summarized in figure 22. The diagram posits that change in minority employment over some time period (t-1 to t) is a function of two factors that have independent effects on the change in minority employment: parity

[8]The second form of response, in which minority political factors are capable of producing gains in minority employment even if parity gap is small or zero, or even if minority employment is greater than minority population already, is the stronger of the two kinds. In the long run it produces higher levels of minority employment. In contrast the first kind of responsiveness posits an interaction between parity gap and minority political factors, such that stronger minority political factors will increase city response to a substantial parity gap but will not produce employment gains if parity gap is small, zero, or negative.

In this group of cities minority political factors have produced significant gains in minority employment independently of parity gap. Two cities—San Francisco and Berkeley—have already passed through the parity value and have continued to increase levels of minority employment (figure 20). Whether other cities where minority groups are strong will show the same behavior as

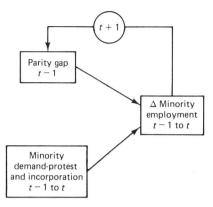

FIGURE 22   A Model of Change in Minority Employment

gap (the magnitude of the problem) at the beginning of the period (*t*-1) and levels of minority demand-protest and incorporation during the period. Changes in minority employment levels of course affect parity gap for the next period, as do changes in minority population from *t*-1 to *t* (not shown).

In spite of the role of minority population in both parity gap and minority political strength, these two factors are virtually unrelated in any period, with relationships (*r*) that fluctuate around zero (−.17 to .24) for both blacks and Hispanics. Chapter 3 discussed other factors, in addition to the percent minority of city population, that determined levels of minority demand-protest and incorporation during the 1960s and 1970s. It is apparent that factors other than percent minority so shaped the process of minority mobilization and incorporation as to eliminate the relationship between parity gap and the minority political factors that we would expect if both variables were simply the consequence of minority population. The data indicate that we must again reject the simple notion that levels of minority population can satisfactorily explain the processes at work here.

---

they reach the parity level is, of course, uncertain. What was politically and fiscally feasible in the 1970s may not be realizable in the present decade.

Gains in Black Employment

Our basic data on black employment extend from 1966 to 1978, and we are able to analyze patterns of change for the three periods 1966–70, 1970–74, and 1974–78. Table 22 shows the average change in black employment for these periods, the resulting average parity gap for black employment, and mean levels of two black political-strength factors. We see the steady progress toward parity in rapidly shrinking mean parity gap figures and sustained strength in the ever larger average increases in black employment. These gains were accomplished with increasingly strong black incorporation and with demand-protest that peaked in the late sixties and then declined.

Because of the small number of observations, both cities and years, the pooled time-series analysis that otherwise might have been preferable is not called for. Also, preliminary analysis showed that functional relationships were not constant over these periods, further indicating against pooled time series. We present instead cross-sectional analyses of change in black employment in each four-year period.

Relative Effects of Political Factors: Demand-Protest and Incorporation

We know from the data discussed to this point that demand-protest peaked in the late 1960s, that the incorporation of blacks continued to spread in the 1970s, and that external enforcement pressures for minority employment became significant for the first time in the mid-1970s. We should expect to see these patterns confirmed in the regression analysis. Various models were analyzed, using parity gap with the two political-strength variables (demand-protest and incorporation) separately, together in the same equation, and as the average of the two. Models with both variables separately were not entirely satisfactory because of collinearity and small N. However, those models did suggest that demand-protest had a relatively large impact on black employment gains in the late sixties, the peak period of demand-protest, whereas incorporation was the primary factor in the early seventies, when demand-protest was on the wane but black incorporation was spreading rapidly. Because the case

TABLE 22   Increase in Black Employment in City Government, Parity Gap, and Minority Political Factors, Ten Cities, 1966–78

Years	Black employment, percentage points increase, t-4 to t			Parity gap[a]			Demand-protest[b]	Incorporation[b]
	Low	Mean	High	Low	Mean	High		
1966				-5.0	7.1	27.7	2.4	0.9
1966–70	0.1	2.6	8.7	-7.6	6.4	29.2	4.4	1.5
1970–74	0.4	3.6	11.4	-10.5	4.3	22.4	3.3	2.2
1974–78	0.4	3.9	11.1	-16.4	1.8	18.6	2.5	2.4

[a]Percent black of city population minus percent black of city government employment; negative values indicate black employment greater than parity with black population.
[b]Mean for ten cities over four years ending at t.

TABLE 23   Increase in Black Employment in City Government as a Function of Parity Gap, Demand-Protest, and Incorporation

Period	Average, black demand-protest and incorporation	Parity gap	Adjusted R^2
	Standardized regression coefficients (betas)		
1966–70	.63	.45	.60
1970–74	.67	.60	.87
1974–78	.65	.69	.77
	Unstandardized regression coefficients		Intercept
1966–70	0.93	0.13	−1.00
	(2.97)	(2.13)	(−0.90)
1970–74	1.15	0.22	−1.03
	(5.47)	(4.96)	(−1.35)
1974–78	1.03	0.24	0.36
	(4.06)	(4.31)	(0.42)

NOTE: Numbers in parentheses are *t* values.

studies indicated that both political variables had an impact on minority employment, and because the data do not support consistent use of models with three independent variables, we use the average of demand-protest and incorporation as the measure of black political strength.[9]

The regression data presented in table 23 support the general model of figure 22. Given the possibilities for measurement error and for other factors that might influence the rate of

[9]From a measurement point of view, we are more comfortable with incorporation than with demand-protest. The latter measure, although based on survey evidence and on a great deal of case material, is probably a less reliable measure than incorporation, which depends on representation and coalition data. It is also likely to be easier for practical reasons to replicate the incorporation measure across a large number of cities than to gather the sort of information necessary to replicate demand-protest ratings. For these ten cities, one could explain black employment gains reasonably well with incorporation and parity gap alone, except for the 1966–70 period. The basic analysis may be replicable in a larger number of cities even if one cannot measure demand-protest directly.

increase in black employment, the data fit the model surprisingly well, and the model appears to capture the main structure of the process.

Relative Effects of Parity Gap and Political Factors

Because parity gap and measures of black demand-protest and incorporation are so completely independent of each other, we can take regression coefficients as reasonably accurate indications of their effects on black employment gains. The coefficients for the political variable are similar over the three periods, indicating that this factor has remained about equally important for black employment gains in spite of substantial shifts in the levels of black demand-protest and incorporation.[10] Other studies of the relation between political variables and black public employment also find that political variables are important, but they obtain different results depending on the particular variables used (Conyers and Wallace, 1976; Dye and Renick, 1981; Eisinger, 1980, 1982).

Parity gap had a substantially stronger effect on black employment gains in the seventies than in the late sixties. By the seventies parity gap was about as important as black political factors in generating greater black employment gains, in terms of the standardized coefficients.[11]

[10]Specifically, the unstandardized coefficient for the political variable suggests that an increment of one point on the combined incorporation/demand-protest scale generated about one percentage point greater increase in black employment. In concrete terms several important shifts in levels of incorporation translate into two-point increments on the incorporation scale. These include placing two minority representatives on the city council, incorporating two minority councilmembers into a newly dominant coalition, and electing a minority mayor (3 points). On the basis of the regression results, each of these conditions may be seen as generating on the average about two percentage points' increase in black employment in each four-year period, independently of the magnitude of the black employment problem in parity-gap terms.

[11]The unstandardized regression coefficients suggest a shift toward greater responsiveness to parity gap from the 1966–70 period to 1970–74. A given difference in parity gap generated about twice as much difference in black employment gains in the seventies as it did in the late sixties. A 10 percent difference in black parity gap was associated with about two and a half percentage points in greater black employment gains during the seventies.

How can we interpret these results in terms of the relative effects of local and external pressures? Although it would be convenient to be able to ascribe all the local pressure to minority political variables and all the external pressure to parity gap, this is probably not valid. A city's response to parity gap almost certainly includes effects that are locally generated rather than simply the result of external pressure. For example, minority political pressure on the hiring process is very likely to increase when there is a big parity gap.[12] Then, too, surely part of the parity-gap effect is the result of the size of the minority population. The larger the minority population, the greater the parity gap, on the average, and the more minority applicants can be expected for city jobs. However, the correlation between percent black population and parity gap declines steadily from 1966 to 1978: $r = .79, .73, .60,$ and $.51$.

Even if some of the effect of parity gap is locally generated, all of the effects of external enforcement efforts of state and federal agencies should appear, if at all, in connection with parity gap. Successful external enforcement should increase responsiveness to the magnitude of the minority employment problem in city government, in parity-gap terms. As we have seen, responsiveness to parity gap did increase substantially

---

Our confidence that these equations are correctly specified is strengthened by the fact that the estimated intercepts for these equations are very close to zero. This is precisely what we would expect—zero change in black employment—if incorporation and demand-protest were nonexistent and there were no parity gap, hence no political problem, either local or external, to be dealt with. To be sure, this expectation is based on the optimistic assumption that decreases in black employment would not occur under such conditions. If the structure of these relationships is sustained as some cities approach zero parity gap, these values suggest that decreases will not occur.

[12]And once the processes of change in government hiring practices are set in motion, effects may cumulate over many years as personnel administrators and governing ordinances are changed; as recruitment, testing, and hiring procedures are rewritten; and as minority people learn that chances of employment are good and are mobilized to apply for city jobs. Typically, these developments took place following significant minority incorporation into city government, but their effects in subsequent years operate to increase responsiveness to the magnitude of the problem, that is, to parity gap. Our separate equations for each time period ignore the historical cumulation of minority hiring policies; therefore, they probably understate the effects of minority political factors and overstate the effects of parity gap as a measure of external pressures only.

from the late sixties to the seventies. This is consistent with effects of general external pressures such as the passage of the Equal Employment Opportunity Act of 1972. However, enforcement efforts targeted at minority hiring practices in particular cities were concentrated in the 1974–78 time period, in which there was little increase in the overall effect of parity gap on black employment gains.

Of the three cities—Daly City, Stockton, and Vallejo—where California FEPC investigations or surveys were carried out, examination of deviant case residuals in successive time periods shows some shifts that might be attributable to these enforcement efforts. Stockton went from one of the largest negative residuals in 1970–74 (2.5 percentage points increase in black employment, 1.4 points below the regression estimate) to one of the highest in 1974–78 (5.9 points increase, 1.0 point above the regression estimate). Daly City increased from a minuscule 0.5 percent gain in black employment and a residual of −0.4 in 1970–74, to 3.2 points gain and a residual of 1.3 in 1974–78, a substantial improvement. Only Vallejo shows no improvement relative to the other cities over this period. Vallejo continued to increase its employment of blacks (by 1.9 and 1.4 percentage points), but this was still low relative to other cities, given Vallejo's parity gap. The findings are consistent with significant positive effects of FEPC efforts in two of the three cities.

Gains in Hispanic Employment

As noted earlier in this chapter, Hispanics are some years behind blacks in city government employment (figure 21). Table 24 replicates for Hispanics the employment gains, parity gap, and political factors data reported for blacks in table 22, except only two periods can be analyzed given the lack of consistent Hispanic population figures prior to 1970. Although the average gain in employment increased for both groups, Hispanics in 1978 were only approaching the rate of gain blacks achieved in 1970, and the magnitude of the average parity gap, although declining for both groups, was considerably higher for Hispanics than for blacks at the end of the period under study.

TABLE 24   Increase in Hispanic Employment in City Government, Parity Gap, and Minority Political Factors, Ten Cities, 1970–78

| Years | Hisp. employment percentage points increase, t-4 to t | | | Parity gap[a] | | | Demand-protest[b] | Incorporation[b] |
	Low	Mean	High	Low	Mean	High		
1970				1.4	6.2	11.9	2.6	0.3
1970–74	−0.5	2.0	5.3	1.2	5.6	8.8	2.8	1.3
1974–78	0.3	2.4	6.4	0.6	4.7	10.5	2.2	0.9

[a]Percent Hispanic of city population minus percent Hispanic of city government employment.
[b]Mean for ten cities over four years ending at t.

It is apparent that the Hispanic employment process, compared to the process for blacks, was greatly constrained in many ways. Comparison of standard deviations shows that Hispanic parity gap varies less from city to city than the equivalent figure for blacks, which is partly a reflection of the more even distribution of Hispanic population in these cities. Hispanic demand-protest and incorporation and the employment gains variable are all at lower levels and less variable from city to city than the same figures for blacks.

The Hispanic data show high correlations between Hispanic population size (percent of total population) and Hispanic parity gap: $r = .86$ in 1974 and $.84$ in 1978; for blacks, these variables were not related. Like Welch, Karnig, and Eribes (1983), we find a close relation between Hispanic employment and the proportion of Hispanics in the city. For blacks, in contrast, we saw lower and steadily declining correlations between these variables, registering the effects of gains in black employment associated with black political effort both preceding and during the period under study.

Analysis of the Hispanic data provides no evidence of effects of the Hispanic political variables on Hispanic employment gains. Bivariate correlations of Hispanic employment gains and the political variables hover around 0; for blacks they are in the range .60 to .75 in every time period. Nor does any discernible effect of the political variables appear when effects of Hispanic population and parity gap are taken into account. Welch, Karnig, and Eribes (1983) also found Hispanic representation on councils was not related to Hispanic employment, but Dye and Renick (1981) did find a relationship.

No other variables available to us explain additional variance in Hispanic employment gains in any substantial, meaningful, and consistent manner. Parity gap (X) alone—the magnitude of the Hispanic employment problem—explains employment gains (Y) in R^2 terms as well as parity gap and Hispanic population together. The results of the parity-gap model are

$$1974 \qquad Y' = \begin{matrix} .075 \\ (0.63) \end{matrix} + \begin{matrix} .316X \\ (3.05) \end{matrix} \qquad r^2 = .54$$

$$1978 \qquad Y' = \begin{matrix} .213 \\ (0.33) \end{matrix} + \begin{matrix} .396X \\ (1.86) \end{matrix} \qquad r^2 = .30$$

Adding Hispanic population to this model does not improve R^2 and results in partial regression coefficients that fall far short of statistical significance. The results suggest a modest and increasing responsiveness to the magnitude of the problem, more than to size of Hispanic population. Because these factors are so closely correlated, however, it may well be that city governments were responding to size of population as well.

It is worth noting also the fact that in no city had Hispanic employment exceeded parity, whereas two cities, Berkeley and San Francisco, where blacks were especially strong politically relative to population size, have achieved black employment levels substantially above parity. In no city have Hispanics generated the combination of demand-protest and incorporation that propelled black employment to such high levels, nor can this difference be explained away in terms of size of minority population—several cities had Hispanic populations nearly as large as Berkeley's black population and larger than San Francisco's.

Again, the point is that political mobilization and incorporation were much stronger for blacks than for Hispanics and had demonstrable effects on black employment gains, whereas effects of Hispanic political effort were at best scattered and inconsistent. Even so, we can show some effects of both demand-protest and incorporation on Hispanic employment in particular cities.

The Impact of Hispanic Demand-Protest—San Jose, 1966–70

The late 1960s saw a surge of Hispanic demand-protest effort in San Jose, focused on Model Cities and employment issues. Protest tactics—marches, rallies, and disruption of public meetings— were common. This period of peak pressure on city government was accompanied by a spurt in the employment of Hispanics by city government. Over the four years 1966–70, Hispanics increased from 2.2 to 10.1 percent of the city's permanent employees. Clearly, unprecedented efforts were made to hire Hispanics. It was the greatest four-year increase in Hispanic employment in any of the cities.

Although Hispanics have been represented on the city council, they were clearly incorporated in a moderately liberal dominant coalition for only a brief period in the early 1970s. Subsequent to 1970, Hispanic employment continued to increase, though at a slower rate, to 13.0 percent in 1974 and 14.6 percent in 1978. In the late seventies, over the protests of Hispanic groups, the city adopted a conservative stance on parity criteria, choosing to measure progress relative to percent Hispanic in the occupationally relevant labor force. By this criterion the city had nearly reached parity; by the population criterion it fell short. When early successful demand-protest was not followed by sustained incorporation, Hispanics lost their initial momentum in city government hiring.

The Impact of Hispanic Incorporation—Sacramento since 1970

Sacramento is the only city in this group with clearly effective incorporation of Hispanics into the dominant coalition and effective demand effort sustained over a long period of time. The organization Concilio has managed to combine social service programs and political mobilization. Hispanics gained a seat on the city council in 1969 and have been incorporated in the dominant coalition since then. This coalition hired a personnel director known for affirmative action achievements, and as a consequence, Hispanic employment in city government increased steadily from 6.6 percent (1970) to 12.3 percent (1978). In Sacramento Hispanics made more rapid gains than blacks over this period.

Gains in Employment with Little Mobilization—Hayward, 1974–78

Hayward exemplifies the possibility of responsiveness even with minimal incorporation and demand-protest on the part of a minority group. With no Hispanic representation on the city council and with very little demand activity, a coalition led by the white liberal mayor and city manager nevertheless pushed affirmative action in city hiring and a variety of other social programs. As a consequence, in the four years 1974–78 the employment of Hispanics in Hayward city government increased from 7.9 to 14.3 percent of the work force. Thus it is possible—though Hayward is the only instance in this group of cities—that significant responsiveness to minority interests can occur as a result of a shift in the ideological commitments of the dominant coalition, a shift that does not involve incorporation or elected minority representatives.

Barriers to Hispanic Employment

As we noted in chapter 3, the mobilization of Hispanics was not so closely related to the basic resource of relative size in the population, and the mobilization movement has diffused less effectively and pervasively for Hispanics than for blacks. These conditions mean that sizeable numbers of Hispanics in some cities were virtually unmobilized and lacking in influence over city programs. If, as was usually the case, the dominant coalition in city government was not strongly committed to affirmative action, employment gains were slow even if the parity gap was large. Daly City is a case in point. In spite of some affirmative action effort, Daly City managed to increase the percentage of Hispanics in its work force only from 6.2 to 7.4 percent between 1974 and 1978. This is one of the smallest increases in this set of cities, even though the parity gap for Hispanics was 15.0 percent in 1974, the largest in the group. The weakness and unevenness of Hispanic political mobilization left resistant dominant coalitions free to drag their heels in employment and other areas of potential responsiveness to minority interests.

In addition to the general weakness of Hispanic incorporation and demand-protest, the relatively stronger position of blacks in some cities appeared to slow the responsiveness of city government to Hispanic interests.[13] In Richmond blacks were by far the larger minority group; they mobilized much earlier and gained control over programs such as Community Development Block Grants. In San Francisco similarly, even

[13]Welch, Karnig, and Eribes (1983) found an inverse relation between Hispanic employment and black employment.

though the census shows virtually equal numbers of blacks and Hispanics (we estimate 12.9 and 11.8 percent in 1978), blacks mobilized much earlier and more effectively and persistently and were well established in city government employment and other program areas early on. For example, only 9 percent of the members of major city commissions were Hispanics in 1977, whereas blacks were above parity at 15 percent. Even though Hispanics have been represented on city councils in both of these cities and have shown some continuing capacity for organized demands on city government, their gains in employment were about what we would expect in the absence of representation. It seems likely that responsiveness to Hispanics in these cities has been reduced by the stronger incorporation of blacks in the dominant coalition.

This is not to imply that black interests in these cities always held Hispanic employment back. In Sacramento and Stockton, for example, cities with substantial proportions of both groups in their populations, progress in city government employment has proceeded at roughly the same pace for the two groups. And in Oakland and Berkeley Hispanic employment showed persistent, steady gains, even though blacks were by far the largest minority in both cities; the commitment to affirmative action benefitted Hispanics as well as blacks.

Minority Administrators and Professionals

Changes in the overall level of minority employment in city government have been dramatic, as we have shown, and the changes reflect both the magnitude of the problem and political characteristics of the cities. Another important indicator of city government responsiveness to minorities is the distribution of minority employment within the city government hierarchy.

Are minorities moving into top positions in the proportions one would expect given their presence in the populations or are they underrepresented at those levels? This would seem to be a stricter test of responsiveness. It is likely that there would be more white resistance to redistribution of top jobs than to a

TABLE 25   Levels of Black and Hispanic Employment, City
Government Officials and Total, 1974–78

| | | Mean percent minority, ten cities | |
		1974	1978
Officials	Black	8.6	11.1
	Hispanic	3.7	4.5
Total	Black	12.7	16.9
	Hispanic	6.5	8.9

SOURCE: Copies of city government EEO4 submittals to the U.S. Equal Employment Opportunity Commission, obtained from city personnel offices.

minority presence in lower level jobs. Thus newly incorporated minorities might find it easier to push successfully for minority hiring in the general work force than for minority hiring in top positions. Finally, to what extent are the dynamics of black and Hispanic employment change, explored earlier, applicable to employment at higher levels?[14]

Changes in the percentage of minority administrators and professionals in city employment are similar to those for minority employment generally. Comparison between the two types of employment reveals what we would expect. Employment of minorities in the higher positions is lower than total minority employment in city government, and both groups are moving into top positions at a slower rate than into city government employment generally. Blacks again fare better than Hispanics, though as table 25 indicates, both groups have increasingly entered administrative and professional positions in these cities.

In cities with comparably sized black and Hispanic populations, the percent of black administrators and professionals

[14]Our data on minority employment in higher positions come from the information cities submit to the U.S. Equal Employment Opportunity Commission (EEOC). (See appendix C-6.) We use data from 1974 and 1978 for two EEOC occupational categories: officials/administrators and professionals. In our interviews we also collected data on the number of blacks and Hispanics serving as department heads or in professional positions in the city manager's office in 1966, 1970, 1974, and 1978. That information generally confirms the trends revealed in the EEOC data.

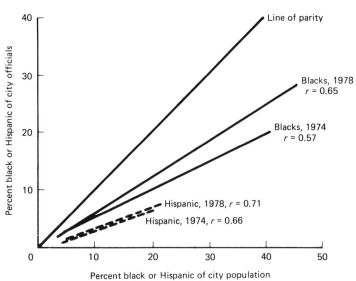

FIGURE 23   Relationship of Minority Officials to Minority
Population. (Blacks and Hispanics, 1974–78)

was substantially higher than the percent Hispanic. Figure 23
shows the regression estimates for both blacks and Hispanics
for 1974 and 1978 in relation to the size of the groups in the
cities. At 20 percent black population in 1978, the regression
estimate is an average 12 percent black administrators and professionals; for Hispanics the corresponding estimate is 6.2 percent. The average gain in employment of black officials from
1974 to 1978 was three times that of Hispanic officials during
this period.

The parity gap for top officials in 1978, indicating the ratio
between percent minority in the top occupational categories and
percent minority in the population, correlates very closely with
overall employment parity scores (r = .93 for blacks, .85 for Hispanics). Cities that had a good record in hiring minorities also
had a good record in hiring minorities at the higher levels. Comparison with figure 21 reveals that both blacks and Hispanics
were farther from parity in employment in these higher positions than they were in total city government employment.

The models that explain change in the percent of black and
Hispanic administrators and professionals between 1974 and 1978

are virtually identical in structure and in values of coefficients to those that explain overall black and Hispanic employment. For both groups, the factors that explain their employment overall also shaped their employment in the higher positions.

Responsiveness—Some Implications

The findings of this chapter and chapter 4 should help to dispel some of the pessimism expressed by observers about the effects of minority officeholding or about the ability of city governments to control their own policies at all. The question has been raised whether "aside from symbolism and some patronage jobs, it really matters" if minority voters choose minority candidates over white candidates. Many scholars have asserted the negative; for example, George Sternlieb: "The fact is that race hasn't made any difference" (*Wall Street Journal*, October 29, 1980). We find to the contrary that black and Hispanic representation and incorporation have increased governmental responsiveness to those groups in many areas. The higher the levels of minority incorporation, the greater the impact of the minority presence. Councils with minority incorporation did vote the interests of minorities more than those without it. Minority representatives and the more liberal coalitions in which they played significant roles did remain committed to minority interests, did promote programs to meet minority concerns, and did produce a shift in local policy making. Race and ethnicity did make a difference.[15]

Another school of thought is even more pessimistic, suggesting that cities in general and their elected officials in particular are so powerless that there is nothing they can do to shape policy in a favorable direction. The argument goes that officials are so busy trying to find revenue, following (or trying to evade) federal and state guidelines and regulations, filling potholes or deciding they cannot afford to fill them, and getting

---

[15]These findings confirm and extend the conclusions of many other scholars: Cole (1976, pp. 87, 126, 157); Eisinger (1980); Fainstein and Fainstein (1976); Henderson (1978); and Keller (1978).

reelected, that they cannot govern, cannot use discretion in shaping and implementing urban policy. Although all of that is to some extent true and may become increasingly so, our research shows that in the last twenty years at least, a really committed set of people on councils did develop policies responsive to blacks and Hispanics and did bring about significant change in the behavior of city governments.[16]

Using different data and different methods of analysis, we support Karnig and Welch's conclusion (1980) that the presence of minorities in city government is associated with responsiveness to minorities. Karnig and Welch found a rather weak relationship in a much larger and more heterogeneous sample of cities; they used aggregate expenditure data instead of measures of responsiveness that tap more directly the issues in which minorities expressed strong interests (see also Gruber, 1979). In our analyses the relationships between the minority presence (especially as measured by incorporation) and responsiveness are very strong statistically, and the statistics are supported by a wealth of qualitative evidence. We attempted to replicate Karnig and Welch's work with a similar analysis of aggregate expenditure data. Knowing what we did about each city quickly led us to the conclusion that the use of aggregate expenditure data to assess responsiveness to minority interests is quite problematic. The data are often too distant from the real objects of minority concern, and it is often the case, as Larkey suggests, that "there are simply too many confounding factors and sources of bias ever to get interpretable, usable results" (1979, p. 87).[17]

We find little support for the hypothesis that socioeconomic or demographic variables are more important than political variables in explaining policy (Dye, 1966; Hawkins, 1971); variations in city government responsiveness are not well explained by the proportion of minorities in the population.

[16]Cf. Peterson (1981) and Browning, Marshall, and Tabb (1983). Levine, Rubin, and Wolohojian (1981, pp. 71 and 83) found that increases in black political power influenced not only city government employment, but also retrenchment strategies.

[17]Examples of studies using aggregate expenditure data to assess responsiveness to minorities include Clark and Ferguson (1983, chap. 5); Gruber (1979); and Karnig and Welch (1980).

Cities with relatively small proportions of minorities were sometimes more responsive than cities with larger minority populations. Other factors more directly political in nature, namely minority incorporation and related minority political activity, yield a much stronger explanation.[18]

Our variables do not allow us to address directly the hypothesis that bureaucratic decision rules are the primary determinants of policy responsiveness as manifested in service delivery and distribution.[19] However, the primacy of political incorporation in explaining responsiveness in the areas examined in these chapters suggests that studies of service delivery may not have paid enough attention to political variables. We do not deny the importance of bureaucracies in shaping city policy, but minority incorporation in dominant coalitions was clearly a preeminent factor in these issue areas. Our findings suggest the primacy of bureaucratic decision rules only in areas where there is little concern on the part of mobilized groups, little conflict, and little interest in the dominant coalition in changing city policy.

Where minority incorporation was weak, to be sure, as it remained in many of these cities, administrators continued to determine service delivery rules within the framework acceptable to the dominant coalition. But where minority interests were strongly incorporated, policies, programs, and service delivery were in fact altered to meet those interests. Minority interests did not always prevail against strong bureaucracies, but they often did. Bureaucratic control over service delivery really depends on the sufferance of the dominant coalition. A determined coalition that controls a city council over a period of years can change the delivery of services throughout city government.

[18]Aiken and Alford (1970) also argue against the sufficiency of demographic and socioeconomic variables. So do Schumaker and Getter (1983), who stress effective organization of interest groups, strong Democratic parties, and competitive elections as important in producing responsiveness to blacks.

[19]Some of the studies supporting these positions are B. Jones (1980); Levy, Meltsner, and Wildavsky (1974); Lineberry (1977); Lipsky (1980); Mladenka (1980). See also Gruber (1981) for a discussion of bureaucratic resistance to external constraints and Aberbach, Putnam, and Rockman (1981) for a discussion of bureaucratic/political interaction.

Responsiveness and the Decline of Reform Institutions

In addition to the changes in policies discussed in chapters 4 and 5, minority incorporation is also associated with another change in our ten cities—the decline of reform institutions. This illustrates structural responsiveness. It is an institutional reform that strengthens the ability of new dominant coalitions to control city government. The gradual weakening of reform structures in our cities parallels the trend in other U.S. cities (Adrian and Sullivan, 1979). The old reform tradition is itself being reformed as more liberal Democratic coalitions that include minorities gain control of city councils. These new elites have different values and goals than the "good government" elites who instituted the reform tradition. Indications of this trend are the increasing power of city councils and mayors, the decreasing power of city managers, and the change from at-large to district elections.

The role of elected officials has been strengthened in more than half of the cities (Berkeley, Oakland, San Jose, Sacramento, Stockton, and San Francisco). Sacramento, San Jose, and Hayward moved to popular election of mayors; Oakland, San Francisco, Berkeley, and Vallejo already had such systems. City managers are increasingly subject to direct council control. When the group in control of the council changes, the city manager is replaced similarly to the way prime ministers are shifted when legislative control changes in parliamentary systems. When liberal dominant coalitions replaced conservative ones, the old city manager was always let go and a new, more liberal manager hired. The view that managers are neutral professionals would suggest that when councils change, city managers simply adapt their behavior to accommodate the new council. But in our cities new liberal coalitions saw the old manager as part of an earlier regime and thus not amenable to a new direction. Clearly, city manager positions in many of these cities are now highly politicized. The earlier assumption that city managers could be neutral professionals depended on a degree of consensus in local politics that was destroyed by minority mobilization and the replacement of conservative coalitions. (Cf. Loveridge, 1971.)

Another striking move away from reform structures is the decline of at-large elections. In 1960 all of our cities had at-large or district at-large systems. By 1980 five of the cities had switched to district elections. The first district elections were held in Sacramento and Stockton in 1971. San Francisco changed in 1977 (reverting to at-large in 1980); San Jose in 1980; and Oakland in 1981.[20]

In general, groups trying to change city government, such as neighborhood groups, liberals, and minority groups, proposed a change to district elections as a strategy for initiating or institutionalizing shifts favorable to their interests. Minority groups played a central role in pushing for district elections in three of the cities (Sacramento, Stockton, and Oakland). In the other two cities, San Francisco and San Jose, minorities were involved but were not the prime factors in the coalition pushing for district elections. The impetus came from neighborhood groups that saw district elections as a way of decreasing the representation of downtown interests and strengthening neighborhood interests. Minority representation increased in two of these five cities (Stockton and Oakland) after the institution of district elections; in both cities minorities had been key to instituting the new system.[21] In Stockton no minorities had been elected until after district elections, when three were successful. In Oakland black representation jumped from three to five members of a nine-person council in the first district election. The adoption of district elections in Sacramento led to no increase in minority representation. In San Francisco, although there was no increase in total minority representation after district elections, black representation did increase. The Hispanic councilmember lost, leaving Hispanics without representation, and blacks increased their representation from

[20]For recent studies of the causes and consequences of district elections, see Heilig and Mundt (1981); and Morgan and Pelissero (1980).

[21]Several studies have found district elections to be causally related to increases in minority representation, even when controlling for socioeconomic characteristics of the cities and for size of minority population. See Engstrom and McDonald (1981); Hamilton (1978); and Robinson and Dye (1978). These contrast with Karnig (1979) and MacManus (1978).

one to two. Thus in Stockton, Oakland, and San Francisco black representation increased; district elections created an advantage for black candidates.

Summary

City government employment of minorities has increased substantially but much more in some cities than others. Both blacks and Hispanics are advancing toward population parity, but blacks have achieved more than Hispanics. This chapter has shown that the gains depended upon the level of minority demand-protest and incorporation and on the size of the parity gap, that is, the magnitude of the problem. Minority political factors generated employment gains regardless of the size of the parity gap. This model provides a better explanation than one that attributes changes simply to differences in the size of minority populations.

For blacks, parity gap had a substantially stronger effect on black employment gains in the seventies than in the late sixties, and by the late seventies it was about as important as black political factors in generating greater black employment gains. This change is partly a reflection of the growing importance of state and federal enforcement efforts. For Hispanics the employment process is greatly constrained compared to blacks. Hispanic parity gap varies less from city to city, and Hispanic demand-protest and incorporation and the employment gains variable are all at lower levels and show less variation than the same figures for blacks. Hispanic employment gain is modestly related to parity gap and percent Hispanic, but Hispanic political variables had no detectable impact on Hispanic employment gains. The general weakness of Hispanic demand-protest and incorporation slowed the responsiveness of city governments and so did the relatively stronger position of blacks.

Turning to minority employment in top city government positions, we have shown that employment at that level is lower than total minority employment in city government, and minorities are moving into top positions at a slower rate than into city employment generally. Again, blacks fare better than Hispanics.

For both groups the factors that explain their employment over-all also explain their employment in the higher positions.

In all policy areas examined in chapters 4 and 5, we find that minority incorporation has increased governmental respon-siveness. Minority representatives and the more liberal coali-tions in which they played significant roles did make a differ-ence in local policy. Our work underscores the importance of political variables, namely, minority incorporation and related minority political activity, in explaining policy. We find little support for the hypothesis that socioeconomic or demographic or bureaucratic variables are more important than political var-iables in explaining responsiveness. Minority incorporation is also associated with the decline of reform institutions in our ten cities as indicated by the increasing power of city councils and mayors, the decreasing power of city managers, and the change from at-large to district elections.

PART THREE

Federal Programs and the Future of Responsiveness

6

Federal Programs: Their Implementation and Effects on Incorporation and Responsiveness

> If it ain't a federal dollar, you can hang it up as far as minorities are concerned. (Oakland respondent)
>
> Model Cities helped people understand what's possible and what's not possible with respect to community self-determination. It created organizations. It created aspirants for higher office. It raised expectations, perhaps too much in a sense, but it was still better that it raised them. . . . Model Cities was worth every cent. (San Francisco respondent)

Throughout the preceding chapters we have alluded to the effects of the national civil rights movement and federal programs on minority mobilization, the political incorporation of minorities, and the policy responsiveness of city governments. This chapter directly addresses the role of selected federal social programs. We discuss the impact of social programs across all our cities and examine variations in the local implementation and effects of the programs, specifying how the local systems produced variations in program implementation and effect and how the programs changed local policy-making processes.

We argue that in our ten cities the programs have played an important role in the mobilization of minorities (both demand-protest and electoral) and thus their incorporation into political systems, and in facilitating city policy responsiveness to minorities. We support the view that the Great Society programs stimulated minority demands (Piven and Cloward, 1979) and the revisionist view that these programs were successful in promoting changes in the direction of increased city government responsiveness to minorities (Williams, 1980b).

The chapter first assesses the influence of federal social programs (poverty, urban renewal, and Model Cities) on demand-protest, electoral mobilization, incorporation, and policy responsiveness in our ten cities. Next we consider variations across cities in local implementation of these programs in the sixties. Then we ask whether differences in the strength of federal statutes made any difference in the federal influence on the local policy-making system, comparing local implementation of General Revenue Sharing (GRS) and Community Development Block Grants (CDBG) in the seventies. The final section summarizes our findings and their implications for increased city government responsiveness to minorities and for the study of implementation.

Influence of Federal Social Programs

In the course of our research we collected a variety of data on the implementation and effects of three federal social programs in our cities: poverty programs, urban renewal as it was implemented in minority neighborhoods, and Model Cities. The data came from structured and semistructured interviews, reports on the programs, newspaper articles, and published analyses. Although we originally thought we would concentrate on Model Cities, respondents referred to the programs almost interchangeably, seeing them, at least from the vantage point of the seventies, as a package of federal social programs that were closely intertwined at the local level primarily because they had impact on poor people, a category that in our cities was largely indistinguishable from minorities.

Thus, as we examined the data in order to understand the influences on mobilization, we came to see that for many types of analyses, the programs are best treated as functional equivalents. In one city, renewal programs were the focus of most minority activity; in another, minority political effort focused on a different program such as Model Cities. Although we can distinguish the formal structures and activities of the programs, we found similar impacts such as the stimulation of minority organizing connected with formally dissimilar programs. Therefore, we often refer to the federal social programs of the sixties as a group, though in the last half of the chapter we give special attention to Model Cities programs because certain data are available for them that facilitate comparison with two programs in the seventies, General Revenue Sharing and CDBG.

There are competing hypotheses about the relationship of the programs to mobilization. One hypothesis is that locally implemented federal programs increased minority mobilization, especially demand-protest.[1] Another view is that the programs actually served to quiet discontent, to co-opt minority mobilization by directing it toward running programs rather than pressuring city hall. The implication is that demands would have increased much more in the absence of programs.[2]

There are also competing views concerning the success of the programs in promoting policy responsiveness. Some argue that the federal social programs of the sixties—poverty, urban renewal, and Model Cities—failed because they did not eliminate poverty, create decent housing for the poor, or revitalize central city neighborhoods. Social scientists making these evaluations typically accept the grandiose goals written into the statutes as their criteria for measuring success and, predictably, find that the programs fall short. This kind of evaluation is associated with the view that implementation is a problem in control, a view that is an extension of the rational approach to decision making. Statutory goals are given, and the problem is to maximize com-

[1] Authors associated with this view include Ambrecht (1976); Lamb (1975); Marshall (1971a and b); May (1969); Mollenkopf (1973); and Piven and Cloward (1979).

[2] See Gittell (1980); Katznelson (1981, p. 179); Kerstein and Judd (1980); and Piven and Cloward (1979, pp. 274–77).

pliance with them.[3] But students of evaluation and implementation have gradually developed different perspectives as they have gained a more sophisticated understanding of the complexity involved. Implementation is now more often viewed as a problem in bargaining, as an interaction in which organizational learning takes place as the policies evolve.[4] Along with this has come an increased willingness to evaluate the programs according to different standards than those in the statutes.

One revisionist interpretation of Great Society programs views much of the early evaluative work as using unrealistically high standards.[5] The argument is that the programs should be considered successful if they contributed to stimulating local governments to provide services for the poor and increased the ability of the poor to organize to promote local government responsiveness. This view stresses the assessment of the long run indirect effects of the programs on social systems and on the political strength of poor people at the local level, rather than just an examination of compliance with official regulations or with the lofty goals set forth in the statute.[6]

In our work the standard of evaluation is movement in the direction of increasing city government responsiveness to the interests of minority groups. What then were the effects of the three federal social programs on minority mobilization and incorporation, and on city government responsiveness?

Respondents were virtually unanimous in perceiving federal social programs as important in shaping both the mobilization and incorporation of minorities, and city government responsiveness. In regard to mobilization and incorporation, they said that federal social programs had played a major role in the wave of demand-protest that occurred between 1966 and 1970 (see chapter 3, figure 9). Respondents indicated that rather than quieting demands, the programs generated them

[3]See Marshall (1975); Mazmanian and Sabatier (1980); Montjoy and O'Toole (1979); and Pressman and Wildavsky (1979).

[4]See Bardach (1977); Berman (1978); Elmore (1978); Ingram (1977); Rein and Rabinovitz (1977); Thomas (1979); and Van Horn (1979).

[5]See Aaron (1978); Marshall (1982); and Pressman and Wildavsky (1979, pp. 163–64.

[6]Such a perspective obviously complicates the problem of evaluation, because each evaluator must then specify standards of evaluation, and relevant "hard" data may be difficult, if not impossible, to obtain.

by providing issues, a staff, and resources for organizing efforts. Demand-protest focused on issues that might not have arisen in the absence of the programs. Citizen participation activities associated with federal grants were frequently cited as sources of demand-protest and electoral mobilization. As a respondent in San Jose described it:

> Originally through its Model Cities program, San Jose organized advocacy groups. They continue to be politically active. With increased visibility and city assistance they have become a strong political force.

The programs were seen as creating opportunities for minority leaders to develop a political base through formulating issues and gaining media attention. Program funds facilitated further community organizing and leadership development (Ambrecht, 1976; Marshall, 1971a and b).

Our respondents also thought that federal programs contributed in a major way to increased policy responsiveness. As shown in table 26, when asked to rate the importance of eleven factors in explaining changes in minority programs in their cities, respondents as a group ranked federal pressures as the third most important factor, after city officials and minority mobilization (see appendix C-8). Federal programs were seen as providing the resources for local minority-oriented services. And federal requirements in such programs as affirmative action, housing rehabilitation, manpower, poverty, Model Cit-

TABLE 26   Factors Perceived as Most Responsible for Minority-Oriented Programs of City Governments, 1980

Factor	Percent of respondents mentioning	Importance, mean rating
City officials (council, mayor, city manager)	39	2.4
Minority pressure	29	2.8
Federal pressure	21	2.3

SOURCE: See appendix C-8.

TABLE 27   Perceived Importance of City Officials and Federal
Pressure in Bringing about Minority-Oriented Programs

	City	Perceived importance (mean rating)		Difference
		City officials	Federal pressure	
Liberal dominant coalitions	Berkeley	2.9	1.8	+1.1
	Oakland	2.6	2.1	+ .5
	Sacramento	2.8	2.3	+ .5
	Richmond	2.4	2.1	+ .3
	Hayward	2.6	2.3	+ .3
	San Francisco	2.1	2.4	− .3
Resistant dominant coalitions	San Jose	2.0	2.1	− .1
	Stockton	2.2	2.5	− .3
	Vallejo	1.6	2.6	−1.0
	Daly City	2.7	2.5	+ .2

SOURCE: See appendix C-8.

ies, and community development were seen as forcing city
governments to take further actions that benefitted minorities.

Although respondents stressed the importance of federal
programs for policy responsiveness in all our cities, the importance attributed to the programs varied between cities with liberal and those with resistant dominant coalitions (table 27). In
three out of four cities in the latter group (San Jose, Stockton,
and Vallejo) federal pressure received a higher rating than city
officials for bringing about minority programs. In five of the six
cities with clearly liberal dominant coalitions (Berkeley, Oakland, Sacramento, Richmond, and Hayward), the ratings for city
officials were higher than the ratings for federal pressures. The
ratings indicate the significance of local dominant coalitions for
minority programs. When the dominant coalition was opposed

or less committed to minority interests, respondents perceived federal pressure as more important than city hall in bringing about minority programs. It is interesting to note that minority mobilization was typically viewed as more important than either city hall or federal pressure in both kinds of cities—those with liberal and those with more resistant dominant coalitions.

Respondents' perceptions of the importance of federal programs in shaping minority mobilization, incorporation, and policy responsiveness are entirely consistent with our analyses in chapters 3–5, where we explained variations as a function of local characteristics. As we indicated there, we were really tapping the interaction of local characteristics with the national movement and social programs. They created opportunities and resources that were potentially common to the cities but which were used differently, depending on local city characteristics.

Another way of assessing the impact of federal programs on city responsiveness is to determine what proportion of the programs listed by respondents as benefitting minorities is supported from the cities' own funds. We asked respondents, "About what percent of the general fund budget goes to minority-oriented programs?" with the presumption that other minority-oriented program funds came from intergovernmental grants. Respondents indicated the difficulty of making accurate estimates, but there was wide agreement that not more than 5 percent of general funds went to minority-oriented programs. Berkeley was an exception: most of the respondents estimated that 11–20 percent of general funds were allocated to minority-oriented programs. Thus programs benefitting minorities were generally funded by federal grants, not by city revenues.[7]

[7]Respondents' perceptions of the importance of federal pressure and money in stimulating local policy responsiveness are supported by budgetary data, which show increased reliance on federal grants in the ten cities. A major contributor to the overall increase in city expenditures per capita between 1960 and 1980 was the rapid growth of federal grants to cities. As in other American cities increasing proportions of revenues have come from federal grants, though this trend has leveled off in recent years (Harrigan, 1981; Pressman, 1975; Reagan and Sanzone, 1981; U.S. Advisory Commission on Intergovernmental Relations, 1980 and 1981; Wright, 1978, pp. 68–70). If there had been no federal programs, minorities might have focused more effort on local fund allocations and made a somewhat greater dent on the local general fund budget and on the traditional city agencies.

In sum, the programs created a new arena in these ten cities, the arena of federal social programs, in which minority concerns received greater attention than had previously been the case in other arenas. This arena involved interest groups, city bureaucrats, and elected officials in a new "game," a new domain—and this changed the behavior of those who had been operating in old games and stimulated the emergence of new players in each of these roles. The programs provided the functional equivalent of earlier forms of patronage, offering new bases of power for the politicians and organizations allocating program funds and directly or indirectly generating political activity (Piven and Cloward, 1979, pp. 274–77; Rossi, Berk, and Eidson, 1974, p. 421).

Even though our respondents perceived the programs as increasing mobilization, incorporation, and responsiveness, we cannot adequately address the issue of whether these same changes in mobilization and responsiveness would have occurred in the absence of the programs. Because all ten cities participated in them, we do not know what changes would have occurred without them. Perhaps the civil rights movement alone could have served as a mechanism for activating minorities, and the resources of group size and white support could have operated in the absence of the federal social programs to generate demand-protest and electoral mobilization. We cannot reject the alternative hypothesis to program effect—namely, that mobilization and incorporation of minorities and governmental responsiveness would have occurred at the same rate in the absence of the federal social programs reflecting conditions independent of and existing prior to the programs. But clearly none of our respondents thinks that is true and neither do we.

Variations in Local Implementation in the Sixties

Federal officials and students of program implementation in the sixties held a vastly simplified picture of city governments in the United States. No one, of course, really thought all cities were alike, but few realized that the differences would be so crucial to the results of the Great Society programs. Gradually urban complexity has been rediscovered, and analysts have realized that even though federal programs have important local impact, they are changed in an almost infinite number of ways as they make their way through the intergovernmental system toward delivery by the thousands of local governments in the United States. Our research underscores the importance of local political factors in shaping the implementation and effects of federal programs (Berman, 1978; Wirt, 1970).

In our cities, chosen to be less diverse in demographic, regional, and political structures than the universe of American cities, the ideology of the dominant coalition is a very important factor in shaping local implementation but it is not the only one. Some argue that grants can facilitate change in local governments where officials are willing to change but that grants cannot compel substantive program change where officials are not committed to change (Ingram, 1977). However, we find that the dominant coalition is not the only group that can shape programs. Grants also provide resources to interest groups (in our case, minority organizations) and to potential challengers to coalitions that control local government (Derthick, 1970; Pressman, 1975; Wirt, 1970). Local actors use federal grants as leverage to pursue their own agendas. Grants change the odds favoring certain local participants rather than others by influencing their political and economic resources.

Where local government favors the kind of change required by the grant, the additional federal resources facilitate the efforts of the government to bring about the change. Where local government opposes the kind of change required by the grant, modest program development may nevertheless come about in the short run because the additional resources made available by the federal programs can strengthen the local actors pushing for the change—that is, groups opposed to the coalition that dominates local government—and thus enhance their efforts to extract concessions from the dominant coalition. In the longer run the federal programs may strengthen local interests that seek to replace a resistant dominant coalition. If these interests are eventually successful, substantial policy changes may be brought into being. Thus federal programs become one of many factors in a dynamic of initiative, resources, and interaction that may eventually result in "compliance" with federal goals.

The key elements, then, in the local policy-making system influencing the implementation and effects of the programs are the ideology of the dominant coalition and the activities of groups pushing for change. We elaborate on this idea by comparing program-related mobilization and responsiveness in our ten cities, and identifying some of the processes that translated minority population size and white support into mobilization and incorporation, and then into policy responsiveness.

We distinguish three groups of cities based on the ideology of the coalitions dominant in 1968 when the federal social programs were at their height:

1.   Cities with resistant dominant coalitions where the programs generated policy responsiveness, demand-protest, and electoral mobilization.

2.   Cities with liberal coalitions where the programs generated policy responsiveness and demand-protest.

3.   Cities with resistant dominant coalitions where the programs generated only minimal policy responsiveness and minimal demand-protest.

In the first group of cities—Oakland, San Jose, and Sacramento—resistant coalitions were dominant and attempted to control the programs to prevent changes in city government, but minority groups used program resources to increase mobilization, both demand-protest and electoral, and this eventually led to increased incorporation and, subsequently, to institutionalization of responsiveness beyond the life of the programs.

In the second group of cities—Berkeley, Richmond, and San Francisco—liberal coalitions were in power at the time of the programs and favored some increased responsiveness to minority needs. Because they used the programs to satisfy some minority demands—that is, because they were somewhat responsive—demands generated by the programs did not directly stimulate electoral mobilization. Federal social programs focused minority demand-protest on the programs and also led to some responsiveness. With minority demands partly satisfied, incentives for increased demand-protest and electoral mobilization were reduced.

Like the first group of cities, the third group—Stockton, Vallejo, Daly City, and Hayward—had resistant dominant coalitions in 1968, which attempted to control the programs to prevent changes in city government. But in this case minority groups did not use the resources from the programs to increase mobilization as they did in Oakland, San Jose, and Sacramento. The demand-protest generated through programs was not translated into electoral mobilization. And in all four, demand-protest efforts led only to minimal increases in policy responsiveness either directly as a result of programs or indirectly as a result of incorporation.

Implementation and Resistant Dominant Coalitions with Electoral Mobilization

In Oakland, San Jose, and Sacramento federal social programs became the central focus for minority mobilization efforts, involving minorities in the operation of social service programs and demand-protest activity. (In Sacramento the programs were simply poverty programs, in Oakland and San Jose both poverty programs and Model Cities.) This mobilization generated issues, leaders, and organizations that were partly channeled into electoral mobilization, which, in turn, achieved some success in increasing incorporation and then program responsiveness.

In the mid-sixties dominant coalitions in these three cities opposed the redistribution of power to minorities by resisting their incorporation into the dominant coalition. They favored the vigorous use of government to undertake large-scale economic development efforts but opposed using government to redistribute benefits to minorities except as that might be necessary to achieve economic objectives. Instead of using the programs to build positive support for the dominant coalition and to incorporate minority interests via some degree of mutual exchange, the dominant coalitions in Oakland, San Jose, and Sacramento used the programs to insulate city hall from minority demands, to minimize opposition rather than transform it into participation and support, and to divert minority discontent away from city hall toward the leaders of the programs. The dominant coalitions saw little or no positive value in the programs; the goals of the programs did not coincide with the coalition's agenda, so the programs were viewed simply as necessary evils until passions cooled. The program organizations were kept separate both formally and informally from city hall. The leaders of the programs and the minority community were not a significant base of support for the dominant coalition and were not included in the city's policy-making process.

It would be easy to conclude that the programs simply co-opted minorities, that the programs were used to decrease minority unrest without resulting in any benefits for minorities. However, the programs did promote change over the longer run by increasing the resources available for minority mobilization in opposition to the dominant coalition. And in all three cities the programs became the focus for intense minority mobilization efforts, involving both minority participation in the operation of social service programs and vigorous demand-protest activity, which translated into electoral mobilization as well.

Although the immediate effects of this mobilization were minimal (apparent victories actually being minor concessions granted by city hall), the long run effects were more important. Mobilization of minorities around the programs generated issues, leaders, and organizations, which increased the strength of the opposition to the dominant coalition and, when channeled into electoral mobilization, contributed to changing the dominant coalition. Experience with the programs helped convince minorities that other efforts, in particular electoral mobilization, were necessary.

For example, in Oakland the same black leadership cadre that formed first around the poverty program and then around the Model Cities program became active in electoral politics. Mayor Reading was conservative, cautious, and not ambitious for higher office. Although he sought to win support from blacks with the programs, he lacked the incentive to try for a strong co-optive effort that might have fragmented moderate black leadership (Pressman, 1972). Running conflict between city hall and black leaders over program issues helped keep black mobilization alive. The programs created issues, organizational funding, and potential leadership positions that would not have been available otherwise. Black leaders were able to apply these resources to electoral mobilization, ultimately contributing to the coalitional effort that elected Lionel Wilson mayor in 1977. Wilson himself had been an important leader in the programs since the early sixties.

In San Jose Hispanics linked with Model Cities have not been as successful in electoral politics, but demand-protest on program issues did lead to the appointment of a Model Cities leader, Al Garza, to the council.[8] Backed by Model Cities groups, he had run unsuccessfully for the council in 1971. He was subsequently appointed to fill a vacancy due to the growing demand-protest and electoral mobilization of Hispanics in the Model Cities areas. Garza then won reelection to the council and later succeeded in getting into a run-off election for mayor, which he did not win.

In Sacramento demand-protest and electoral activity developed more or less simultaneously, often but not always with the same organizations and leaders participating. A network of Hispanics associated with a loose organization called Chicanos Organized for Political Action (COPA) was a focus for both kinds of Hispanic mobilization. The long-term goals of mobilization remained constant but were manifested in different kinds of activity in different settings as issues, opportunities, and leadership evolved. Demand-protest mobilization increased the visibility of minority leaders and issues. This enhanced the capacity of minority groups to mobilize for elections and stimulated the interest of the white liberals—interest in including minorities in the emerging coalition, which was successful in 1969 in replacing the resistant dominant coalition.

Thus, the effect of the programs in these three cities with resistant dominant coalitions was eventually to strengthen minorities and allied groups challenging the dominant coalition. However, these positive effects were not strong enough or soon enough to promote the institutionalization of the programs. The

[8]The combined minority population in San Jose, unlike that in Oakland and Sacramento, is probably insufficient to support a liberal dominant coalition in the absence of strong white support, so the difference in success is not unexpected.

extent to which the programs were maintained and institutionalized paralleled the ideology of the coalitions in control when
programs ended. The more supportive the existing dominant
coalition, the more the program was institutionalized. The less
supportive the coalition was, the less institutionalization occurred. In Oakland the Model Cities program ended long before
a liberal coalition took office. The director of the Model Cities
agency was fired, the agency abolished, and its programs largely
terminated. In San Jose city hall also moved decisively to eliminate Model Cities, which it saw as a thorn in its side. This contrasts with the fate of Model Cities in cities with liberal dominant coalitions.

Implementation and Liberal Dominant Coalitions

In Richmond, San Francisco, and Berkeley federal social
programs did not become the focus for minority electoral mobilization efforts. But the programs did contribute directly to
some increases in policy responsiveness because they permitted the dominant coalition to expand services to minorities and
produced some institutionalization of minority interests.

The clearest example is Richmond, a city of 79,000 with a
minority population of 46 percent in 1970, where blacks are by
far the largest minority. A liberal administrative coalition was
led by the city manager, a white, and his top staff, with acquies-
cence from a liberal-to-moderate majority on the council, on
which blacks typically held one-third of the seats. They used
Model Cities to promote modestly redistributive programs,
which were responsive to blacks but which also served to avoid
disruptive conflict.

The Model Cities structure and staff were chosen to facilitate
these goals. The Model Neighborhood Area was drawn to include virtually all of the mainly black areas of the city. Even
though the Model Cities Agency (MCA) was formally separate
from city hall, it was seen by the city manager, key staff within
the city hall, and the MCA as directly complementing already
established functions of city government. City hall saw defer-

ence to the MCA board (which had veto power) as a positive good rather than a necessary evil; similarly, the leadership of MCA saw the program as a way of institutionalizing processes, programs, and personnel, which would increase city hall responsiveness to minorities. City hall leaders were trying to tie an emerging black leadership and informed citizenry to a cooperative city government. Minority mobilization was skillfully channeled into cooperative participation in the Model Cities program. When Model Cities ended, many features were institutionalized in city government. Model Cities personnel were brought under civil service, the director of Model Cities became assistant city manager, and many of the programs were continued. Model Cities had appeared on the horizon just as it was becoming urgent for city officials to bring the city's black population peaceably into city government, and Model Cities proved to be the vehicle by which that could be accomplished.

As attention and energy focused on the implementation of Model Cities, electoral mobilization fell somewhat and has never approached the kind of tightly organized, sustained coalition effort found in Berkeley. Although blacks have secured significant advantages from Richmond's city government, on several indicators they do less well than Berkeley's considerably smaller black population. The development of black incorporation in Richmond has something of a cast of co-optation — blacks brought into an administrative and political process that might not provide the strongest base for a continuing rise in influence. Nevertheless, rapid changes did occur in Richmond city government, the struggle for control over Model Cities programs did produce notable gains, and the Model Cities agency was eventually brought completely into the government. In an alternative scenario the leading coalition might have been less forthcoming, and strong electoral mobilization might have finally seemed the only feasible strategy, eventually building a stronger electoral base, a more active city council, and greater gains for blacks. But, of course, still other scenarios are less optimistic.

In Berkeley and San Francisco the federal social programs played a more limited role in expanding services to minorities, but, as in Richmond, the programs did not become a focus for electoral mobilization. In San Francisco protests early in the sixties against discrimination and plans for downtown urban renewal and freeways were not successfully transformed into cohesive electoral mobilization. In response to the demands, Mayor Alioto used federal programs, Model Cities in particular, to meet some demands and to build his electoral support in minority neighborhoods. As a result minority groups became deeply involved in running programs. The way these programs were distributed, the resulting struggles for power and competition for resources, the demands of grantsmanship and financial accountability, and the clear expectation of loyalty to the mayor contributed to the fragmentation of minority leadership and made unified electoral activity less likely. Consequently, black electoral mobilization in San Francisco was less cohesive than expected, given the estimated level of support for black interests in the city and the strong relationship between support and mobilization in the ten cities as a group. Because the mayor needed minority support to win elections and could as a Democrat make appeals for it without alienating his electoral base, the co-optive effort was vigorous and successful in conciliating and diverting minority organizations and in disrupting minority mobilization (see pp. 54–58 and 114–17 above). But some of the Model Cities programs were institutionalized in San Francisco. The elements of the program that the dominant coalition found useful were continued, and other elements, such as neighborhood citizen participation structures, were dropped or transformed when citywide CDBG advisory processes were established.

Opportunities for program-generated demand-protest and electoral mobilization were minimized in Berkeley, not because program implementation was managed by a government official (be the official a city manager as in Richmond or a mayor in San Francisco) and not because of the needs of the official to elicit some level of minority support, but because electoral mobilization had already reached very high levels and had already led to significant levels of incorporation. Thus the demand-protest that was generated by the programs was a supplement to electoral mobilization rather than a stimulus for it. In Berkeley a liberal coalition of blacks and whites had already gained control before Model Cities and had firm electoral support from the black population. This coalition rejected demands for community control of the programs, choosing instead to keep them in city hall. Model Cities enabled the city to offer new services, continuing an already established trend toward increased responsiveness. The program was not a central issue to the dominant coalition and not the primary focus of political mobilization for the minority population. But, as in San Francisco and Richmond, some policy responsiveness followed from the availability of program funds.

Implementation and Resistant Dominant Coalitions without Electoral Mobilization

The remaining four cities—Stockton, Vallejo, Daly City, and Hayward—like the first group of cities had resistant dominant coalitions in 1968, which opposed the redistributory aspects of the programs, but the effects of the programs were different. They stimulated only low levels of demand-protest, and the issues, leaders, and organizations associated with the programs never were channeled into electoral mobilization. There was no discernible program impact on political incorporation.

The dominant coalitions were characterized by the most resistant conservative ideologies. They were generally hostile to federal grants for local governments, alleging that the federal government had no business interfering in the governance of cities. Compared to our other cities with resistant dominant coalitions, they participated in fewer programs, more grudgingly, and on smaller scales. None of them participated in Model Cities, only two had downtown urban renewal projects in the sixties, and none had city-run poverty programs, participating instead in countywide poverty agencies. The federal social programs that did operate in the cities temporarily expanded services to minorities during the life of the programs, but they were distant from city halls and had minimal impact on policy responsiveness.

Minority groups focused attention on the operation of the programs, contending over structures, personnel, and distribution of funds. They mounted protests and occasionally filed complaints of noncompliance with federal agencies. But the minority organizing efforts stimulated by the programs remained fragmented and did not cumulate into strong pressure on city hall. They were an annoyance to be endured, but they were not viewed as a serious challenge. Moreover, the mobilization stimulated by the programs was not transferred to electoral efforts. Minority candidates were not typically active in the programs or supported by program people. This may be because the level of program-related demand-protest never reached the levels it did in the first group of cities with resistant dominant coalitions or because electoral politics was less coalitional. Minority groups did not create sustained coalitions behind minority candidates, and liberal multiethnic challenging coalitions did not form. Stockton is the one exception in that a multiethnic coalition formed, but it was not linked to program networks. The organizing strategy was to avoid any contacts with the poverty program people because competition over funds had created so many divisions.

An examination of these three groups of cities based on the dominant coalitions that existed in 1968—cities with resistant dominant coalitions where the programs generated electoral mobilization, cities with liberal coalitions, and cities with resistant dominant coalitions where the program did not generate electoral mobilization—shows that program implementation was shaped by the interaction of dominant coalitions and minority organizations. At any given point, minority mobilization was at quite different stages in different cities, and coalitions with very different positions on minority-oriented programs controlled city government. Therefore, federal programs impinged on different local structures and movements. Their responses to or uses of the programs shaped local implementation and effects. The timing of a federal program in relation to the development of minority mobilization and to the replacement of resistant dominant coalitions largely determined how the program was used. We will see that this is also true of programs in the seventies, and we expect that this pattern is relevant to federal programs generally. Local systems develop partly according to their own evolutionary dynamic and partly by adapting to external interventions such as federal programs. They set the parameters within which local factors operated and thus had important influence on local political change, but that influence was shaped by local factors, which, in turn, produced variations in program implementation and effect.[9] Implementation is a process in which dispositions embodied in policies are continuously transformed by implementing actions, in which both policy content and policy context are important (Pressman and Wildavsky, 1979, p. 183; Williams, 1980b). Wildavsky sees implementation from a national perspective as "continuous adjustment of objectives" and "modification of instruments for obtaining them" (p. 176). We see implementation from the local perspective as a similar process of organizational learning in which local officials' responses to shifting national policies are shaped both by federal pressures to comply with the policies and pressures to meet local demands.

Variations in Local Implementation in the Seventies

Apparently federal social programs had significant effects in a direction anticipated in the statutes since liberal dominant coalitions used these programs to increase governmental responsiveness to minorities, and since minority leaders in some cities with conservative dominant coalitions used the programs to mobilize against those coalitions. So far we have

[9]As seen in chapter 3, variations in demand-protest and electoral mobilization are well explained by local characteristics. In this chapter we argue that federal programs had an influence on demand-protest and electoral mobilization. However, the programs did not have a large effect independent of these local characteristics. Otherwise, we would not have been able to explain intercity differences in demand-protest and electoral mobilization so well solely with population and other local characteristics. Although the programs changed the agendas of minority mobilization, it is not clear that they had an independent effect on the level of either electoral mobilization or demand-protest. As shown in figure 11, cities with active federal programs in the 1960s did not experience either more or less than expected electoral mobilization overall (on the basis of percent black and percent white support) than cities with less federal program activity in the 1960s. In figure 10, it may be that cities with more federal programs in the 1960s had more black demand-protest overall, but those were also generally the cities with more liberal dominant coalitions.

examined the influence of federal social programs in the sixties that were based on strong statutes vis-à-vis minorities. The Economic Opportunity Act and the Model Cities statutes were strong because they required resources to be targeted toward poor people and/or poverty areas in order to improve their living conditions. The statutes mandated significant citizen participation (Frieden and Kaplan, 1975) and gave federal agencies the power to choose which applicants were funded and how much money each selected applicant received. This was an inducement for applicants to plan activities that complied with the statute, giving priority to the needs of the poor and poverty neighborhoods.

In addition to collecting data on the sixties social programs, we also examined the implementation and effects of General Revenue Sharing and Community Development Block Grants in the seventies. Thus we can compare how the same local government responded to grants based on weaker statutes or statutes that entailed less federal control to benefit minorities. Again we show the interaction between the federal programs and local political variables in the implementation process. Changes in federal statutory requirements generate shifts in the behavior of local governments. Different types of grants favor different local actors and thus different outcomes. This reality must not get lost in the despair (or joy as the case may be) about the limited capacity of the federal government to direct local political change. The capacity is limited but still important. The more the statute coherently structures the implementation process, the more difficult it is for local actors to resist or distort the thrust of the legislation (Sabatier and Mazmanian, 1979).

General Revenue Sharing

In General Revenue Sharing the federal statute is very weak. The administering agency has no discretion over which cities receive funds or the size of the allocation to cities; all cities receive GRS and the allocations are set by a formula. Local governments have wide discretion over the way funds are used within some very broad categories. The only restrictions concern compliance with the civil rights and Davis Bacon laws and the reporting and publication provisions of the legislation. The sanction for violations is withholding payments and this has rarely been exercised. No specifications are made about target constituencies, structures, or decision processes (except a requirement to publicize reports of planned and actual use of funds). The legislation simply gives financial assistance to local governments and lets them use the money in whatever way they desire. The money comes to city hall without strings and the dominant coalition uses it according to its own agenda.

In spite of the numerous methodological problems in identifying the fiscal impact of GRS, the general outlines are clear. Our cities fit the pattern identified in studies of GRS nationally (Nathan, 1975; Nathan and Adams, 1977). In cities that were hard pressed fiscally, the money was used to operate existing city programs that would have been cut or that would have necessitated an increase in taxes in the absence of the new resources. Cities in a better financial position used the new money to initiate programs that had previously been on a waiting list until sufficient funds appeared. But these new programs only rarely included social services or other activities directed primarily toward minorities.

Thus in our sample, as in other U.S. cities, GRS, which was not oriented toward benefitting minorities, was not typically used locally to benefit minorities. However, it is still interesting to examine variations in the way our ten cities used GRS. Even though the legislation did not favor local actors oriented toward minorities in the same way as the sixties' social programs, where dominant coalitions favored redistributive effort, a little of that occurred. Whether a city had had a Model Cities program was less important than the minority orientation of its dominant coalition. In two of the Model Cities and two of the non-Model Cities, GRS was used to fund limited program innovations beneficial to minorities. In all four cities this was a reflection not of federal requirements but of the ideology and interests of the local dominant coalitions.

In two of the three Model Cities with dominant coalitions favoring redistribution to minorities (Berkeley and San Francisco), portions of GRS were used to increase funding for social services and community-based organizations (CBOs). In the third Model City with a favorable dominant coalition, Richmond, where one might also have expected a "minority tilt," GRS was used to protect the solvency of the police and fire pension fund. The two non-Model Cities that targeted some

GRS money for minorities were Sacramento and Hayward. In these cities liberal dominant coalitions had replaced conservative coalitions by 1972. Although they probably would not have funded a new minority-oriented program out of local tax revenues, GRS created a surplus, and other needs were not perceived as urgent. GRS made additional resources available at precisely the time when dominant coalitions wanted to do something for minority groups. Hayward, like Berkeley and San Francisco, used part of its GRS funds for social services and CBOs, and Sacramento used some GRS money for public works in minority areas—for example, sidewaiks and sewers.

Did GRS contribute to mobilizing opposition to resistant dominant coalitions the way the sixties' social programs did? Evidence from our cities suggests that it did not. Insofar as there was minority mobilization to influence GRS allocations, it was the result of prior social program activities. In the Model Cities, particularly, citizen groups were more active in the GRS process than they had ever been in previous budget processes. In four of the Model Cities, the revenue sharing hearings in 1972 were described as the largest public meetings in city history, with attendance ranging from 250 to 1,400 people. The non-Model Cities did not report any marked increase in attendance. Another indicator of activity that revealed differences between the Model Cities and the non-Model Cities was the number of requests for revenue sharing funds made by groups. Many more groups made requests in Model Cities than in non-Model Cities. In addition to group activity in the Model Cities, there were direct links between GRS activity and the Model Cities program. Groups associated with Model Cities were especially active in attending hearings and urging the allocation of revenue sharing money to social services. However, this mobilization at the onset of GRS was not sustained and did not develop into the continuing networks of organizations and leaders that had formed around Model Cities programs.

Community Development Block Grants

The Community Development Block Grant program fits midway on the continuum of statute strength. There is more federal control in CDBG than in GRS and less than in the social programs. The Housing and Community Development Act of 1974 combined several HUD categorical grant programs—including Model Cities, urban renewal, open space, and water and sewer—into one block grant that is distributed to cities over 50,000 by formula after they submit applications. The objectives, eligible programs, and target populations are stated more specifically than they are in GRS but more generally than in the social programs. According to the statute, the primary objective of CDBG was "the development of viable urban communities, including decent housing and a suitable living environment and expanding economic opportunities, principally for persons of low and moderate income." But until 1978 HUD did not specify the proportion of funds that had to be targeted for low and moderate income groups. The structure and processes to be used in allocating the money were largely left to local discretion, although the recipient jurisdictions were required to certify compliance with a longer list of requirements than in GRS, including holding two public hearings and providing citizens an "adequate opportunity to participate in the development of the application." Thus in CDBG the odds were slightly more favorable to the local actors supporting minorities than they were in GRS because the funds had to be used for housing and community development rather than a wider range of functions. But the odds were less favorable than in Model Cities and poverty programs, which required targeting on the lowest income groups.

Studies of the implementation of CDBG stress the "spreading effect" of the grant at the local level. They find that funds are spread to citywide uses as well as to low and moderate income tracts. Analysts using different methods come up with similar estimates of the proportion of CDBG funds allocated to low and moderate income tracts in their national samples. A Brookings study of the first-year allocations found that 52 percent of the program benefits went to low and moderate income areas—with central cities targeting 60 percent to those areas and satellite cities targeting 29 percent.[10]

We are able to examine the spreading effect in our cities in

[10]Nathan, Dommel et al. (1977). The NAHRO study (1976) found that 51 percent of the funds were allocated to low and moderate income tracts. See also Dommel (1982).

two ways. First, we compare the amount of money that went into Model Neighborhood Areas (MNAs) under the Model Cities program with the amount of CDBG money going into these same census tracts. Second, we compare the percentage of CDBG funds allocated to minority census tracts with the percentage of city population in those tracts.

MNAs had been designated by the five Model Cities as their most needy areas. We defined a tract to be in the MNA if at least one-fourth of it was in the MNA. Minority tracts we defined as those with 20 percent or more black and Hispanic population in 1970. The starting point for determining the allocation of CDBG funds was each city's CDBG application; most of these list the dollar amount and target census tracts for each project. Sometimes both MNA and non-MNA or minority and non-minority tracts are listed as target, and it is necessary to use some criterion to distribute the allocation between the categories. Where possible we obtained a more detailed breakdown of the distribution of funds to target tracts from interviews with CDBG staff or from supplementary city publications. When no informed estimate of the actual distribution of project impact was available, we divided project funds between categories in proportion to population.

Table 28 shows that in all five of our Model Cities the MNA received smaller annual allocations under CDBG than under Model Cities, even though the amount of money coming into the cities from HUD did not decrease (due to the hold harmless provisions). Once the cities were not forced by the federal requirements to target the grant money to the areas they had identified as most needy, they spread the money to other areas, thus reducing the amount of money to the MNA.

Many local factors influenced the spread of funding to non-MNA areas, in addition to the statutory relaxation of criteria for eligibility and need. Most of San Francisco's very high continued allocation to the MNA under CDBG (82 percent of the Model Cities amount) was the by-product of a commitment to complete large-scale urban renewal projects in the largely black Bayview-Hunters Point MNA. Richmond and Berkeley, smaller cities, had been able to draw MNA boundaries so as to include a high proportion of their needy populations, in contrast to both San Francisco and Oakland, where large low income populations were not in the MNAs. Some of the spread-

TABLE 28   Allocations to Model Neighborhood Areas under Model
Cities and CDBG in Five Cities

	Model Cities funding to MNA[a] (thousands)	CDBG funding to MNA[b] (thousands)	CDBG $ to MNA as percent of MC $ to MNA	CDGB $ to MNA as percent of city's total CDBG $
San Francisco	$13,504[c]	$11,038	82	41
Richmond	2,424[c]	1,322	55	39
Berkeley	1,403	747	53	26
San Jose	3,086	1,452	47	23
Oakland	4,092	439	11	3

Note: These cities are the five that participated in the Model Cities program.
[a]Annualized average grant data provided by U.S. Department of Housing and Urban Development, "Data Affecting Hold Harmless Calculations," Washington, D.C., n.d.
[b]Average of allocations for four years, 1975–78 CDBG applications.
[c]Figures for HUD allocations to Model Cities have been augmented to include HUD urban renewal allocations to neighborhood development projects (NDP) to achieve comparability because city allocated CDBG money to preexisting NDP projects in its MNA.

ing effect of CDBG was the result of city efforts to allocate CDBG benefits to low income areas that had not benefitted from Model Cities.

Although it is impossible with these five cases to disentangle all of the influences on the spread of CDBG allocations away from MNAs, the data are consistent also with the hypothesis that the strength of minority incorporation in the dominant coalition was a factor. Cities dominated by relatively liberal coalitions continued to allocate a higher proportion of funds to the Model Neighborhood Areas in the CDBG program than did cities with conservative dominant coalitions. The three cities that rank the highest in CDBG dollars to MNA as a percentage of Model Cities dollars to MNA (column 3 of table 28) are the three cities with the most liberal dominant coalitions. The identical city rankings emerge if we take as our measure the proportion of CDBG funds targeted to MNAs (column 4 of table 28). The three cities continued to target funds to those areas even when not required to do so by the federal government. Still the level of funding to MNAs declined, because when the federal requirements were loosened, the ability of the coalition to resist other demands for those funds was lowered. In San Francisco, for example, Chinese groups stepped forward to claim a share of the new CDBG benefits. Oakland, where the most resistant coalition in this group of cities engaged in a bitter and destructive conflict with the Model Cities neighborhood board, allocated by far the smallest proportion of CDBG funds to the MNA. Both by objective criteria of group need and by the political incentive to respond to organized demand, much of it from needy groups not benefitted by Model Cities, the Model Cities were led to respond to a broader set of interests when they made their CDBG allocations.

So, comparison of dollars going into MNAs under Model Cities and CDBG indicates that CDBG spread federal dollars. How did the amount of spreading vary across cities? The Brookings study of CDBG found that (1) the higher the poverty rate, the higher the proportion of CDBG funds a city allocated to low and moderate income persons; (2) Model Cities allocated higher proportions of CDBG funds to low and moderate income groups than non-Model Cities; (3) where low and moderate income groups made demands and officials were sympathetic, benefits to those groups tended to be higher (Nathan, Dommel et al., 1977).

The first step in our analysis was simply to determine the proportion of CDBG funds targeted to minority tracts averaged over 1975 – 78 (in our cities minority tracts, 20 – 100 percent minority, are also the low and moderate income tracts and constitute a large proportion of all such tracts). Then we compared that figure with the percent of the city's population residing in the minority tracts to see which cities were targeting more money to those needy tracts than one would expect the tracts to get solely on the basis of population. The results are displayed in figure 24.

Figure 24 shows two distinct groups of cities: one group of four cities (Group I) allocating substantially higher proportions of CDBG funds to minority tracts than the other (Group II). With both groups the CDBG allocation to minority tracts is at least as great as the proportion of the city's population resid-

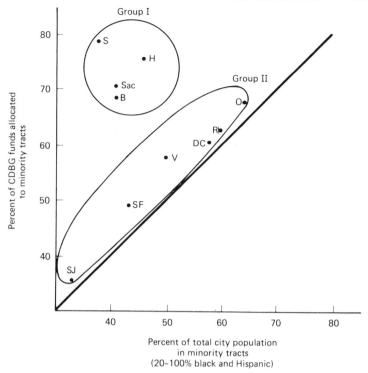

FIGURE 24   CDBG Targeting to Minorities

(B = Berkeley; DC = Daly City; H = Hayward; O = Oakland; R = Richmond;
Sac = Sacramento; SF = San Francisco; SJ = San Jose; St = Stockton; V = Vallejo)

ing in those tracts, as it should be if city governments are not discriminating against their minority populations. But the CDBG allocations of the Group II cities, though related across cities to population in minority tracts, were barely greater than what we could expect on that basis. Because these are also the lower income tracts, the implication is that the responsiveness of Group II cities either to the statutory income criterion or to the nonstatutory racial and ethnic criterion was not great. These cities spent more CDBG funds in minority tracts than we would expect from population size alone, but not much more.

What factors distinguish the two groups of cities? Again, the explanation is in the timing of minority group mobilization and incorporation in relation to the initiation of a program — CDBG — and the opportunities for the distribution of resources that it created. Three of the four Group I cities — Sacramento, Stockton, and Hayward — did not participate in the Model Cities program. Cities that participated had experienced intense mobilization of blacks and Hispanics prior to CDBG. In these cities the peak of black and Hispanic demand-protest had passed by the time CDBG became available and other claimants were pressing for a share. But in the three non-Model Cities in Group I, CDBG presented itself as the first major opportunity to respond effectively to recent gains in minority mobilization and incorporation.

Sacramento had not participated in Model Cities, and CDBG was an obvious way of responding to the substantial black and Hispanic role in the liberal coalition that took office in 1969. In Stockton, although the dominant coalition had not been replaced, minorities had gained two of nine council seats in 1971 and were for the first time a force to be reckoned with on the council. The liberal coalition that dominated Hayward city government beginning in 1972 was also seeking ways to demonstrate its responsiveness, even though Hayward's Hispanics were not represented by Hispanic council members.

Thus the responsiveness of the Group I cities resulted largely from CDBG funds becoming available at a time when those city governments perceived themselves under new pressure to provide benefits to previously ignored black and Hispanic groups and when they had a new commitment or incentive to do so.[11] In contrast to the Brookings study, we do not find that poverty rate or participation in Model Cities distinguishes the two groups of cities (Nathan, Dommel, et al., 1977). Cities with low and high poverty rates are found in each group

[11]Berkeley, in the responsive Group I in figure 24, fits this general description in part. Blacks were so strongly incorporated that city government was always searching for new ways to be responsive, but they had most certainly not been ignored prior to CDBG. There was a modest allocation to a few Hispanic organizations under CDBG, and some grants or contracts were made to other programs supported primarily by whites. Still, Berkeley's CDBG funds were spent, as figure 24 shows, very largely in low-to-moderate income tracts with at least 20 percent minority population.

and so are Model Cities (in fact, more Model Cities are found in Group II than Group I). But the third factor cited by Brookings, demands from low and moderate income groups and sympathetic response from officials, is consistent with our finding that the timing of minority group mobilization and incorporation influences officials' targeting of CDBG funds.

In sum our CDBG data support the generalization that the grant had a "spreading effect" at the local level. When federal requirements for targeting decreased, so did the extent of targeting to the most needy areas and to minority populations. When the federal statute suggested but did not require targeting to low and moderate income areas, some cities chose to spread their resources to other areas and some did not, depending on when minority mobilization and incorporation occurred in relation to the availability of CDBG funds. However, both our GRS and CDBG data show that federal grant money, even with weaker federal strings, can provide resources for local actors with liberal orientations to minorities if those actors have enough power in the local arena to pursue their agendas successfully. However, CDBG and GRS, unlike Model Cities and other federal social programs, have not contributed to the mobilization of liberal prominority opposition to conservative dominant coalitions.

Summary

This examination of the role of federal programs in our ten cities over the last two decades suggests that the federal presence has had an important positive influence on the struggle by blacks and Hispanics for political equality. Looking at the general impact of federal social programs—poverty programs, urban renewal as it impacts on minority neighborhoods, and Model Cities—across all our cities, we find that they stimulated minority mobilization and thus incorporation and that they contributed to increased policy responsiveness to minorities by city governments. In our view, then, the programs have been more successful than commonly realized. When seen in the proper time dimension and with regard for the latent impacts, the programs had substantial, long-term, positive effects on the political position of minorities in cities.[12]

The chapter has also demonstrated that local characteristics produce variation in the implementation and effects of federal social programs from city to city. National programs interact strongly with local conditions. Federal grants had important but limited influence on the direction of local political change. Local coalitions attempted to use the grants to pursue their own agendas. Dominant coalitions that shared the goals of the federal programs used the additional resources to promote some degree of policy responsiveness. Resistant dominant coalitions used program resources to minimize the potential opposition from minorities. Groups challenging resistant dominant coalitions used program resources to strengthen their efforts and push for increased policy responsiveness. In some cities with resistant dominant coalitions, the programs generated electoral mobilization and incorporation as well as demand-protest. The timing of federal programs in relation to minority mobilization and to replacement of resistant dominant coalitions shaped program implementation and effects. Our ten cities vividly illustrate the way that local political contexts shaped program implementation and effects while at the same time being changed by the programs.

Our comparison of grants characterized by strong statutes, such as Model Cities, to grants with less federal control directed to benefitting minorities, such as GRS and CDBG, shows that the implementation processes were clearly and importantly affected by the strength of the statutes as well as by the local conditions. In particular the Model Cities statute set forth less ambiguous objectives than either GRS or CDBG and provided stronger opportunities for local groups to participate in the implementation process, and these differences in statute generated significant differences in outcomes. Yet when federal statutes such as GRS and CDBG do not require targeting to minority areas, some cities target funds more than others. More minority group-responsive allocations were a function of the timing of minority group mobilization and incorporation in relation to the availability of federal resources.

[12]Salamon (1976) illustrates the importance of considering long-term effects.

With regard to the study of policy implementation, our findings sustain the view that implementation of intergovernmental programs is complex and problematic, involving multiple political as well as administrative factors, with diverse effects not understood at the formulation stage. Policy implementation and effects are shaped by both the policy content and the policy context, and the latter involves both a federal and a local dimension. The study of implementation must consider the policy and the implementors (both federal and local), but also the time dimension so that the evolutionary adaptations, which occur as the various levels of government contend in the intergovernmental system, are not overlooked. Likewise the study of urban politics must integrate the federal with the local dimension and must comprehend the vertical context of national programs and movements that shape the evolution of cities over time. Efforts to consider elements of this complex web in isolation from other elements have too often led to simplistic and misleading conclusions. The optimistic view of policy as an easily manipulable lever and the naive hope for simple, static explanations of social systems are fading away. We are left with the realization that there is no easy way to understand and no substitute for basic research into the processes of change in political systems—processes of mobilization, incorporation, and responsiveness—and their interaction with federal policies.

In the concluding chapter, which follows, we engage in some speculation about emerging trends in our cities in an era when federal intervention in local politics on behalf of minorities is decreasing. Our understanding of the dynamics of local politics over the last two decades leads us to be apprehensive but not despairing. Strong federal statutes are not a panacea for minorities. Statutes are at least partly a reflection of the larger political climate so they cannot be relied on as an easily manipulable variable that will transform society. Efforts to benefit minorities, like efforts to improve the environment or achieve any other desirable end, must balance the benefits of high federal control to achieve that end against the disadvantages. However, strong federal statutes and a commitment to redressing injustice have been important contributors to the gains of the last two decades. The question is whether that federal role was necessary to those gains even if not sufficient to produce them.

It is possible that the interaction of federal and local forces has produced enough local changes and that increasingly influential minority political roles have been institutionalized enough to withstand a federal reversal. But just as the changes would not have come about without the national thrust, they may not be able to withstand a national abdication.

7

The Prospects for Political Equality: Is Protest Enough?

Without the wonderful props of the sixties and seventies, without the highs and lows, without the dramatic rhetoric, without the mass approval, with only the nation's best ideals, with a fresh and unscarred sense of the possible, with an often lonely sense of mission, with these and not much more—what has been begun must somehow be finished.

(Eleanor Holmes Norton, former Director of the U.S. Equal Employment Opportunities Commission, October 17, 1981)

This book has analyzed the struggle by blacks and Hispanics for political influence and the response of local governments in ten cities during two turbulent decades. The empirical findings have been used to develop a theory of political incorporation, which has important implications for the study of urban politics and of politics more generally.

Now we pull together the main elements of the theory and return to the study's central questions:

1. How open are urban political systems?
2. How did political incorporation occur?

3. Did political incorporation of minorities make a difference for policy?

We highlight our contribution to current thinking on these issues and consider future prospects for political mobilization, incorporation, and responsiveness, using these elements of our theory to suggest strategies for capitalizing on resources in different types of cities.

Theory of Political Incorporation

Our theory of the political incorporation of minorities is a theory of minority mobilization and white response in which electoral mobilization is a key to incorporation, and incorporation in liberal dominant coalitions is central to policy responsiveness. The stronger forms of incorporation—including the replacement of conservative coalitions on city councils and minority participation in new, more liberal coalitions—are necessary and sufficient for sustained policy responsiveness to the interests of minority groups.

Incorporation, in turn, depends on the determined mobilization of minority resources in the electoral arena. Although demand-protest often contributes to electoral mobilization, demand-protest alone is not enough to produce strong incorporation of minority interests in city government. And although demand-protest yields some measurable gain in responsiveness from city governments, the incorporation of the group yields much more.

We assume the existence of a widely diffused movement in which demands for group access and representation and for governmental responsiveness are prominent and intense. The theory posits a simple structure of resources that shape the pattern and the magnitude of local mobilization. These resources are the size of the minority population (both percentage and numbers are important, in different ways), the amount of support for minority interests among the rest of the electorate (among whites or, for Hispanics, among blacks), and the organizational development and political experience of the group. A group that is large in number is more likely to engage in demand-protest; a group large in percentage terms is more likely to mobilize strongly in the electoral arena.

These basic resources of group size and support largely determine the local form and intensity of a national mobilization movement. They create strong incentives for mobilization where they are present, strong constraints where they are not. However, the evolution of group mobilization and the response of dominant coalitions is contingent on other political factors, in particular on traditional local ways of dealing with demands on city government (cf. Clark and Ferguson, 1983) and on the nature of the dominant coalition at the time of peak demand-protest. Conservative coalitions tend to resist minority demands and to oppose their efforts to gain access to city government; liberal coalitions tend to co-opt.

The theory of incorporation developed here defines and measures the extent to which a group has been able to achieve a position from which strong and sustained influence can be exercised. The theory identifies three steps that are necessary if excluded groups are to move toward political equality: they must get elected, they must become part of a coalition, and the coalition must be dominant—able to shape the policies of city government. Political incorporation, in our view, is a much better indicator of access and potential influence than the more frequently used percentage measure of representation; or, to focus on the relationship between the concepts, incorporation redefines representation, emphasizing and making explicit the stronger forms of representation.

The theory also gives special prominence to electoral effort and to the role of coalitions in electoral mobilization and in governmental decision making. The theory calls attention to the need to describe their makeup, their formation, and their development over time. In particular, we emphasize the relevance of ideology. Conservative and liberal coalitions responded very differently to minority mobilization and demands.

In most of these reform cities, politics no longer fits the friends-and-neighbors pattern associated with nonpartisanship (Lee, 1960) but bears much closer resemblance to a partisan pattern. This increases the likelihood that the theory of incorporation is generalizable to other medium-to-larger cities with sizeable black and Hispanic populations.

Students of national government have always focused on

the development and impact of coalitions, both electoral (party realignment) and policy making (for example, the conservative coalition in Congress). The theory of incorporation offers a way of studying group access and influence at any level. In urban politics in particular, the theory suggests that coalitions are central to questions of group access. Like Peterson (1981), we acknowledge the many external, intergovernmental constraints on urban politics. However, we find that political coalitions, ideology, and conflict are significant in urban politics as in national politics, and they are necessary to any satisfactory explanation of urban responsiveness to blacks and Hispanics. Economic interests and economic competition between cities set undeniably important constraints on urban policy, but these constraints allow a great deal more room for local discretion than Peterson would have us believe—discretion that is shaped by the interests and ideologies of the changing coalitions contending for control over city government.

How Open Are Urban Political Systems?

Blacks and Hispanics are no longer totally excluded from influence over government policy. They have made themselves heard, they have achieved significant incorporation, and city governments are more responsive to their interests. Our principal findings are:

1. By 1980 there was at least some minority representation in seven of the ten cities. Whereas no blacks or Hispanics served on city councils in 1960, by the late 1970s minority council representation, on the average over all ten cities, was 55 percent of the size of the minority population, with blacks closer to parity than Hispanics.

2. From near zero in 1960, blacks and Hispanics had made enormous gains in political incorporation by 1980. Beyond simple representation, this meant that minority councilmembers participated in the coalitions that dominated city policy making on minority-related issues. Minority participation in domi-

nant coalitions produced far more policy change than did simple representation.

3. Blacks achieved stronger incorporation than Hispanics. Black incorporation started earlier, increased more steadily, reached higher levels, and extended over more cities and people.

4. Minority incorporation was associated with the replacement of conservative dominant coalitions by liberal coalitions, with more Democrats on city councils, and with the growth of minority populations.

5. Progress, however, has been uneven from city to city. There has been little or no minority representation or incorporation in one-third of the cities, all of them relatively small.

These findings provide evidence with which to evaluate the openness of American urban politics. A group that is intensely concerned about government policies but has not gained access to the policy-making process has not achieved significant political equality. A group that achieves substantial incorporation—beyond the right to vote and simple representation—is in a strong position to change government policy in areas of special concern to them. Substantial incorporation, including partnership in a dominant coalition, provides an especially strong form of access to policy making, bringing with it opportunities to affect every stage of the policy process.

To paraphrase Schattschneider (1960, p. 35), in 1960 the flaw in the pluralist heaven was that the heavenly choruses in these cities sang with a strong Honky/Anglo accent. In some cities the heavenly chorus now sings in more diverse accents. If we focus on the successes, some cities were open to political access by blacks and Hispanics. On the other hand, some were closed to minority participation. The variations in what was accomplished are as significant as the fact of progress overall.[1]

Whether the pattern of changes we report is significant or negligible, substantive or symbolic, depends on one's ideologi-

---

[1]Other authors who emphasize variations across city political systems are Agger, Goldrich, and Swanson (1964); Greenstone and Peterson (1973); and Kirby, Harris, Crain, and Rossell (1973).

cal position. Measured against the idealistic standard of absolute access and political equality, the openness exhibited in our ten cities clearly falls short. Measured against the preexisting situation in the United States (or other countries with white majorities and large racial or ethnic minorities), the incorporation of minorities in local government, although not a revolution to be sure, is nevertheless a great step forward.

Some scholars have argued that blacks and Hispanics are following much the same path that earlier waves of European immigrants followed. The European immigrants used local governments to gain a political foothold and access to government jobs and contracts. Blacks and Hispanics are the successors to the earlier claimants for political position and governmental benefits, hence the term *ethnic succession*.[2] The term is unfortunate because it implies inevitability. Although it is true that such a succession is occurring in some cities, as we have shown, the wide variation from city to city in the extent to which it has occurred shows that ethnic succession is scarcely inevitable.

Though there are undeniable parallels between blacks and Hispanics and the earlier immigrant groups, there are also clear differences in the groups and in the conditions they faced. These differences are in the cultures, in the circumstances in which they came to the United States, in the times they arrived, in the economic opportunities available, in the attitudes of dominant groups toward them, and in the structure and operation of governments.[3] These differences and our findings lead us to conclude that the process of mobilization, incorporation, and responsiveness is problematic rather than automatic. Just because blacks in Oakland and Berkeley have attained political strength, it does not follow that shortly thereafter they will achieve similar political strength in Vallejo and Stockton. Just because blacks made progress, it does

[2]Scholars disagree about the amount of assimilation that has taken place for such groups as the Irish, the Italians, and the Jews. Some stress the integration of immigrants and others stress the persistence of ethnic identities. See Dahl (1961); Glazer and Moynihan (1963, 1975); Lieberson (1980); Lipset (1979); Lowi (1964); Parenti (1967); Wolfinger and Field (1966).

[3]See Marguerite Ross Barnett's distinctions between the black experience and white ethnic groups (1982, pp. 48–52).

not follow that Hispanics will make the same progress. And just because some "ethnic succession" is occurring does not mean that it will continue, that it cannot be reversed. Later in this chapter we will discuss the increasingly hostile conditions that could make succession even more problematic and reverse some of the positive changes that have taken place.

How Did Political Incorporation of Minorities Occur?

Our findings on incorporation reflect gains won by dint of hard struggle over many years. Triggered by the national civil rights movement, the struggle for political equality diffused strongly but unevenly through these ten cities. The local strength of the movement depended mainly on the political resources available in the cities. Where the resources were present, mobilization was vigorous; where they were not, it was weak. Our principal findings are:

1. For both blacks and Hispanics, demand-protest was very closely related to the absolute size of the minority group.[4] It depended more on numbers of people than on the percentage of the group in the population. Blacks tended to generate slightly higher levels of demand-protest where whites were supportive. Hispanics tended to generate slightly higher levels of demand-protest where black demand-protest was high.

2. For both blacks and Hispanics, electoral mobilization was related to the relative size of the minority population rather than absolute size.[5] Black electoral mobilization was also closely related to white support. Hispanic electoral mobilization was most closely associated with prior levels of Hispanic demand-protest.

[4]Our findings here parallel Spilerman's (1970, 1971, 1976).

[5]The difference may be significant. For demand-protest the resource of absolute size was relevant to the generation of the mobilization activity itself— that is, to the production of mass rallies, demonstrations, and the like. For electoral mobilization the resources of relative size and of electoral support were relevant to the ability to control the outcome—that is, to win elections.

3. Overall, demand-protest and electoral strategies did not interfere with each other and were often used effectively together.[6] Demand-protest strategies by themselves produced limited results in most cities; when combined with electoral strategies, the results were much better in the long run.

4. For both blacks and Hispanics levels of political incorporation were closely related to electoral mobilization and the resources that shaped it. For blacks these resources were black population and white support. For Hispanics they were Hispanic demand-protest, the size of the Hispanic population, and the formation of liberal coalitions including blacks. Political incorporation was more closely related to these political factors than to simple percentages of black or Hispanic populations alone.

Although cumulative levels of mobilization and incorporation were shaped by a few major political resources, there were significant differences from city to city in the evolution of minority mobilization and incorporation, as we saw in chapters 2 and 3. These differences may be attributed to particular local conditions.

We identify four main patterns of mobilization and incorporation that resulted from the interaction between minority mobilization and white response. Levels of incorporation achieved depended not only on the resources of or pressures exerted by blacks and Hispanics, but also on the context in which they mobilized, on the response of the dominant coalition, and the amount of support for challenges to resistant coalitions.[7] The four main patterns of incorporation and mobilization are:

1. *Biracial electoral alliance.* Strong incorporation was achieved early as a result of leadership by blacks and whites in forming a liberal electoral alliance prior to the peak of demand-protest activities.

---

[6]Here we support Mollenkopf (1973, 1983) and Piven and Cloward (1979).

[7]Others who stress the interaction between catalyst and context include Coleman (1971); Heclo (1974); and Tilly (1978).

2. *Co-optation.* Partial incorporation was achieved where minorities had less control over issues and candidates in liberal electoral coalitions led by whites and formed prior to or during periods of high demand-protest. These coalitions used co-optation strategies to respond to minority demands, which limited the levels of incorporation achieved.

3. *Protest and exclusion.* The level of incorporation in these cities varied. All the cities experienced intense demand-protest and tenacious resistance by conservative dominant coalitions over a long period of time. In Oakland, with its sizeable black population, strong incorporation was eventually achieved after a delayed but dramatic victory by a challenging coalition led by a black mayoral candidate. In other cities no such breakthroughs occurred, and incorporation was either transitory or very weak.

4. *Weak minority mobilization.* No incorporation was achieved in cities where little or no demand-protest or electoral effort occurred and where the dominant coalition was extremely resistant.

In no city was minority incorporation increased without sustained and substantial effort—early electoral mobilization and the formation of victorious challenging coalitions in a few cities and sustained, intense demand-protest and electoral mobilization in most of them. Demand-protest and electoral mobilization were often used effectively together; they were reinforcing rather than contradictory strategies in most cities. And in some cities mobilization was enhanced by the implementation of federal social programs. Of the five cities with substantial black populations (25,000 or more), strong protest was avoided only where blacks had already achieved strong incorporation prior to the wave of protest of the mid-sixties—in Berkeley and Richmond, with the election of black councilmembers and their inclusion in a liberal dominant coalition. In these two cities blacks were clearly in the dominant coalition, and the expectation was that their interests would be met in some substantial way. These conditions explain their inclination to work with city hall.

In other cities determined resistance by whites in control of city hall prevented or delayed minority incorporation in spite of sustained minority effort. Group mobilization—demand-protest and electoral—and the responses of resistant dominant coalitions interacted to define paths of conflict and cooptation that severely constrained minority access to city government. There was often a considerable lag between minority mobilization and incorporation; between weak incorporation heavily influenced by white leaders and stronger, autonomous incorporation; and between incorporation and responsiveness. Minority populations in several cities failed to achieve any representation on city councils.

Although minority population was the basic political resource for mobilization, other political factors were also critical for minority incorporation into city government,[8] especially the pattern of white support and opposition to minority interests. In conjunction with the size of the black population, the number of whites willing to give electoral support to minority oriented coalitions determined whether such coalitions could form and whether they could win elections. In no city was the ability of minorities to achieve incorporation unaffected by the pattern of white support and opposition.

In our ten cities where blacks and Hispanics did not constitute a majority of the population, the strongest incorporation of minority groups occurred only in liberal, biracial or multiethnic coalitions. Challenging coalitions could form only when there were liberal whites whose ideology and/or interests led them to work with minority groups to replace a more conservative coalition. Thus the ideological leanings of the population and of the network of activists and leaders in a city were a crucial factor in the success of the mobilization movement. Many urban analysts have assumed or argued that political ideology is irrelevant in nonpartisan settings. At least in regard to minority issues, our work shows that this is patently absurd. Liberals on race issues are very different from conservatives, and ideology has an important influence on the nature and outcome of the minority struggle for access to local government.[9]

Where blacks and Hispanics achieved strong and lasting in-

[8]Contrast with Karnig and Welch (1980).

[9]Agger, Goldrich, and Swanson (1964); Crain (1968); Eulau and Prewitt (1973); and Greenstone and Peterson (1973) also emphasize the importance of political ideology in city politics.

corporation into city government, they did so by forming coalitions with like-minded whites and challenging the more conservative coalition in power.[10] But if white support was essential for minority incorporation, minority mobilization and support were also necessary for the rise of successful liberal coalitions. In the classic pattern (Lowi, 1964), groups that wanted to challenge the dominant coalition on city councils attempted to broaden their base of support by appealing to new constituencies. Or perhaps it is more accurate to say that the civil rights movement created newly mobilized constituencies that thrust themselves into local political arenas and thereby created opportunities for coalition.

In sum, incorporation did not come easily. In no city was minority incorporation increased without sustained and substantial effort, and in some cities incorporation was contained or delayed for years in spite of such efforts. To say that some cities were open to minority demands for access and influence may be misleading. It is more accurate to say that minorities in some cities were able to pry the system open in the face of opposition. Lowi's characterization applies: "The price has always been paid by those who are *out*, and when they do get in they do not always get in through a process of mutual accommodation under a broad umbrella of consensus" (1971, p. 53). Where minority incorporation occurred in these cities, it was not consensus that made it possible but pressure and the defeat of the opposition to minority interests. Peaceful mutual accommodation between group interests was more the result of incorporation than a precondition for it.

Our evidence supports Gamson's conclusion that "entry is not prohibited for those with the gumption, the persistence, and the skill to pursue it long enough" (1975, p. 143)—at least in settings where conditions are relatively favorable. But in some cities these facilitating conditions were absent. Interfering with the ability of blacks and Hispanics to turn concern into effective mobilization and incorporation were conservative dominant coalitions, lack of support from whites in the electorate, conflict

[10]Katznelson (1981) describes the emergence of new minority-oriented coalitions and the struggle for influence between old and new coalitions in New York City.

about goals and strategies within and between minority groups, co-optation and manipulation by white leaders, and the relatively small size of a minority group in the population (or the small size of other minority groups who would be potential allies). Persistence, skill, and gumption, though necessary, were not sufficient conditions for substantial incorporation.

Did Political Incorporation Make a Difference for Policy?

When challenging groups were successful in replacing the old coalition on the council and achieving high levels of minority incorporation, policies changed. Simple minority representation on city councils resulted in smaller gains than when minority groups were incorporated into coalitions that successfully challenged older, more conservative groups that had dominated the councils. When liberal coalitions composed of minorities and whites (typically Democrats) gained control of councils, city employment of minorities increased, police review boards were created, more minorities were appointed to commissions, more minority contractors were utilized by the cities, and minority-oriented programs were established. The new dominant coalitions also tended to strengthen mayors and city councils at the expense of city managers, to push for district elections rather than at-large elections, and to promote other changes designed to undermine the older reform structures that had previously characterized city government.

Our political process model of city government responsiveness to blacks and Hispanics is relevant to several theses about determinants of urban policy. One thesis is that socioeconomic variables are more important than political ones in shaping urban policy; the other is that the implementation of federal social programs contributes to positive changes in city policies of interest to minorities. We challenge the first and support the second.

In our ten cities political incorporation of blacks and Hispanics led to increased policy responsiveness to minorities. This political variable best predicts policy responsiveness, and it is a better predictor of policy responsiveness than minority population. Minority population, of course, is also a political variable. The civil rights movement made it into a political variable by increasing the probability that local minority groups would mobilize. Minority population was obviously the most important resource for mobilization, but we can explain changes in policy and/or differences from city to city only by reference to other political factors that influenced minority incorporation. Population characteristics set the parameters within which political processes unfolded; that is, they provided the resources upon which leaders and organizations capitalized. In spite of the close relationship of minority mobilization to minority population, however, there were many points at which other local political factors affected emerging patterns of responsiveness. Policy responsiveness was not likely in cities with small minority populations, but neither was it automatic in cities with large minority populations.

The importance of political variables changed over time in policy areas, such as employment, where federal and state governments also exerted pressure.[11] Incorporation had the most impact in the earlier periods before federal and state agencies pushed urban policies to adapt to the level of minority population and to achieve some equilibrium with the social context (Eulau and Prewitt, 1973).

The primacy of political incorporation in shaping city policy suggests that studies of service delivery may have overemphasized bureaucratic routines and paid too little attention to political variables (Jones, 1980; Lineberry, 1977).[12] In several of our ten cities political incorporation was responsible for dramatic changes in bureaucratic decision rules in many policy areas. We do not doubt the importance of bureaucratic routines; we simply assert that minority political incorporation shaped the governmental response to interests. The implication is that the political incorporation of a newly mobilized interest is likely to change the delivery of services and the associated bureaucratic decision rules that have grown up around

[11]Clark and Ferguson (1983) also stress the changing importance of variables over time.

[12]Boyle and Jacobs (1982) make a similar point.

earlier governmental policy choices. Although local bureaucracies often successfully resist efforts to change their habits, a conclusive, lasting change in dominant coalitions, with a clearcut ideological shift and strongly mobilized interests, can overcome that resistance.

Our findings on city government responsiveness to blacks and Hispanics highlight not only the local political factors but also national ones: the civil rights movement and federal policies. Employment and social programs of the federal government, as implemented in our ten cities, had important effects on minority mobilization and incorporation, and on local policy responsiveness (Greenstone and Peterson, 1973; Mazmanian and Sabatier, 1980; Van Horn, 1979; Williams, 1980a and b). The social programs stimulated demand-protest and electoral mobilization by increasing the resources available to minorities and the cadre of minority leaders committed to mobilization. The programs also supported dominant coalitions sympathetic to minorities, stimulated cities to offer more services to minorities, and, like earlier forms of patronage, provided new bases of power for established and aspiring political leaders. Variations in the local implementation and impact of these federal programs depended on the timing of the programs in relation to the development of minority mobilization and to the replacement of resistant dominant coalitions.

The national civil rights movement was clearly an important force behind both the changes in national policies and the local mobilization of blacks and Hispanics. The very closeness of the statistical relationships between size of local minority population and the level of minority mobilization establishes, rather than disconfirms, the strength of the national movement.

Thus city politics and policy must be viewed in a national context. City governments are indeed constrained in many ways by the intergovernmental system in which they are embedded.[13] However, local political processes can still produce

[13]See also Berman and McLaughlin (1976); Kirp (1982); and Wirt (1970). Peterson (1981) argues that variations in city policy are primarily shaped by city size and fiscal strength, and he downplays the importance of local political processes, issues, and groups. However, in his earlier work with Greenstone (1973), he stressed such factors as mobilization of minorities and ideologies of competing city groups. We think that attention should continue to be given to local political processes, issues, and groups.

significant change and important differences in city policies, including differences in the local implementation of national programs.[14]

The Past and the Future: What Now?

We have depicted recent minority political development in these ten cities. Our concepts, measures, and models for the period 1960–80 should illumine political developments in other cities. The components of the processes—mobilization, formation of challenging coalitions, replacement of dominant coalitions, minority incorporation, and policy responsiveness—are universally applicable, though, of course, the outcomes will vary in different contexts.[15]

Our work also can be used to inform considerations about future developments in cities in the 1980s and beyond. It is not appropriate to assume that the patterns of the sixties and seventies will apply in any simple way to the eighties. Instead it is necessary to consider the situations that minority groups now face, what kind of mobilization might occur and what sort of response it might receive when many of the relevant conditions have changed.

It is easy enough to sketch the main features of the national setting that have changed. The civil rights movement, which generated enormous passion and dramatic rhetoric in the sixties, has less access to national governmental circles and is now more hesitant, less clear about goals and strategy, and certainly less visible. Although the number of minority officeholders, blacks especially, has continued to grow nationwide, the dramatic protests that so occupied public attention in the sixties now surface much less frequently. The most eloquent voice

[14]See Peterson (1981) on the limits of cities. We also agree with Stone (1980) and Barnett (1982) that there are structural conditions that limit city government effectiveness in reallocating economic benefits and that threaten to undermine "seeming advances won through electoral politics" (Barnett, 1982, p. 52).

[15]Preston (1982) discusses the advantages and disadvantages of the emphasis by blacks in Chicago on electoral politics and electoral power. Eisinger analyzes black rule in Detroit and Atlanta (1980).

was stilled by assassination, and other leaders too were killed or have been the object of assassination attempts. It is small wonder that the leaders of the movement now speak to smaller audiences and receive less attention (Estrada et al., 1981; Jones, 1981). There has also been a decline in black and Hispanic registration and voting in presidential and congressional elections since the sixties (International City Management Association, n.d.; U.S. Bureau of the Census, 1979, p. 147). But in particular elections such as the 1983 mayoral race in Chicago, there have been dramatic increases in black and/or Hispanic registration and voting. And in the November 1982 elections the twenty-year trend of declining voter participation in midterm contests was reversed (*New York Times*, Nov. 14, 1982; Scuros, 1982.) We may be seeing the resurgence in minority turnout predicted by analysts who said that minority voting would increase when minorities believe voting will achieve specific goals (Hamilton, 1980). Reapportionment brought about by the 1980 census will also have an impact on minority voting strength.

Obviously the political context of the movement has changed in other critical ways as well. The strong leadership of the Johnson administration on civil rights issues and on a broad array of redistributive programs that aimed to satisfy minority demands gave way to retrenchment and withdrawal under Presidents Nixon and Ford, and the accession of a Democratic president in Jimmy Carter did nothing to rebuild the momentum of the earlier years. By the mid-seventies countermovements that centered on opposition to taxes and government spending and on increasing resistance to affirmative action, welfare, and other minority-oriented programs had arisen nationally. These pressures pushed the Democratic party to the right and, through limits on taxation and expenditures, greatly reduced the ability of cities in California and many other states to respond positively to new demands; cities generally were faced with cutbacks, layoffs, and severe fiscal constraints. In addition, more recently President Reagan and a largely acquiescent Congress have dismantled many of the federal programs of special concern to minorities and have voiced an interest in cutting back many more. Because in most cities minority-oriented programs depended largely or entirely on federal funds, these trends have forced the elimination of some programs already and threaten to reduce drastically or eliminate entirely many of the programs cities had established (Ellwood, 1982; Palmer and Sawhill, 1982).

These adverse trends, both in the movement for minority political mobilization and in the strength of the opposition to government spending and minority-oriented programs, threaten the gains in governmental responsiveness and political incorporation recorded in earlier chapters. Is it possible that we are entering a second post-Reconstruction period, when policies favorable to minorities will be rescinded both locally and nationally (Jones, 1981)? Or have the core elements of minority political strength been so well institutionalized that the most important gains will be preserved (Piven and Cloward, 1982)?

Minority gains in the last twenty years may be part of a cumulative evolutionary process that is essentially irreversible (Bendix, 1964, pp. 76–101; Heclo, 1974; Wilensky, 1975). On the other hand, they may be transitory concessions that will be withdrawn once the pressures for them recede (Gough, 1979; Piven and Cloward, 1971). Tarrow (1981) has suggested that

> scholars who see reform cycles as the outcome of objective socioeconomic processes or of elite enlightenment tend to be evolutionists, while those who see reform as the outcome of social and political conflict are more impressed with the reversibility of reform.

We have shown that the responsiveness of city governments came about as the result of all three kinds of factors: growth in minority population (socioeconomic processes), white liberal support (elite enlightenment), and minority mobilization (the national movement, leading to social and political conflict). Because minority mobilization and incorporation are driven in part by the potential resource of minority population, it is unlikely that we will see the complete dismantling of the minority position; the process is at least in part evolutionary, not completely reversible. On the other hand, both "elite enlightenment" and minority mobilization are variable and potentially reversible. The kinds of minority political goals and strategies that emerge now will surely have an impact both on minority mobilization and on the attitudes of potentially supportive whites, both elite and mass, and on responsiveness to minority interests in the 1980s.

Strategies

In the face of so many adverse national trends, what strategies
might be most effective in the drive for local political incorporation and responsiveness? What will it take to sustain the political gains achieved so far and to strengthen the minority position in cities where it is still weak? The variables of the models
we have developed, the basic building blocks of incorporation
and responsiveness, suggest different strategies depending on
the level of incorporation achieved in a given city and the resources available.

The basic resources relevant to incorporation are size of minority population (the number and percent black and Hispanic), supportive white population, and minority demand-
protest and electoral mobilization. These resources facilitate
the formation and success of multiethnic liberal challenging
coalitions. What are the trends in our cities on each of these
dimensions?

Both black and Hispanic populations have been growing in
most of our ten cities over the last decade and this trend is expected to continue. Between 1970 and 1980 the median increase
in black population was 3.6 percentage points and in Hispanic,
4.3. The percent black increased in seven of the cities, percent
Hispanic in all ten. Recent projections of population trends in
California indicate that Hispanics will increase from the current 19.2 percent to more than 25 percent of the population by
the year 2000, nearly doubling in number (Center for Continuing Study of the California Economy, 1982). Estimates as to the
rate of growth in the eighties vary (Office of the Lieutenant
Governor, 1977), but only in two cities will blacks approach a
majority position (Oakland and Richmond). And although in
some cities Hispanics may achieve sizeable proportions similar
to blacks ten years ago (San Jose, Stockton, Hayward, and Daly
City), they will not constitute majorities in any of the cities.
Both groups will continue to need support from and coalitions
with others to maximize their political impact.

The prospects for white support of minorities in our cities
are not so clear. Nationally there has been a reduction of white
hostility to blacks over the past decades (Campbell, 1971;

Jones, 1981, p. 87; Pettigrew, 1981, pp. 249–52). However, whites and blacks continue to differ markedly on a variety of race-related policy issues (Jennings and Niemi, 1981, pp. 320–22). Whites are much more supportive of President Reagan and more optimistic about black progress than blacks are (*San Francisco Chronicle*, Feb. 2, 1981; Sept. 28, 1981). The situation has been described as one in which "white Americans increasingly reject racial injustice in principle, but are reluctant to accept the measures necessary to eliminate the injustice" (Pettigrew, 1981, p. 252). In the absence of data on current trends in white attitudes in our cities, we can only speculate that the decrease in support for minority-related policies occurring nationally is reflected locally, but variations across the cities in white support will probably continue. The actual support elicited will depend heavily on the mobilization strategies used by minorities (National Urban League, 1982, p. 102).

The decline of the national civil rights movement discussed earlier obviously makes local minority mobilization more difficult. The growth of a black and Hispanic middle class may also increase the likelihood of splits within the groups and hinder mobilization (Joint Center, 1980, pp. 240–41).[16] However, blacks in our cities have continued to achieve stronger incorporation since 1980, paralleling national trends (*New York Times*, Nov. 21, 1982; *San Francisco Chronicle*, Oct. 25, 1981). Organizational resources and leadership developed during the past twenty years are continuing to be used to organize minority political effort in the eighties. Even in the face of declining federal funds, community-based organizations continue to adopt a wide range of tactics and supply a cadre of leaders linked by informal networks. Electoral leadership, often connected with community-based organizations, continues to organize candidacies and campaigns. Resources for incorporation, then, are still present, though some are diminishing and others—particularly the size of minority populations—are increasing.

Given the growing obstacles, it is clear from the evidence that neither incorporation nor responsiveness can even be sus-

---

[16]Nevertheless, some evidence (Hamilton, 1980, 1982) suggests that middle-class blacks continue to identify with black concerns and on economic matters are as liberal as (and sometimes more liberal than) lower-class black voters.

tained, let alone increased, without continued effort. Incorporation is still very fragile, especially for Hispanics (in no city is there more than one Hispanic councilmember). Any lapse of attention to candidate selection and campaigns is likely to be followed by the loss of minority seats on city councils. Where the interests of a group are clearly accepted by the dominant coalition, a temporary loss of group representation will probably not diminish the responsiveness of city government—for instance, in Sacramento, where these conditions obtained from 1979 to 1981, it did not—but repeated failure to secure representation would surely do so. Interests opposed to local programs for minorities are active and vocal in almost all of our cities and will capitalize on signs of weakness in liberal coalitions to dismantle those coalitions and the affirmative action, social, and neighborhood programs they have supported. And liberal coalitions will undoubtedly have to make choices among those programs, saving the ones that serve the greatest need and have the strongest demonstrated performance. Their leaders must make renewed efforts to persuade citizens of the importance of such programs in improved forms, to link them to widely shared values, and to justify local government action and expenditures for them.

Aside from the necessity for sustained effort, what can be done to strengthen incorporation in cities where significant incorporation has already been achieved? What can be done to promote the inclusion of minority groups in dominant coalitions where they are presently excluded or unrepresented? What strategies can capitalize on the resources existing in the different cities?

Cities with Strong Incorporation and Sizeable Black Populations

Berkeley and Oakland are cities with sizeable black populations that have achieved strong incorporation and policy responsiveness. Nevertheless, minority groups in such cities need to develop unified efforts to maintain and even strengthen that incorporation to meet present threats, but splits among minority leaders after electoral success at times make that difficult.

Differences in political ideology that were deemphasized during electoral challenges become more visible after victory. Black elected officials in both Berkeley and Oakland disagree over the best means for promoting black interests, particularly over the priority that should be given to economic development as opposed to traditional social service and neighborhood development programs. Mayor Wilson, for example, is often criticized for aligning himself with business interests, but he asserts that economic growth is necessary in order to solve the problems of poverty and unemployment (*Grassroots*, June 22, 1977; *New West*, Nov. 17, 1980, p. 66; *San Francisco Chronicle*, April 17, 1981).

Nevertheless, competing liberal coalitions in Berkeley ("moderates" and "progressives") were able to unite in an effort to minimize cuts in minority-oriented programs. They agreed in early 1982 that, even to preserve reduced program levels, they would need to increase local taxes. Such reunification is possible if leadership is able to submerge conflicts and unite behind a common goal. (However, the vote in a referendum on the tax proposal fell far short of the two-thirds required.) A united effort would appear also to be needed and feasible in Oakland. The explicit inclusion of Hispanics might increase the size of the supportive majority in Oakland.

Cities with Partial Incorporation

Richmond, Sacramento, and San Francisco fall in this category. Richmond, like Berkeley and Oakland, has a sizeable black population, but it has not achieved strong incorporation or strong policy responsiveness, especially in employment. Minority leadership in Richmond has apparently not been able to capitalize upon the available population resources to gain strong incorporation and influence on policy. There seems to be slack in the coalitional structure in the absence of a well-defined, cohesive liberal coalition. To become better institutionalized in the political system, minority groups need stronger articulation of their interests and more cohesive organization of electoral activity and coalitions. As in Oakland, if Hispanics were included in this coalition, the coalition would constitute a majority of the population.

Sacramento and San Francisco have relatively small black populations, and the combined percent black and Hispanic in each city is smaller than Richmond's black population alone. The key vehicle of incorporation has been the formation of multiethnic coalitions. White liberal challenging coalitions included both blacks and Hispanics, demonstrating that black and Hispanic coalitions are possible, if fragile. Blacks and Hispanics were important components of the successful electoral coalitions of mayors in both cities. In spite of the intense antagonisms between the two minority groups as they compete for the same limited benefits, coalitions are possible and desirable (Garcia and de la Garza, 1977, p. 125).[17] In such cities prevention of reversals in incorporation will require preservation of these multiethnic coalitions. It is possible that the increasingly adverse conditions facing both blacks and Hispanics will facilitate unity by increasing their awareness that both groups are poorly treated.[18]

Cities with Weak Incorporation

Stockton and San Jose have had minority representatives on the city council, but they have not been part of a sustained liberal dominant coalition, and policy responsiveness has been very uneven. In such cities minority groups clearly need to continue mobilization efforts in order to become part of a lib-

[17]For discussions of the antagonism between older and new immigrants like the Irish and Italians, see Wilson (1960, p. 24); Wolfinger (1974). Interviews in our cities revealed a great deal of mistrust between blacks and Hispanics. Blacks said: "Hispanics want us blacks to do it for them." "The Chicano style was 'me too,' to watch how blacks do it, but hold back until the blacks had won something, and then come in and demand a part of the winnings." Hispanics felt that blacks talked as if they favored cooperation but actually were preventing Hispanics from getting what they deserved.

[18]Arias (1980); Calhoun (1980). One study (Ambrecht and Pachon, 1974) found that the proportion of Hispanics willing to consider coalitions with blacks increased between 1965 and 1972. (See also Ambrecht, 1976, p. 181; Fremstad, 1982; Henry, 1980.)

eral dominant coalition. Both cities have sizeable Hispanic populations and a long history of mobilization efforts, which together could be used by skillful leaders finally to overcome resistant dominant coalitions, which have been weakening gradually, even though they have not yet been clearly replaced.

These cities offer a test of whether Hispanics can be mobilized where they are present in much larger proportions than blacks. In one view Hispanics are much more difficult to mobilize than blacks because they have higher median family incomes, less political consciousness, less geographical concentration, and more divisions among various nationalities, and they are more conservative politically (Garcia and de la Garza, 1977). In another view these conditions are not insurmountable barriers to Hispanic mobilization, and more mobilization and incorporation will occur as their numbers increase. In this view political consciousness and the cadre of experienced leaders will follow the black pattern with a lag.

In both San Jose and Stockton problems in Hispanic leadership are apparent. The first Hispanic elected to the council in each city was perceived as weak—either because of personality characteristics or questions about conflict of interest. These initial selections set patterns that were difficult to change. Thus demand-protest and electoral mobilization have not been very successful in achieving incorporation or responsiveness.

Stockton has not only a sizeable Hispanic population but also a significant black population. In fact, even though blacks make up only one-third of Stockton's minority population, they have typically taken the lead in mobilization efforts and establishing transitory coalitions with Hispanics. An obvious strategy in Stockton is not only to increase Hispanic mobilization but to forge more lasting coalitions with blacks and other minority groups.

Cities with No Minority Incorporation

Blacks and Hispanics are still completely unrepresented in three of the ten cities—Vallejo, Daly City, and Hayward—although one minority councilmember was elected for a single term in Vallejo and Hayward between 1960 and 1980. In such cities, too, minority groups need to continue to push for inclusion in a liberal dominant coalition, but the prospects—at least in Vallejo and Daly City—are not very promising because of the small size of the supportive white group.

Vallejo and Daly City are similar in the demonstrable conservatism of their dominant coalitions and of the white population generally. Efforts to develop liberal challenging coalitions will have to start at the very basic level of identifying issues and creating linkages among activists. But presently, the occasional demands that are made, sometimes with help from outside organizations like the California FEPC, are resisted so strongly that the incentives for leaders are small. In these cities where little progress has been made toward minority incorporation and responsiveness and when all the talk is of retrenchment, it will be very difficult to mobilize the energies needed to make substantial progress toward a liberal challenging coalition. This is true even though Vallejo has a sizeable black population and Daly City has a sizeable Hispanic population, and coalitions with the other group in each city would contribute substantially to the size of the minority population being mobilized.

In Hayward minority mobilization would not meet with the same kind of opposition. Since 1972 a rather loose liberal coalition has dominated the city council, and an attractive Hispanic candidate might well succeed in gaining both election to office and entry into this coalition—at least in the sense of supporting it and getting support from it. Another positive resource is Hayward's relatively strong fiscal position. Hayward is a city with a sizeable Hispanic population but a small black population (the proportions are similar to those in San Jose), and Hispanic mobilization has proved to be difficult. If Hispanic leaders were inclined to focus efforts on city politics, the prospects for improvement would seem more positive than in Vallejo and Daly City.

The Continuing Struggle for Political Equality

The strategies suggested here for different types of cities emphasize the importance of leadership—of choices made by political actors—in the struggle for political equality. Our findings for the period 1960—80 suggest that these choices are constrained by societal conditions and political structures, but they also suggest that choices made by leaders can have substantial impact on the way group resources get translated into political action and, in particular, on the formation and nature of coalitions. Also, if the national mobilization movement is weaker and the call to local action less insistent than in the sixties, the initiatives of local leaders will be more important and more variable than before.

We cannot say for certain, of course, whether different choices or different leaders would be able to overcome the obstacles in a particular city. Would black leadership or strategies from Berkeley or Oakland be able to mount a sustained organizing effort and contribute to incorporation in Vallejo? Or is white opposition so great there that no leaders or approaches can succeed? Would different Hispanic leadership or strategies be able to achieve mobilization in cities with sizeable Hispanic populations comparable to that in cities with sizeable black populations?

There is no way to answer such questions except by the attempt. We believe that more could be done to mobilize minorities in each city and that such increased effort would probably have some impact. We also know that obstacles persist and are looming larger, so that to call for minority leadership is to ask people in the weaker position to make the most heroic efforts. But they have done it in the past, and although their work has not led inevitably to increased equality for blacks and Hispanics, progress does not occur in the absence of such effort.

We know that protest is not enough. Protest alone is not sufficient for representation and the stronger forms of access and responsiveness. Something more is needed, and electoral effort is the key. Protest must be translated into electoral organizing, the traditional political activity of recruiting candidates, controlling the number who run, and developing support and coalitions.

But those who said that protest inevitably hinders the struggle for political equality were wrong. Protest was frequently used successfully to stimulate electoral mobilization and to reinforce the positions of elected minority councilmembers and mayors in the legislative process. Without protest, the impact of incorporation would surely have been much weaker.

If the trend toward political equality is not irresistible, as de Tocqueville thought, it will continue—provided that both protest and electoral struggle are carried on and engage all those who support the cause.

Appendices

APPENDIX A

Selected Characteristics of the Ten Cities

City	Population		Percent minority of population				Percent below poverty level			
	1970	1980	1970		1980		1969		1979	
			Black	Hispanic[a]	Black	Hispanic[a]	Black	Hispanic[b]	Black	Hispanic[a]
Berkeley	116,716	103,328	23.5	3.5	20.1	5.1	19.7	18.2	21.4	25.1
Daly City	66,922	78,519	5.4	12.2	10.7	19.3	11.6	5.3	7.6	6.1
Hayward	93,058	94,167	1.8	14.1	5.7	20.2	9.8	9.4	11.4	13.0
Oakland	361,561	339,288	34.5	6.7	46.9	9.6	25.2	19.2	24.9	20.3
Richmond	79,043	74,676	36.2	6.4	47.9	10.3	21.0	16.5	23.7	19.7
Sacramento	254,413	275,741	10.7	9.4	13.4	14.2	29.9	20.8	25.6	21.8
San Francisco	715,674	678,974	13.4	9.7	12.7	12.3	24.6	14.1	25.1	17.1
San Jose	445,779	636,550	2.5	15.1	4.6	22.1	19.3	14.3	15.4	13.5
Stockton	104,644	149,779	11.2	17.3	10.4	22.1	36.0	25.1	31.6	25.1
Vallejo	69,238	80,188	16.6	4.2	19.1	8.5	17.7	11.0	20.0	10.7
Mean	230,705	251,121	15.6	10.6	19.2	14.4	21.5	15.4	20.7	17.2

SOURCES: U.S. Department of Commerce, Bureau of the Census, 1970 and 1980 censuses of population and housing. For 1970: vol. 1, *Characteristics of the Population*, part 6, *California*, tables 6, 23, 81, 95, and 101, respectively. For 1980: population data from *General Population Characteristics*, part 6, *California*, table 14; poverty data for 1979 from *Advance Estimates of Social, Economic, and Housing Characteristics*, part 6, *California*, table P-5.

[a]Persons of Spanish origin or descent. The Hispanic population data for 1970 and 1980 were obtained with the same question, in which people identified themselves as of Spanish origin, but the 1970 data are estimates based on a relatively small sample (5 percent); also, the Census Bureau acknowledges an undercount of Hispanics in 1970 (California State Census Data Center, 1981). Spanish surname was the only census criterion for "Hispanic" in 1960 and was one of the criteria, along with Spanish language, for most of the data on "Hispanics" reported in the 1970 census. All of the Hispanic data analyzed in this book are based on the Spanish-origin criterion (except see fn. b), and comparisons back to 1960 are not attempted (except in table 16).

[b]The 1969 Hispanic poverty data are for persons of Spanish language or Spanish surname rather than for persons of Spanish origin. Poverty status was reported for persons of Spanish origin for only three of our ten cities in the 1970 Subject Report, *Persons of Spanish Origin*, table 16. The percentages given there are very close to those for persons of Spanish language or surname in the same three cities. In this case, the Spanish language-or-surname data appear to be reasonably good estimates of the Spanish-origin data.

Data

Intensive fieldwork conducted in ten cities over a period of approximately five years produced both microlevel and aggregate data. The following are the major sources of data utilized in the analysis.

1. Structured Elite Interviews

The majority of the indices used in the study are based on a survey conducted in 1980 consisting of eighty structured elite interviews. Selected questions from the interview schedule can be found in appendix C. The full interview schedule can be obtained by contacting the authors. The interviews, lasting approximately an hour each, constituted the final round of fieldwork and were designed to produce data to measure systematically phenomena identified in an earlier round of semi-structured interviews. The focus was on city programs that affected minorities and on their relationship to minority mobilization and city politics.

Eight respondents were interviewed in each city—two elected officials, two administrators, two leaders of organizations promoting minority interests, and two local reporters. The intent was to obtain diverse perspectives on each city. Selection of respondents within these categories was based on decision rules identifying people holding comparable positions in each city. This was facilitated by the previous interviews, which had identified main actors and their views on minority issues. In cases where more than one person fit the criteria, the person with the longest investment in and knowledge of these issues was chosen.

The elected officials interviewed were the mayor and/or councilmembers—one identified as an active, knowledgeable leader of those supporting minority positions on issues and one as a leader among those less supportive or opposed. The administrators included one person from the city manager's office and one top administrator in the community development unit. The leaders from minority organizations were from groups at the center of minority mobilization activities; these included such groups as Spanish-speaking unity organizations, Mexican American political associations, citizen participation units connected with federal programs such as Community Development Block Grants, ministerial associations, and neighborhood improvement groups. The reporters selected were those who had covered a city hall for the longest time and were familiar with minority issues. The actual number of blacks and Hispanics interviewed in any one city varied depending upon the ethnic identification of the people holding the positions chosen for the interviews. For example, in some cities, the councilmember interviewed as a supporter of minority issues was black or Hispanic. Care was taken to ensure that in every city black or Hispanic perspectives were included, and in cities where both groups were sizeable, both perspectives were obtained.

2. Semistructured Interviews

The initial phases of this study, 1976–79, collected data by means of a variety of semistructured interviews. These focused on many different topics, including the implementation of federal programs such as urban renewal, poverty, General Revenue Sharing, and Community Development Block Grants; minority demand-protest and electoral activities; electoral campaigns and the composition of city councils; the decision-making process in city hall regarding minority issues, including the roles of minority representatives and the relationship between the council and mayor, on the one hand, and the city manager and administrators on the other; and personnel practices and affirmative action activities.

Background materials for the semistructured interviews came from secondary analysis of publicly available studies of cities and programs and a systematic collection of newspaper clippings, city hall reports, memoranda, and records. Initial respondents were identified in the course of this research, then additional respondents were identified by the snowball method. Respondents held leadership positions in organizations linked with the federal programs and in city government, including city managers, mayors, councilmembers, and department heads. More than 300 semistructured interviews were conducted, varying in length from half an hour to three hours.

At about midway in the study, findings from the interviews and other sources of data were integrated as case studies. These studies identified key events, turning points, and trends in each city since 1960: levels of minority demand and protest activity, major mobilization events, the evolution of issues and conflicts, changes in city councils and city administrations and in minority leadership, and the pattern of city response to minority demands. The case studies provided a base for the formulation of alternative hypotheses and for the construction of measures to test them. These measures were obtained in the final round of structured interviews.

3. Other Sources

We collected information on city council elections since 1950, identifying voter turnout; the number, characteristics, and success rate of minority candidates; and the composition and characteristics of councils. Efforts to use precinct data to identify minority voting behavior over time were unsuccessful due to the difficulty of matching precincts with census tracts to determine percent minorities in precincts—a difficulty compounded by frequent changes in tract and precinct boundaries.

We also collected information on city revenues and expenditures, including federal grants, taxes, tax rates, assessed valuation, measures of fiscal strain, and allocations to various city functions. Information on the implementation of federal grants, including reports on Model Cities, General Revenue Sharing, and Community Development Block Grants was assembled. Employment figures were collected, including city reports on the ethnic composition of the work force prior to 1974; the annual city reports to the U.S. Equal Employment Opportunity Commission, which were initiated in 1974; and other affirmative action surveys. City hall records were used to assemble information on appointments to commissions. Information on minority contracting was obtained from the area office of the U.S. Department of Housing and Urban Development.

We drew upon all the standard sources of demographic data and supplemented these with data generated by local planning, Model Cities, and community development offices.

Indices and Measures

1. Incorporation

Minority political incorporation scores were produced for each city for each year, 1960 – 79. The scale of incorporation is based on three aspects of minority position on the city council: the number of minority councilmembers; the minority role, if any, in the dominant coalition; and minority occupancy of the mayor's office. First, one point was assigned for each minority councilmember.[1] Two additional points were assigned if minority representatives (regardless of number) were part of the dominant coalition on the council. Three additional points were assigned if a black or a Hispanic held the mayor's office.

[1]But where minority representatives were not part of the dominant coalition, a maximum of two points was assigned even if there were more than two minority councilmembers. This limit slightly reduces the incorporation score in only one city (Stockton) where three minority councilmembers held office 1975 – 78 but were not part of the dominant coalition. In the other cities with as many as three minority councilmembers, they were major factors in liberal coalitions that had successfully challenged more conservative predecessors. The limit was based on our hypothesis that having one minority councilmember in a dominant coalition that clearly supported minority interests was better than having three minority representatives on a council dominated by a coalition hostile to minority interests.

(The two minority mayors, both blacks, were also leaders of dominant coalitions.) For example, Berkeley in 1978 had two black councilmembers (+2) who were part of the dominant coalition (+2), and a black occupied the mayor's office (+3), for a total score of 7. The additional points for minority occupancy of the mayor's office were assigned only to independently elected mayors, who played much stronger leadership roles and exercised much more influence than mayors selected by city councils from their own members (the two minority mayors in our cities were both independently elected).

The scoring scheme has certain consequences. One minority councilmember who is part of the dominant coalition is weighted three times as heavily $(1 + 2 = 3)$ as a minority member not in the dominant coalition (1). If one or more minority councilmembers is already in the dominant coalition, then electing a minority person to the mayor's office is worth three times as much (+3) as an additional minority councilmember (+1). The weighting scheme was chosen to be consistent with our informed impressions of the impact of minority representatives on issues of particular concern to them, depending on whether they were inside or outside the dominant coalition and whether they were mayors or ordinary councilmembers, but we do not argue that these particular ratios correspond to relative influence in a precise way. The concept requires some weighting for participation in dominant coalitions and for control over the mayor's office. Several weightings were tried. They were closely correlated, but this one is simple and replicable and produced no obvious anomalies.[2]

We did not conduct analyses of alternative measures of incorporation with other variables, then select the measure that performed best statistically. Rather, we evaluated the way each measure, both in its components and in toto, fit our qualitative knowledge of the strength of the minority position across cities and over time within each city. Subsequent analysis of rela-

[2]The measure does not control for variations in the number of councilmembers, but all of the cities except two had seven or nine councilmembers including the mayor (Daly City had five, San Francisco twelve in all), and we detect no evidence that the effects of minority incorporation as measured were different in cities with larger councils in this size range than in cities with smaller councils.

tionships between variables was carried out only with the measure described here.

With a considerably larger number of cities, one might estimate the weights for three components of the measure separately. With ten cities this is not feasible. Establishment of a plausible measure of incorporation overall seemed to us more fruitful than an effort to estimate precise weights for the components of incorporation in any case.

Like the ordinary percentage measure of representation, this measure of incorporation counts minority persons, on the widely held perception that minority interests are most likely to be effectively represented by minority persons (Greenstone and Peterson, 1973; see Pitkin, 1967, for an elaboration of concepts of representation). Unlike simple representation, the measure of incorporation includes the minority position in the coalitional structure of city council politics—that is, the minority position vis-à-vis the opposition to minority interests—and in relation to the single most powerful office in city governments. (See also chapter 1, pp. 25–27 and table 2.)

We used the 80 structured interviews and city case histories based on 300 semistructured interviews to identify dominant coalitions, their ideologies, and the role of minorities in the coalitions over time. From the case histories we rated the ideologies of dominant coalitions and the role of minorities in these coalitions. These ratings were then validated by the structured interviews. Respondents were asked whether there was a group of top officials in city government that was usually able to shape policy on minority-related issues. There was a high level of agreement about the existence of such groups, as shown in table 1A. Respondents were then asked to name the members of dominant groups, to indicate whether they typically supported or opposed minority interests, and to rate the amount of support for minority interests by various regimes over the past twenty years. Again, there was wide agreement about which dominant coalitions were resistant to minority interests and when less resistant dominant coalitions replaced them. Minority representatives never belonged to coalitions that opposed minority coalitions. They were always associated with liberal dominant coalitions or excluded from resistant coalitions.

TABLE 1A   Existence of a Dominant Coalition on Minority-
Related Issues

City (ranked by level of agreement)	Percentage of respondents agreeing that such a dominant coalition exists
Berkeley	100
Oakland	100
Stockton	100
Daly City	88
Richmond	88
Sacramento	88
Vallejo	88
Hayward	75
San Jose	75
San Francisco	50[a]

SOURCE: Positive responses to questions 17a and 17e, structured interview schedule.

[a]The relatively low level of agreement in San Francisco may reflect what Wirt (1972) calls San Francisco's hyperpluralism.

The structured interview questions were as follows:

17. In each city we are interested in finding out whether there is a group of top officials in city government which is usually able to shape policy on minority-related issues. Is there such a group in (city)?

 a.   No   Yes

 If YES, ask:

 b. Considering the mayor, councilmembers, and top administrators, what officials are part of this group?

 c. Does this group typically support or typically oppose the minority position on minority-related issues?
 support
 oppose
 sometimes support, sometimes oppose

 d. If you had to make a choice, would you say they tend to oppose or tend to support more?

     tend to support   tend to oppose

If NO, ask:

e.   Among top officials, does support for and opposition to minority-oriented policies tend to involve the same people or different people from issue to issue?

   same people   different people

f.   If same, who typically supports?
 Who typically opposes?

g.   If different,
 Does anyone typically support minority-oriented policies?
 Who?
 Does anyone typically oppose minority-oriented policies?
 Who?

18. Who is usually able to shape city policy on minority-related issues, those who support or those who oppose the minority position?

   Support Oppose Neither Don't know

2. Ideology and Interests

The scale of ideology and interests distinguishes primarily along the dimension of support for governmental redistribution to minorities. The top position on the scale, orthodox liberal, refers to an ideology in which the highest commitment is given to the redistribution of advantages to disadvantaged minority groups. The bottom position on the scale, orthodox conservative, is characterized by opposition to government action to redistribute benefits to minorities. The middle three positions on the scale—liberal pragmatist, administrative liberal, and economic development conservative—also refer to two other dimensions, namely, regime and economic development interests. Administrative liberal and liberal pragmatist ideologies are distinguished on the regime dimension. Like Greenstone and Peterson (1973), we use regime interests to mean adherence to particular governmental structures and processes. We distinguish between a commitment to pluralist bargaining, held by liberal pragmatists, and a commitment to more hierarchical rational planning, held by administrative liberals (Agger, Goldrich, and Swanson, 1964; and Greenstone and Peterson, 1973, refer to them as community conservationists). Economic development and orthodox conservative ideologies are distinguished on the economic development dimension, which refers to the use of government to promote economic development. Economic development conservatives support the use of governmental authority to intervene in large-scale economic development efforts such as urban renewal, industrial parks, and port development. (Greenstone and Peterson refer to them as progressive conservatives.) Orthodox conservatives may be no less committed to business interests but favor more limited, routine government and expect to be able to achieve their economic interests using more passive instruments of government such as zoning powers (compare with Marshall, 1979).

We used material in the city case histories including a variety of documentary and interview sources to rate the ideologies of dominant coalitions. Responses to the structured interviews were then used to validate the ratings. There was typically a clear consensus on the positions held by coalition leaders. The ratings of ideology and interests of dominant coalitions for the 1977–79 period were closely related to minority political incorporation ($r = .86$ for blacks and Hispanics combined). In most of our analysis the ideology scale was actually dichotomized into liberal and conservative ideologies. The distinctions between different types of liberal and conservative ideologies were useful in explaining deviations from general patterns—variations that occurred in individual cities due to the preferences of the specific sets of actors.

Structured interview questions on ideology included the following:

15. Now I'd like to ask some questions about the commitment to minority interests of various participants in city government. Please rate the level of commitment to minority-oriented policies of the following: the mayor, majority of the city council, the city manager/CAO, and city department heads.

	Mayor	Majority of city council	City manager/ CAO	Department heads

a. strongly opposes

b. tends to oppose minority-oriented policies

c. only supports a few such efforts

d. supports some such efforts

e. supports many efforts to establish such policies

TABLE 2A   Scale of Ideology and Interests of Dominant Coalitions

---

Liberal ideologies

Orthodox liberal

Strong support for redistribution. Broad scope of govenment to redistribute benefits to minorities.

Liberal pragmatist

Moderate support for redistribution. Consistent with pluralist bargaining. Gains for minorities bargained rather than following from a liberal program.

Administrative liberal

Moderate support for redistribution. Consistent with rational planning combining social and economic considerations and consultative participation.

Resistant or conservative ideologies

Economic development conservative

Little support for redistribution. Vigorous use of government to undertake large-scale economic development. Opposed to redistribution but may have incentive to bargain to achieve economic objectives.

Orthodox conservative

Opposition to redistribution. Narrow scope of government to maintain current distribution of benefits.

---

f.   strongly supports efforts to establish such policies

g.   leads efforts to establish minority-oriented programs, policies, and allocations

16.   Now I'd like you to think back to 5 years ago. Please rate the commitment of the same participants to efforts to establish minority-oriented policies then.

	Mayor	Majority of city council	City manager/ CAO	Department heads

a.   strongly opposes

b. tends to oppose minority-oriented policies

c. only supports a few such efforts

d. supports some such efforts

e. supports many efforts to establish such policies

f. strongly supports efforts to establish such policies

g. leads efforts to establish minority-oriented programs, policies, and allocations

21a. We have found that in some cities, support of top officials for minority-oriented policies reflects different priorities. How would you *rank* the priorities of the top officials who support these policies in (city)?

a. professional human service planning

b. redistribution of resources to meet minority needs

c. maintenance of political support

21b. In some cities, top officials who generally support minority-oriented policies give priority to large-scale city economic development rather than to programs of more direct benefit to minority groups. In (city) if forced to choose would these officials decide in favor of more direct benefit to minorities or in favor of city economic development?

a. economic development

b. programs of more direct benefit to minorities

21c. In most cities there are some top officials who are not supportive of minority-oriented programs. Which best describes the reasons for not supporting minority-related programs in (city): economic development priorities or a belief in limiting city government to basic services?

a. economic development priorities

b. limit city government to basic services

c. other

21d. Here is a list of city government administrations since 1960. Please rate each in terms of its stance toward minority influence in city government.

resisted minority influence in city government	supported some minority influence in city government	supported strong minority influence in city government

3. Demand-Protest

Demand-protest covers a wide range of activity including violent and nonviolent protest (sit-ins, boycotts, pickets, demonstrations, riots) and more traditional demand articulation tactics such as mass turnout at city meetings, press conferences, neighborhood meetings, petitions, and formal and informal exchanges with city officials. Ratings were based on responses to a structured interview question about the level of black and Hispanic demand-protest directed at city hall and on the reconstruction of events from interviews, newspapers, and other published sources. Respondents rated demand-protest as extremely high, high, moderate, low, or none (scored 8, 6, 4, 2, 0) for each of twenty years. These responses were combined, and responses for each city were averaged. Missing ratings for some years were reconstructed from interview narratives and from newspaper and other published accounts.

As a check on our ratings, we asked respondents in the structured interviews to rate the level of pressure from black and Hispanic groups in 1978–79 and to describe changes since the late 1960s and the mid-1970s. The ratings for 1978–79 were closely correlated with the measure used for black demand-protest ($r = .71$), less closely for Hispanic ($r = .50$).

The structured interview questions were as follows:

22.   For black (or Hispanic) groups, we would like to know how vigorously they press city government to respond to their needs and interests. Which of the following best describes the pressure from black groups in (city) over the last year or so?

HIGH:	MODERATE:	LOW:
well-organized and persistent pressure on city government	fairly well-organized and persistent pressure	poorly organized not persistent pressure, not involved in many issues

23.   Compared to the late 1960s, is the intensity of demands from black (or Hispanic) groups higher, lower, or about the same?

24.   Since the late 1960s, what changes have there been in the *ways* black (or Hispanic) groups pressure city government?

4. Electoral Mobilization

Minority electoral mobilization consists of efforts to elect minority candidates to city council and mayoral positions. Analysis suggested that the extent to which minority groups organized to control minority candidacies was more important for electoral success than other measurable aspects of electoral mobilization such as minority turnout. Our earlier research had shown that, although peaks in turnout were always associated with successful challenges by liberal coalitions, turnout levels typically dropped back substantially after the challenge (Browning, Marshall, and Tabb, 1979). Over time, therefore, turnout is closely related to the large changes in minority incorporation associated with shifts in dominant coalition, but it is not closely related to the level of incorporation. In contrast, the organization of efforts to control minority candidacies is closely correlated with level of incorporation, both over time within cities and across cities at various points in time. The measure used assesses minority control over candidacies. Our ratings for each election were based on interviews, newspapers, election results, statements by candidates, and records of endorsements.

TABLE 3A   Electoral Mobilization Scale

High Control

8	Centralized control over serious[a] minority candidacies by minority organization that put forth slates
6	Negotiations between minority and white organizations over serious minority candidacies on slates
4	Recruitment and endorsement of minority candidates by minority organizations
2	Endorsements of minority candidates by minority organizations
0	No endorsements

Low Control

---

[a]Serious refers to candidates receiving at least 10 percent of the vote.

Further validation of the electoral mobilization ratings was provided by the structured interviews. Respondents were asked in 1980 to rate the level of black and Hispanic organizing for local elections on the electoral mobilization scale. The correlation between this measure of mobilization and our measure for 1979 was high for black electoral effort ($r = .82$) and lower for Hispanic ($r = .46$). The lower correlations for measures of Hispanic mobilization (both electoral and demand-protest) are probably just the result of the relative weakness and inconsistency of Hispanic mobilization in these cities, relative to that of blacks, as shown in chapter 3.

The questions were:

30. This question refers to ways in which blacks (or Hispanics) are organized for local elections in (city). Which of the following best describes black participation in local elections now?

- centralized control over serious black candidacies by black organizations which put forth slates
- blacks and whites work together as a coalition to form slates of candidates and run coordinated campaigns
- black organizations recruit and endorse black candidates for local office
- black candidates run pretty much on their own initiative and are endorsed by black organizations
- black organizations are typically inactive in local elections

31. In the selection of black candidates for the slate, how much influence do blacks have? Do they have a major say, or do black and white leaders have about equal say, or do white leaders have the major say?

5. Electoral Support for Minority Interests

City votes on a 1964 statewide ballot proposition, Proposition 14, are used as a measure of electoral support for black interests, specifically the percentage voting no on Proposition 14. This figure has two components: black votes and nonblack votes. We estimate white support for black interests by subtracting the percent black of the total voting age population in the city in 1964 from the percent voting no on the proposition.

Strictly speaking, white support is a measure of support by nonblacks, including Hispanics, Asians, Filipinos, and other groups. The accuracy of the estimate rests on the assumption that blacks who cast ballots voted virtually 100 percent against Proposition 14 and that they voted at about the same rate as whites on this issue. However, even if these assumptions are not fully met, the estimates probably correctly reflect differences between the cities in levels of white support for black interests. Percent black in 1964 is a linear interpolation between 1960 and 1970.

6. Minority Employment and Minority Officials

The Equal Employment Opportunity Act of 1972, Title VII, requires state and local governments to report figures on minority employment to the U.S. Equal Employment Opportunity Commission. Copies of these EEO-4 reports were obtained from the cities for 1974 and 1978 and were used to calculate the percent black and Hispanic in the total city work force as well as the percent in the top two occupational categories, officials/administrators and professionals.

We also collected minority employment figures for 1966 and 1970 from city ethnic surveys and, when none existed, from personnel directors' estimates (Browning and Marshall, 1976). Information was also obtained on the number of blacks and Hispanics serving as department heads or in professional positions in the city manager's office in 1966, 1970, 1974, and 1978.

7. Other Measures of Policy Responsiveness

Police Review Board

In the structured interview respondents were asked to indicate what action the city had taken on police review boards:

approved, considered but disapproved, under consideration, or not considered. There was near unanimity in responses; the city was coded according to the most prevalent response.

Minority Appointments to Boards and Commissions

From three to ten commissions reported to be important were identified in each city. Efforts were made to select types of commissions present in most of the cities to facilitate comparisons. These typically were the following commissions: city planning, parks and recreation, personnel, housing, redevelopment, economic development or ports, and human relations. City hall records were used to reconstruct membership lists for the selected commissions over a fifteen-year period and to identify which members were black or Hispanic.

Minority Contracting

Three measures of contracting effort were obtained, two of them from the structured interviews. Respondents were shown a list of six elements of a strong minority contracting program and asked to identify which elements the city had. The measure is the count, over all respondents for each city, of the number of elements mentioned.

The six elements were:

a. City specifically targets minority entrepreneurs in advertising its contracting needs.

b. City has ordinance that permits giving preference to local or minority contractors even if they are not the lowest bidders.

c. City sets aside a percentage of federal public-works funds for minority entrepreneurs, greater than the 10 percent required by federal law.

    d. City has an ordinance requiring firms that bid on con-
tracts to meet affirmative action criteria.

    e. City council pushes for higher levels of minority contract-
ing.

    f. City sets specific goals for minority contracting.

The second measure of contracting effort is a respondent rating of program aggressiveness. Respondents were asked to say whether they considered the city's minority contracting program to be very, moderately, or not aggressive.

The third measure of contracting is the percentage of CDBG contract funds that went to minority contractors. The HUD Area Office provided data on minority shares of CDBG contract monies.

We developed an overall measure of minority contracting by calculating the standard score for each measure, then taking the mean of the three standard scores.

Aggregate Measure of Policy Responsiveness

This measure is constructed by calculating the standard scores of responsiveness measures in each of four policy areas: minority employment, police review boards, representation on commissions, and contracting with minority businesses. The aggregate measure is the mean of the four standard scores.

Extent of Minority-Oriented Programs

In the structured interview respondents were asked:

8. Some cities become very involved in running programs for minorities, whereas others focus attention primarily on the traditional basic-service functions. Where would you place (city)

on the continuum between basic-services and minority-oriented policies?

- Primarily a basic-service city, with a few minority-oriented programs
- A basic-service city with some special programs for minorities
- A city with many minority-oriented policies and programs in addition to basic services

The mean response to this question in a given city was used as a measure of that city's reputation for responsiveness to minority interests (compare with the scale of perceived rate of black progress used by Rossi, Berk, and Eidson, 1974, p. 101).

8. Factors Responsible for Minority-Oriented Programs

In the structured interviews respondents were asked two questions about the factors responsible for minority-oriented programs. The questions were as follows:

10. What, in your view, have been the major factors responsible for the city's programs and activities concerning minorities, and for change over the past five years?

11. You've mentioned several factors. How important were these and other factors on this list in bringing about this pattern or level of activity?

Not important	Secondary importance	Primary importance

- pressures from the feds, changes in federal programs & policies

- pressures from state agencies

- pressure from minority leaders and organizations

- pressure from liberal white leaders and organizations

- pressure from conservative white leaders and organizations

- city council members

- city manager

- mayor

- city boards and commissions

- city department heads

- changes in revenues

Bibliography

Aaron, Henry J. 1978. *Politics and the professors: The great society in perspective.* Washington, D.C.: Brookings Institution.

Aberbach, Joel D., and Walker, Jack L. 1973. *Race in the city.* Boston: Little, Brown and Co.

Aberbach, Joel D.; Putnam, Robert D.; and Rockman, Bert A. 1981. *Bureaucrats and politicians in western democracies.* Cambridge, Mass.: Harvard University Press.

Achen, Christopher H. 1982. *Interpreting and using regression.* Beverly Hills, Calif.: Sage.

Adrian, Charles R., and Sullivan, James. 1979. The urban appointed chief executive, past and emergent. *Urban Interest* 1, no. 1: 3 – 9.

Agger, Robert; Goldrich, Daniel; and Swanson, Bert. 1964. *The rulers and the ruled: Political power and impotence in American communities.* New York: Wiley.

Aiken, Michael, and Alford, Robert. 1970. Community structure and innovation: The case of public housing. *American Political Science Review* 64, no. 3 (September): 840 – 64.

Alford, Robert. 1975. *Health care politics: Ideological and interest group barriers to reform.* Chicago: University of Chicago Press.

Ambrecht, Biliana C. S. 1976. *Politicizing the poor: The legacy of the war on poverty in a Mexican-American community.* New York: Praeger.

Ambrecht, Biliana C.S., and Pachon, Harry P. 1974. Ethnic political mobilization in a Mexican-American community: An Exploratory study of East Los Angeles 1965 – 1972. *Western Political Quarterly* 21, no. 3 (September): 500 – 19.

American Civil Liberties Union. 1981. Civil liberties. June.

Antunes, George, and Gaitz, Charles M. 1975. Ethnicity and participation: A study of Mexican-Americans, Blacks, and Whites. *American Journal of Sociology* 80, no. 5 (March): 1192–1211.

Arias, Ron. 1980. The coming black . . . Hispanic coalition: An Hispanic view. *Perspective: The Civil Rights Quarterly*. U.S. Commission on Civil Rights (Spring) 13, 16–18.

Bachrach, Peter, and Baratz, Morton. 1970. *Power and poverty*. New York: Oxford University Press.

Banfield, Edward, and Wilson, James. 1963. *City politics*. New York: Vintage Books.

Bardach, Eugene. 1977. *The implementation game: What happens after a bill becomes a law*. Cambridge, Mass.: MIT Press.

Barnett, Marguerite Ross. 1982. The congressional black caucus: Illusions and realities of power. In *The new black politics: The search for political power*, edited by Michael Preston, Lenneal Henderson, Jr., and Paul Puryear. New York: Longman.

Baskin, Jane A.; Hartweg, Joyce K.; Lewis, Ralph G.; and McCullough, Lester W. 1971. *Race related civil disorders: 1967–1969*. Waltham, Mass.: Lemberg Center for the Study of Violence.

Bass, Jack, and DeVries, Walter. 1976. *The transformation of Southern politics*. New York: Basic Books.

Bendix, Reinhard. 1964. *Nation-building and citizenship*. New York: Wiley.

Berman, Paul. 1978. The study of macro- and micro-implementation. *Public Policy* 26, no. 2 (Spring): 157–84.

Berman, Paul, and McLaughlin, Milbrey. 1976. Implementation of educational innovation. *Educational Forum* 40, no. 3 (March): 345–70.

Betsalel, Kenneth A. 1983. San Jose: Crime and the politics of growth. In *Crime in City Politics*, edited by Anne Heinz, Herbert Jacob, and Robert Lineberry. New York: Longman.

Boyle, John, and Jacobs, David. 1982. The intracity institution of services: A multivariate analysis. *American Political Science Review* 76, no. 2 (June): 371–79.

Broussard, Albert S. 1981. Organizing the black community in the San Francisco Bay Area, 1915–1930. *Arizona and the West* (Winter): 352–54.

———. 1983. A blemish in the California dream: The emergence of protest organizations in San Francisco's Black community, 1915–1950. Paper prepared for presentation at the University of California Symposium "Blacks in the West," 28–29 April, at U.C. Davis.

Browning, Rufus, and Marshall, Dale Rogers. 1976. Implementation of model cities and revenue sharing in ten bay area cities: Design and first findings. In *Public policy making in a federal system*, edited by

Charles O. Jones and Robert Thomas. Beverly Hills, Calif.: Sage.

Browning, Rufus P.; Marshall, Dale Rogers; and Tabb, David H. 1978. Responsiveness to minorities: a theory of political change in cities. Paper prepared for delivery at the annual meeting of the American Political Science Association.

––––––. 1979a. Blacks and Hispanics in California city politics: Changes in representation. *Public Affairs Report* 50, no. 3 (June): 1–9. Berkeley: Institute of Governmental Studies, University of California.

––––––. 1979b. Minorities and urban electoral change: A longitudinal study. *Urban Affairs Quarterly* 15, no. 2: 206–28.

––––––. 1979c. Minority mobilization and urban political change, 1960–1979. Paper presented at the annual meeting of the American Political Science Association.

––––––. 1980. Implementation and political change: Sources of local variations in federal social programs. In *Effective policy implementation*, edited by Paul Sabatier and Daniel Mazmanian. Lexington, Mass.: Lexington Books.

––––––. 1983. Local control over local policies: Can city politics make a difference for minorities? Paper presented at the annual meeting of the American Political Science Association.

Button, James. 1978. *Black violence: Political impact of the 1960s riots.* Princeton, N.J.: Princeton University Press.

Calhoun, Lillian. 1980. The coming black . . . Hispanic coalition: A black view. *Perspective: The Civil Rights Quarterly.* U.S. Commission on Civil Rights (Spring): 12, 14–15.

California Journal. 1982. 13, no. 9 (September): 309.

California State Census Data Center. 1981. *Newsletter.* Spring.

Campbell, Angus. 1971. *White attitudes toward black people.* Ann Arbor, Mich. Institute for Social Research.

Carmichael, Stokely, and Hamilton, Charles. 1967. *Black power.* New York: Vintage Books.

Cayer, Joseph N., and Sigelman, Lee. 1980. Minorities and women in state and local government: 1973–1975. *Public Administration Review* 40:443–50.

Center for Continuing Study of the California Economy. 1982. *Projections of Hispanic population for California 1985–2000.* Palo Alto, Calif.

Clark, Terry N., and Ferguson, Lorna C. 1983. *City money: Political processes, fiscal strain, and retrenchment.* New York: Columbia University Press.

Cole, Leonard. 1976. *Blacks in power: A comparative study of black and white elected officials.* Princeton, N.J.: Princeton University Press.

Coleman, James S. 1971. *Resources for social change.* New York: Wiley.

Conyers, James E., and Wallace, Walter. 1976. *Black elected officials: A study of black Americans holding government office.* New York: Russell Sage Foundation.

Crain, Robert L. 1968. *The politics of school desegregation.* Chicago: Aldine.

Dahl, Robert. 1961. *Who governs? Democracy and power in an American city.* New Haven, Conn.: Yale University Press.

————. 1967. *Pluralist democracy in the United States.* Chicago: Rand McNally.

Derthick, Martha H. 1970. *The influence of federal grants.* Cambridge, Mass.: Harvard University Press.

De Tocqueville, Alexis. 1966. *Democracy in America.* Vol. 1. Translated by Henry Reeve. New Rochelle, N.Y.: Arlington House.

————. 1969. *Democracy in America.* Edited by D.P. Mayer. Garden City, N.Y.: Doubleday Anchor Books.

Dommel, Paul, and Associates. 1982. *Decentralizing urban policy.* Washington, D.C.: Brookings Institution.

Dye, Thomas. 1966. *Politics, economics, and the public: Policy outcomes in the American states.* Chicago: Rand McNally.

Dye, Thomas, and Renick, James. 1981. Political power and city jobs. *Social Science Quarterly* 62, no. 3 (September): 475–86.

Edelman, Murray. 1971. *Politics as symbolic action.* New Haven, Conn.: Yale University Press.

Eisinger, Peter K. 1973. The conditions of protest behavior in American cities. *American Political Science Review* 67, 1 (March): 11–28.

————. 1980. *Politics of displacement: Racial and ethnic transition in three American cities.* New York: Academic Press.

————. 1982. Black employment in municipal jobs: The impact of black political power. *American Political Science Review* 76, no. 2 (June): 380–92.

Ellwood, John William, ed. 1982. *Reductions in U.S. domestic spending.* New Brunswick, N.J.: Transaction Books.

Elmore, Richard. 1978. Organizational models of social program implementation. *Public Policy* 26:2 (Spring): 199–216.

Engstrom, Richard L., and McDonald, Michael E. 1981. The election of blacks to city councils: Clarifying the impact of electoral arrangements on the seats/population relationship. *American Political Science Review* 75, no. 2: (June) 344–54.

Estrada, Leobardo; Garcia, Chris F.; Macias, Reynaldo Flores; Maldonado, Lionel. 1981. Chicanos in the United States: A history of exploitation and resistance. *Daedalus* 110, no. 2 (Spring): 103–32.

Eulau, Heinz, and Prewitt, Kenneth. 1973. *Labyrinths of democracy: Adaptations, linkages, representation, and policies in urban politics.* Indianapolis: Bobbs-Merrill.

Fainstein, Norman, and Fainstein, Susan. 1976. The future of community control. *American Political Science Review* 70, 3 (September) 905–23.

Fisher, Sethard. 1978. Black elected officials in California. San Francisco, Calif.: R & E Research Associates Inc.

Fremstad, Lee. 1982. Political spoils struggle splits blacks, browns. *Sacramento Bee,* May 9.

Frieden, Bernard, and Kaplan, Marshall. 1975. *The politics of neglect: Urban aid from model cities to revenue sharing.* Cambridge, Mass.: MIT Press.

Gamson, William. 1961. A theory of coalition-formation. *American Sociological Review* 26 (June): 373–82.

————. 1975. *The strategy of social protest.* Homewood, Ill. Dorsey Press.

Garcia, Chris F., and de la Garza, Rudolph O. 1977. *The Chicano political experience: Three perspectives.* North Scituate, Mass.: Duxbury Press.

Gittell, Marilyn. 1980. *Limits to citizen participation: The decline of community organizations.* Beverly Hills, Calif.: Sage.

Glazer, Nathan, and Moynihan, Daniel Patrick. 1963. *Beyond the melting pot.* Cambridge, Mass.: MIT and Harvard Press.

Glazer, Nathan, and Moynihan, Daniel P., eds. 1975. *Ethnicity: Theory and experience.* Cambridge, Mass.: Harvard University Press.

Gordon, Margaret. 1978. From liberal control to radical challenge. In *Experiment and change in Berkeley,* edited by Harriet Nathan and Stanley Scott. Berkeley: Institute of Governmental Studies, University of California.

Gough, Ian. 1979. *The political economy of the welfare state.* London: Macmillan and Co.

Grassroots, June 22, 1973.

Greenberg, Stanley B. 1974. *Politics and poverty: Modernization and response in five poor neighborhoods.* New York: Wiley.

Greenstone, David J., and Peterson, Paul. 1973. *Race and authority in urban politics: Community participation and the war on poverty.* New York: Russell Sage Foundation.

Gronbjerg, Kirsten; Street, David; and Suttles, Gerald. 1978. *Poverty and social change.* Chicago: University of Chicago Press.

Gruber, Judith Emily. 1979. Political strength and policy responsiveness: The results of electing blacks to city councils. Paper prepared for delivery at the annual meeting of the Western Political Science Association.

————. 1981. Democracy versus bureaucracy: The problem of democratic control. Ph.D. diss., Yale University.

Hamilton, Charles V. 1979. The patron-recipient relationship and minority politics in New York City. *Political Science Quarterly* 95: 211–28.

————. 1980. On politics. In *The state of black America 1980*. New York: National Urban League.

————. 1982. Measuring Black conservatism. In *The state of black America 1982*. New York: National Urban League.

Hamilton, Howard D. 1978. Electing the Cincinnati city council: An examination of alternative electoral representation systems. Cincinnati, Ohio: Stephen H. Wilder Foundation.

Harding, Vincent. 1981. *There is a river: The black struggle for freedom in America*. New York: Harcourt Brace Jovanovich.

Harrigan, John J. 1981. *Political change in the metropolis*. Boston: Little, Brown and Co.

Hawkins, Bret. 1971. *Politics and urban policies*. Indianapolis: Bobbs-Merrill.

Hawley, Willis. 1973. *Nonpartisan elections and the case for party politics*. New York: Wiley.

Hayes, Edward C. 1972. *Power structure and urban policy*. New York: McGraw-Hill.

Heclo, Hugh. 1974. *Modern social politics in Britain and Sweden*. New Haven: Yale University Press.

Heilig, Peggy, and Mundt, Robert J. 1981. Do districts make a difference? *The Urban Interest* 3, no. 1: 62–75.

Henderson, Lenneal. 1978. Administrative advocacy and black urban administrators. *Annals* 439 (September): 68–79.

Henry, Charles. 1980. Black-Chicano coalitions: Possibilities and problems. *Western Journal of Black Studies* 4, (Winter): 202–32.

Hinckley, Barbara. 1981. *Coalitions and politics*. New York: Harcourt Brace Jovanovich.

Hutchins, Matthew, and Sigelman, Lee. 1981. Black employment in state and local governments: A comparative analysis. *Social Science Quarterly* 62, no. 1: 79–87.

Ingram, Helen. 1977. Policy implementation through bargaining: The case of federal grants-in-aid. *Public Policy* 25, no. 4 (Fall): 499–562.

International City Management Association. n.d. Municipal service delivery in Hispanic communities. Washington, D.C.

Jennings, Edward T., Jr. 1979. Competition, constituencies, and welfare policies in American states. *American Political Science Review* 73, no. 2 (June): 414–29.

Jennings, Kent M., and Niemi, Richard G. 1981. *Generations and politics*. Princeton, N.J.: Princeton University Press.

Joint Center for Political Studies. 1980. *National roster of black elected officials*. Vol. 10. Washington, D.C.

Jones, Bryan D. 1980. *Service delivery in the city: Citizen demand and bureaucratic rules*. New York: Longman.

Jones, Faustine. 1981. External cross-currents and internal diversity:

An assessment of Black progress, 1960–1980. *Daedalus* (Spring): 71–102.

Karnig, Albert. 1979. Black resources and city council representation. *Journal of Politics* 41 (February): 134–49.

Karnig, Albert, and Welch, Susan. 1980. *Black representation and urban policy.* Chicago: University of Chicago Press.

Katznelson, Ira. 1973. *Black men, white cities.* London: Oxford University Press.

———. 1981. *City trenches: Urban politics and the patterning of class in the United States.* New York: Pantheon Books.

Keech, William R. 1968. *The impact of Negro voting: The role of the vote in the quest for equality.* Chicago: Rand McNally.

Keller, Edward J. 1978. The impact of black mayors on urban policy. *Annals* 439 (September): 40–52.

Kent, T. J. 1978. Berkeley's first liberal democratic regime: 1961–1970. In *Experiment and change in Berkeley,* edited by Harriet Nathan and Stanley Scott. Berkeley: Institute of Governmental Studies, University of California.

Kerstein, Robert J., and Judd, Dennis R. 1980. Achieving less influence with more democracy: The permanent legacy of the war on poverty. *Social Science Quarterly* 61, no. 2 (September): 208–20.

Kirby, David T.; Harris, Robert; Crain, Robert L.; and Rossell, Christine H. 1973. *Political strategies in Northern school desegregation.* Lexington, Mass.: Lexington Books.

Kirlin, John J. 1973. The impact of increasing lower status clientele upon city governmental structure: a model from organization theory. *Urban Affairs Quarterly* 8, no. 3 (March): 317–44.

Kirp, David L. 1982. Just schools: The idea of racial equality in American schools. Berkeley: University of California Press.

Kleinwaks, Jay D. 1982. The effects of at-large and district elections on the San Francisco Board of Supervisors. Unpublished M.A. thesis, San Francisco State University.

Kramer, Ralph M. 1969. *Participation of the poor: Comparative case studies in the war on poverty.* Englewood Cliffs, N.J.: Prentice-Hall.

Kranz, Harry. 1976. *The participatory bureaucracy: Women and minorities in a more representative public service.* Lexington, Mass.: Lexington Books.

Ladd, Everett Carl. 1980. Realignment? No/Realignment? Yes. *Public Opinion* (Oct./Nov.): 13–15.

Ladd, Everett Carl, and Lipset, Seymour M. 1980. The United States in the 1980's. Palo Alto, Calif.: Hoover Institution, Stanford University.

Lamb, Curt. 1975. *Political power in poor neighborhoods.* New York: Wiley.

Lapidus, Gail Warshofsky. 1978. *Women in soviet society: Equality, devel-*

opment, and social change. Berkeley: University of California Press.

Larkey, Patrick. 1979. *Evaluating public programs: The impact of general revenue sharing on municipal government.* Princeton, N.J.: Princeton University Press.

Lee, Eugene. 1960. *The politics of nonpartisanship.* Berkeley: University of California Press.

Levine, Charles. 1971. *Racial conflict and the American mayor.* Lexington, Mass.: Lexington Books.

Levine, Charles H.; Rubin, Irene S.; and Wolohojian, George. 1981. *The politics of retrenchment.* Beverly Hills, Calif.: Sage.

Levy, Frank; Meltsner, Arnold; and Wildavsky, Aaron. 1974. *Urban outcomes.* Berkeley: University of California Press.

Lieberson, Stanley. 1980. *A piece of the pie: Black and white immigrants since 1880.* Berkeley: University of California Press.

Lieske, Joel. 1978. The conditions of racial violence in American cities: A developmental synthesis. *American Political Science Review* 72, no. 4 (December): 1324–40.

Lineberry, Robert L. 1977. *Equality and urban policy: The distribution of municipal public services.* Beverly Hills, Calif.: Sage.

Lipset, Seymour Martin. 1979. *The first new nation.* New York: Norton.

Lipsky, Michael. 1970. *Protest in city politics: Rent strikes, housing and the power of the poor.* Chicago: Rand McNally.

———. 1980. *Street-level bureaucracy.* New York: Russell Sage Foundation.

Loveridge, Ronald. 1971. *City managers in legislative politics.* Indianapolis: Bobbs-Merrill.

Lowi, Theodore J. 1964. *At the pleasure of the major: Patronage and power in New York City, 1898 –1958.* London: Collier-Macmillan.

———. 1971. *The politics of disorder.* New York: Basic Books.

———. 1972. Four systems of policy, politics and choice. *Public Administration Review* 32 (July): 298–310.

Lyford, Joseph. 1982. *The Berkeley archipelago.* Chicago: Regnery Gateway.

MacManus, Susan S. 1978. City council election procedures and minority representation: Are they related? *Social Science Quarterly* 59, no. 1 (June): 153–161.

Marshall, Dale Rogers. 1971a. *The politics of participation in poverty.* Berkeley: University of California Press.

———. 1971b. Public participation and the politics of poverty. In *Race, change and urban society,* edited by Peter Orleans and William Ellis. Beverly Hills, Calif.: Sage.

———. 1975. Implementation of federal poverty and welfare policy: A review essay. In *Analyzing poverty policy,* edited by Dorothy B. James. Lexington, Mass.: Lexington Books.

———. 1979. Introduction: The study of urban policy making. In *Ur-*

ban policy making, edited by Dale Rogers Marshall, Beverly Hills, Calif.: Sage.

———— . 1982. Lessons from the implementation of poverty programs in the United States. In *Institutions of rural development for the poor: Decentralization and organizational linkages*, edited by David K. Leonard and Dale Rogers Marshall. Berkeley: Institute for International Studies, University of California.

Marshall, Dale Rogers, and Waste, Robert. 1977. Large city responses to the community development act. Davis: Institute of Governmental Affairs, University of California.

Marshall, T. H. 1964. *Class, citizenship, and social development*. Garden City, N.Y.: Doubleday.

May, Judith V. 1969. Two model cities: Political development on the local level. Paper presented at the annual meeting of the American Political Science Association.

———— . 1973. Struggle for authority: A comparison of four social change programs in Oakland, Calif. Ph.D. diss., University of California, Berkeley.

Mazmanian, Daniel, and Sabatier, Paul. 1980. *Effective policy implementation*. Lexington, Mass.: Lexington Books.

Michels, Robert. 1966. *Political parties*. New York: Free Press.

Milbrath, Lester. 1965. *Political participation*. Chicago: Rand McNally.

Mladenka, Kenneth. 1980. The urban bureaucracy and the Chicago political machine: Who gets what and the limits to political control. *American Political Science Review* 74, no. 4. (December) 991–98.

Mollenkopf, John. 1973. On the causes and consequences of political mobilization. Paper prepared for annual meeting of the American Political Science Association.

———— . 1983. *The contested city*. Princeton, N.J.: Princeton University Press.

Montclarion. March 14, 1979.

Montjoy, Robert S., and O'Toole, Laurence J. 1979. Toward a theory of policy implementation: An organizational perspective. *Public Administration Review* 39, no. 5 (Sept./Oct.): 465–76.

Morgan, David R., and Pelissero, John P. 1980. Urban policy: Does political structure matter? *American Political Science Review* 74, no. 4: 999–1006.

Morgan, William R., and Clark, Terry Nichols. 1973. The causes of racial disorders: A grievance-level explanation, *American Sociological Review* 38 (October): 611–24.

Mundt, Robert J.; Heilig, Peggy; Fleischman, Arnold; Cox, David N.; and Sosa-Riddell, Ada. 1982. *Local representation and the quality of urban life*. Report to Center for Work and Mental Health, National Institute of Mental Health. University of North Carolina.

Myrdal, Gunnar. 1944. *An American dilemma: The negro problem and modern democracy.* New York: Harper and Brothers.

Nathan, Harriet, and Scott, Stanley, eds. 1978. *Experiment and change in Berkeley.* Berkeley: Institute of Governmental Studies, University of California.

Nathan, Richard P.; Marvel, Allen D.; and Calkins, Susannah E. 1975. *Revenue sharing.* Washington, D.C. Brookings Institution.

Nathan, Richard P., and Adams, Charles E. Jr. 1977. *Revenue sharing: The second round.* Washington: D.C. Brookings Institution.

Nathan, Richard; Dommel, Paul R.; Liebschutz, Sarah; Morris, Milton; and Associates. 1977. *Block grants for community development.* Washington, D.C.: U.S. Department of Housing and Urban Development.

National Association of Housing and Redevelopment Officials. 1976. A summary of major findings of NAHRO's community development monitoring project. Washington, D.C.

National Urban League. 1982. *The state of black America.* New York.

Nelson, William E., Jr., and Meranto, Philip J. 1977. *Electing black mayors: Political action in the black community.* Columbus, Ohio: Ohio State University Press.

New York Times. November 14, 1982. November 21, 1982. January 9, 1984.

New West, November 17, 1980.

Office of the Lieutenant Governor, Calif., Council on Intergroup Relations, Intern Research Project. 1977. Third world population in California.

Palmer, John L., and Sawhill, Isabel V., eds. 1982. *The Reagan experiment.* Washington, D.C.: Urban Institute.

Parenti, Michael. 1967. Ethnic politics and the persistence of ethnic identification. *American Political Science Review* 61, no. 3 (September) 717 – 26.

Peterson, Paul L. 1981. *City limits.* Chicago: University of Chicago Press.

Pettigrew, Thomas F. 1981. Race and class in the 1980s: An interactive view. *Daedalus* (Spring): 233 – 56.

Pitkin, Hanna F. 1967. *The concept of representation.* Berkeley: University of California Press.

Piven, Frances, and Cloward, Richard. 1971. *Regulating the poor.* New York: Pantheon Books.

———. 1979. *Poor people's movements: Why they succeed, how they fail.* New York: Vintage Books.

———. 1982. *The new class war.* New York: Pantheon Books.

Polsby, Nelson. 1980. *Community power and political theory.* 2d ed. New Haven, Conn.: Yale University Press.

Pressman, Jeffrey L. 1972. Preconditions of mayoral leadership. *American Political Science Review* 66 (June): 511 – 24.

_____ . 1975. *Federal programs and city politics.* Berkeley: University of California Press.

Pressman, Jeffrey L., and Wildavsky, Aaron. 1979. *Implementation.* 2d ed. Berkeley: University of California Press.

Preston, Michael B. 1982. Black politics and public policy in Chicago: Self-interest versus constituent representation. In *The new black politics*, edited by Michael B. Preston, Lenneal Henderson, Jr., and Paul Puryear. New York: Longman.

Rae, Douglas, 1981. *Equalities.* Cambridge, Mass.: Harvard University Press.

Reagan, Michael, and Sanzone, John. 1981. *The new federalism.* New York: Oxford University Press.

Rein, Martin, and Rabinovitz, Francine. 1977. Implementation: A theoretical perspective. Working paper no. 43. Cambridge, Mass: Joint Center for Urban Studies.

Riker, William. 1961. *The theory of political coalitions.* New Haven, Conn.: Yale University Press.

Robinson, Theodore P., and Dye, Thomas R. 1978. Reformism and black representation on city councils. *Social Science Quarterly* 59, no. 1 (June): 133–41.

Rosenbloom, Robert A. 1976. Pressuring policy making from the grass roots. Ph.D. diss., Stanford University.

Rossi, Peter; Berk, R.; and Eidson, B. 1974. *The roots of urban discontent.* New York: Wiley.

Sabatier, Paul, and Mazmanian, Daniel. 1979. Toward a more adequate conceptualization of the implementation process. Davis: Institute of Governmental Affairs, University of California.

Salamon, Lester. 1976. Follow-ups, letdowns, and sleepers: The time dimensions in policy evaluation. In *Public policy making in a federal system*, edited by Charles O. Jones and Robert D. Thomas, Beverly Hills, Calif.: Sage.

_____ . 1977. Urban politics, urban policy, case studies, and political theory. *Public Administration Review* 37, no. 4: 418–28.

San Francisco Chronicle, September 8, 1979. June 5, 1980. February 2, 1981. April 17, 1981. September 28, 1981. October 25, 1981.

Schattschneider, E. E. 1960. *The semisovereign people.* New York: Holt, Rinehart and Winston.

Schumaker, Paul D., and Getter, Russell W. 1977. Responsiveness bias in 51 American communities. *American Journal of Political Science* 21, no. 2: 247–82.

_____ . 1983. Structural sources of unequal responsiveness to group demands in American cities. *Western Political Quarterly* 36, no. 1 (March): 7–29.

Scuros, Mariana. 1982. The Southwest voter registration education project. *Citizen Participation.* (September/October): 8–10.

Silberman, Charles E. 1980. *Criminal violence, criminal justice.* New York: Vintage Books.

Spilerman, Seymour. 1970. The causes of racial disturbances: A comparison of alternative explanations. *American Sociological Review* 35: 627 – 49.

———. 1971. The causes of racial disturbances: A comparison of alternative explanations. *American Sociological Review* 36: 427 – 42.

———. 1976. Structural characteristics of cities and the severity of racial disorder. *American Sociological Review* 41: 771 – 93.

Steedley, Homer R., and Foley, John W. 1979. The success of protest groups: Multivariate analysis. *Social Science Research* 8: 1 – 15.

Stinchcombe, Arthur. 1968. *Constructing social theories.* New York: Wiley.

Stone, Clarence. 1980. Systemic power in community decision making. *American Political Science Review* 74, no. 4 (December): 978 – 90.

Taebel, Delbert. 1978. Minority representation on city councils: The impact of structure on blacks and Hispanics. *Social Science Quarterly* 59, no. 1 (June): 142 – 52.

Tarrow, Sidney. 1981. Cycles of protest and cycles of reform: Italy (1965 – 1979). Unpublished manuscript.

Thomas, Robert D. 1979. Implementing federal programs at the local level. *Political Science Quarterly* 94, no. 3 (Fall): 419 – 35.

Thompson, Frank J. 1975. *Personnel policy in the city: The politics of jobs in Oakland.* Berkeley: University of California Press.

———. 1978. Civil servants and the deprived: Sociopolitical and occupational explanations of attitudes toward minority hiring. *American Journal of Political Science* 22: 325 – 47.

Thompson, James D. 1967. *Organizations in action.* New York: McGraw-Hill.

Tilly, Charles. 1978. *From mobilization to revolution.* Reading, Mass.: Addison-Wesley.

Trounstine, Philip J., and Christensen, Terry. 1982. *Movers and shakers.* New York: St. Martin's Press.

U.S. Advisory Commission on Intergovernmental Relations. 1980. "Recent trends in federal and state aid to local governments," M-118.

U.S. Advisory Commission on Intergovernmental Relations. 1981. "Significant features of fiscal federalism, 1980 – 1981," M-132, December.

U.S. Department of Commerce. Bureau of the Census. 1973. *1970 Census of population,* General Population Characteristics, U.S. Summary. Washington D.C.: Government Printing Office.

U.S. Department of Commerce. U.S. Bureau of the Census. 1971. Selected characteristics of persons and families of Mexican, Puerto Rican, and other Spanish origin. *Current population reports,* ser. P-20, no. 224. Washington, D.C.: Government Printing Office. March.

U.S. Department of Commerce. Bureau of the Census. 1977. *County and city data book,* Washington D.C.: Government Printing Office.

U.S. Department of Commerce. Bureau of the Census. 1979. The social and economic status of the black population in the U.S.: An historical view. *Current population reports,* ser. P-23, no. 80. Washington, D.C.: Government Printing Office.

U.S. Department of Commerce. Bureau of the Census. 1980. *Census of population and housing,* California. Advance Reports.

U.S. Department of Commerce. Bureau of the Census. 1981a. *1980 Census of population.* Supplementary Report PC 80-S1-1, Age, sex, race and Spanish origin of the population by regions, divisions, and states.

U.S. Department of Commerce. Bureau of the Census. 1981b. *Census of population.* Supplementary Report PC 80-S1-3, Race of the population by states.

U.S. Department of Commerce. Bureau of the Census. 1981c. *Data user news* 16, no. 10 (October).

U.S. Equal Employment Opportunity Commission. 1977. *Minorities and women in state and local government, 1974.* Washington, D.C.: Government Printing Office.

U.S. Equal Employment Opportunity Commission. 1980. *Minorities and women in state and local government, 1978.* Washington, D.C.: Government Printing Office.

U.S. National Advisory Commission on Civil Disorders. 1968. *Report.* New York: E. P. Dutton.

Van Horn, Carl. 1979. *Policy implementation in the federal system: National goals and local implementors,* Lexington, Mass.: Lexington Books.

Viorst, Milton. 1977. *The citizen poor of the 1960's.* Dayton, Ohio: Charles F. Kettering Foundation.

Viteritti, Joseph P. 1979. *Bureaucracy and social justice: Allocation of jobs and services to minority groups.* Port Washington, N.Y.: Kennikat Press.

Wall Street Journal. October 29, 1980.

Warren, Roland L.; Rose, Stephen M.; and Bergunder, Ann F. 1974. *The structure of urban reform.* Lexington, Mass.: Lexington Books.

Welch, Susan; Karnig, Albert; and Eribes, Richard. 1983. Changes in Hispanic local public employment in the southwest. *Western Political Quarterly* 36, no. 4 (Dec.): 660–73.

Wilensky, Harold. 1975. *The welfare state and equality.* Berkeley: University of California Press.

Williams, Walter. 1980a. *Government by agency: Lessons from the social program grants-in-aid experience.* New York: American Press.

———. 1980b. *The implementation perspective,* Berkeley: University of California Press.

Wilson, James Q. 1960. *Negro politics*. New York: Free Press.

———. 1973. *Political organizations*. New York: Basic Books.

Wirt, Frederick. 1970. *Politics of Southern equality*. Chicago: Aldine.

———. 1971. Alioto and the politics of hyperpluralism. *Transaction 7*, no. 6 (April): 46–55.

———. 1974. *Power in the city: Decision making in San Francisco*. Berkeley: University of California Press.

Wolfinger, Raymond E. 1974. *The politics of progress*. Englewood Cliffs, N.J.: Prentice-Hall.

Wolfinger, Raymond E., and Field, J. 1966. Political ethos and the structure of city government. *American Political Science Review 60*, no. 2 (June): 306–26.

Wolfinger, Raymond E., and Greenstein, Fred I. 1968. The repeal of fair housing in California: An analysis of referendum voting. *American Political Science Review 62*, no. 3 (September): 753–69.

Wright, Deil S. 1978. *Understanding intergovernmental relations*. North Scituate, Mass.: Duxbury Press.

Index

Compositor:	Innovative Media, Inc.
Text:	10/12 Palatino
Display:	Palatino
Printer:	Princeton University Press/Printing
Binder:	Princeton University Press/Printing